OCT 3 1 2016

YA 378.1662 ACT 2016

MW01106342

REMAIN CLAM!

Did you notice the title of this book? Did you notice what was wrong with it? Or did you think the title was *Remain Calm*? Don't be embarrassed if you did. MANY people, grown-ups and kids alike, make the same mistake. Why? Well, the brain wants the title to make sense. Remain Calm makes sense; Remain Clam doesn't. Also, most of us only glance at or skim things like titles, instructions or epigraphs [which is what this paragraph is]. If we do read more closely, we might read too quickly or too anxiously and flip letters automatically. This is what some dyslexic people do, and when we're stressed, we all become a little bit dyslexic: letters switch, negatives and positives flip, and up becomes down. So? Why does this matter? It matters because test makers on every level are all too aware of this tendency, which is especially common in young minds. They know if you feel rushed, stressed or distracted that you'll be prone to miss details, get things backwards or answer the question you imagine rather than the one on the page. That means it is VERY important that you find a way to quiet your mind, focus on ALL the words and, by all means, no matter what:

Remain Clam!

Checked for writing	Staff Initials	Date
✓	SA	7-25-17

WITHDRAWN

BLOOMINGDALE PUBLIC LIBRARY
101 FAIRFIELD WAY
BLOOMINGDALE, IL 60108
630 - 529 - 3120

© ibidPREP llc

An ibidPREP Book

2328 Broadway, 3rd Floor

New York, NY 10024

ibidprep.com

© 2016 Stuart Servetar

All rights reserved

1st Edition

ISBN 978-0-9964418-5-8

BLOOMINGDALE PUBLIC LIBRARY
101 FAIRFIELD WAY
BLOOMINGDALE, IL 60108

REMAIN CLAM!
ACT EDITION

1ˢᵗ Ed. © ibidPREP llc

INTRODUCTION
TEST-TAKING AND THE TEENAGE MIND

1ˢᵗ Ed. © ibidPREP llc

As a teenager, I was a classic underachiever, partly because I thought so highly of myself that nothing I could contemplate doing was good enough for me to be doing. Therefore, I often did nothing. I certainly didn't prepare for my standardized tests; I was far too arrogant for that. I know now that a couple of practice tests and some review would probably have helped me gain a lot of points. I don't want my students ever feeling as if they didn't reach for every last point. We may not always reach our goals, but it will never be for lack of trying. The goals we reach for are never soft. Many tutoring courses artificially manipulate their diagnostics to ensure the appearance of gains among their students. I prefer the challenge of challenging my students.

LEARN TO LOVE TESTS—THEY'RE NOT AS EVIL AS YOU'VE BEEN LED TO BELIEVE [AND EVEN IF THEY ARE, WHAT ARE YOU GOING TO DO ABOUT IT?]

Standardized tests have become a pet target for test-prep organizations, educators, parents and, not least, students. The displays of rage and animosity[1] I have seen directed toward tests are nothing short spectacular. Of course, when students act out toward a test there might be other things going on: resentment at being reduced to a number, fear of not getting into the school they want, fear of not getting picked for kickball, but mostly a lot of fear that turns into rage that gets redirected at their tests. Certain test prep organizations have benefited hugely from fanning the flames of victimhood in test takers while at the same time cramming their cynicism into the very fiber of test prep. I do not do that because ultimately it is not effective. Rather than offer my students excuses for sub-par scores, I pride myself on getting them to admit to their own shortcomings and teaching them to get out of their own bad habits.

As fun as it might be, complaining about tests is a waste of your time, and having a negative attitude going into your tests usually leads to a negative result coming out. The best way to use your energy is by studying and learning how to get better at taking the test in front of you, in this case the ACT. Remember that all tests are inherently unfair. Most are skewed toward better prepared, calmer and more confident students. If tests were not unfair or skewed, everyone would excel equally.

Test Taking & the Teenage Mind

Underachievers—Aka The Slackers

Students often come to me with their minds stressed and self-images wobbling. They are filled with notions of what kind of students they are, and what their potential is or isn't; they all dread becoming numbers that don't represent them. Obviously, you are not a number, but neither are you your potential. You are what you are right now.

My job is to convince my underachievers [as I had to convince myself] to try and, in so doing, begin to end their boring cycles. Even though one of the credos[2] of the underachiever is "If I ever did try, I'd ace this test," that isn't always true. No one succeeds every time; once you learn to try, it just means that you must **always** try.

[1] resentment, hostility
[2] statement of beliefs

Though there are no guarantees of success, I can guarantee you one thing: if you **don't** try, then it is certain you **won't** succeed.

THE MIND IS A MUSCLE —USE IT!

EVEN FOR THOSE STUDENTS WHO SEEM TO BREEZE THROUGH TESTS, IT'S NOT BECAUSE THEY NEVER THINK; IT'S BECAUSE THEY'RE USED TO THINKING AND WORKING THROUGH PROBLEMS. THE FINEST PROBLEM-SOLVING METHODS AND APPROACHES WILL NOT HELP UNLESS YOU IMPLEMENT[3] THEM. THE MIND IS INDEED A MUSCLE THAT CAN BE STRENGTHENED AND IMPROVED THROUGH USE. IF MY FLABBY BELLY CAN BE TIGHTENED WITH FEWER BAGELS AND MORE SIT-UPS, YOUR MIND CAN WRAP ITSELF AROUND FRACTIONS.

Overachievers—The Anxious Test Takers

In addition to underachievers, I also work with a lot of students caught in the grip of test anxiety. These students are usually good students and hard workers, but they often, well, stink at tests like these. Why? Because there are certain things for which we cannot prepare, namely questions and topics that require improvisational flair. This is where the slacker excels. He is used to being unprepared and forced to wing it.

All Of You

Almost all students—slackers, overachievers and every student in between—come to me with preconceived notions of their own abilities: "I suck at math," "I'm terrible at grammar," "I'm slow," etc. Most of these preconceptions have been formed through years of parent/teacher conferences or odd family dynamics: "My sister is the smart one," "I'm the reader," "I'm not so mathish." Ugh. Often these diagnoses have only the slightest basis in reality and, if we believe them, lead us into self-fulfilling-prophecy territory. Students are told that they are bad at math, so they stop applying themselves, and then they really do become bad at math. Or students have a little difficulty getting the hang of reading, so they stop reading! Instead of conforming to artificial definitions, keep your mind open to its own possibilities. If you do, who knows where you can go?

If you focus only on the muscle groups you are strong in, then those muscles will get very strong, and the rest of you will turn to flab. It's the same for the brain. Don't avoid what you're weak at; it will only get worse!

[3] put into practice

  1st Ed. © ibidPREP llc

Even into adolescence, most kids' minds are amorphous[4] mushes that have yet to be formed to any reasonable degree. Telling kids that they have math minds or verbal minds is about as productive or accurate as looking at a sack of flour and saying it is only ever going to be bread and then looking at another sack of flour and saying it will only ever be cookies.

IT REALLY IS LIKE EXERCISE!

But I'm Not Good At Test Taking...

Being good at test taking is not an innate[5] trait like having brown eyes or webbed toes. Some students may have done poorly on one or two tests when they were little and have since gotten stuck with the "poor test taker" label. Some may have started out with some test taking anxiety only to see it snowball as they've gotten older and the tests have come to have more consequences. Whatever the case, none of this means you are doomed to a life of underperforming on tests. As you read and implement the lessons in this book, you will begin to fight fear and your preconceived[6] notions with knowledge and experience. The first step in learning how to use your brilliant young mind properly is to find a way to Remain Clam!

NO TURTLING

YOU SEE IT EVERY DAY. WE'VE TURNED INTO A NATION OF TURTLES, AND SOMEHOW WE'RE PROUD OF IT. SOMEONE ON A TALK SHOW MENTIONS MATH, AND SOMEONE ELSE WAVES HER FLIPPERS AROUND LIKE A TURTLE FLAILING ON ITS BACK: "OH, I CAN'T DO ANY OF THAT MATH STUFF. I'M JUST AWFUL AT IT. HAHAHAHAHA!" AND FOR SOME REASON THAT'S OKAY. THAT KIND OF HELPLESSNESS IN THE FACE OF SOMETHING VAGUELY CHALLENGING IS REALLY DOING GREAT THINGS FOR US INDIVIDUALLY AND AS A NATION. NOT. I'M NOT SAYING THAT MATH ISN'T HARD, OR THAT YOU'RE A NINCOMPOOP IF YOU HAVE PROBLEMS WITH IT. WHAT I AM SAYING IS, STOP FLIPPING ONTO YOUR BACK AT EVERY OBSTACLE. TRY!

[4] without a clearly defined shape or form
[5] inborn, natural
[6] predetermined, set

1st Ed. © *ibidPREP llc*

CHAPTER ONE
ACT OVERVIEW

1st Ed. © ibidPREP llc

How to Use this Book

It's about ***process***. As much HOW you do something as WHAT you do. The United States [currently] has no national curriculum; a student in Alabama may not necessarily learn the same things as a student in Iowa. As a result, the ACT can only test students on a relatively narrow range of skills. Therefore, in order to distinguish among students, the ACTs preys on students' tendency to make careless errors, not pay attention, and *RUSH!* **Therefore**, students who learn HOW TO: pay attention, execute properly, and NOT rush – WIN!!!

Read this book, and I do mean READ, in order to prep and guide yourself in the basic knowledge required on the ACTs ***and*** the rigors of HOW TO TAKE TESTS. Then practice, practice, practice, but practice WELL. It doesn't help to do a lot of work if you keep making the same mistakes over and over again. Pay attention to what you're doing and try honestly to evaluate your weaknesses [and strengths!].

Remain Clam! contains exercises for every topic and type of question on the ACT. Once you have worked through every topic and type of question, try a complete practice test section. When you are just starting out, don't worry about time or skipping questions based on your goal scores. Just work your way through the section. Note the time when you start and when you stop. This will give you an idea about how long you need in a relaxed fashion and allow you to get a realistic [non-panicked] feel for time.

Once you have worked through all of the test's sections, try taking a practice test [I recommend one from <u>The Real ACT Prep Guide</u>] under realistic conditions. That means getting out of your bed and off the couch. Find a quiet spot in which you won't be interrupted [this may involve leaving your house entirely and seeking out the sanctuary of the nearest library, school, church or ashram[7]]. It also means admitting at last that in order to properly test, prep, study, read, learn, look or listen to ANYTHING, you must first turn off the computer, phone and TV.

IF YOU CANNOT LEARN TO CREATE A TEMPORARY MEDIA-FREE ZONE IN YOUR LIFE YOU WILL NEVER DO YOUR BEST ON THESE TESTS.

However, before you even start your test, be aware of what you're getting into:

Test Breakdown

Part of mastering this test, and any test, is learning to think formally: gaining an overview of what's in front of you and not diving head first into every swimming pool only to find out too late it may be empty or frozen. *Ow.* So please, if only to save your own skin, learn the shape of the test before starting out.[8] Then we can make a plan to best it!

IF YOU DON'T LIKE SURPRISES
THIS TEST IS FOR YOU!!

---

[7] religious retreat [Hindu]
[8] I can't tell you how many times I've been working with a student for months before he looks up at me blankly and asks, "So does the essay count?" Or she asks, "Is there always a fiction passage?" Don't be that guy or gal!

THE TEST IS NOT YOUR PARENTS.

BY THE TIME YOU ARE READY TO TAKE THESE TESTS, YOU PROBABLY WILL HAVE BECOME EXPERT AT TUNING OUT YOUR PARENTS. THE WORDS OF INSTRUCTION, ADVICE AND DIRECTION YOUR PARENTS HAVE BEEN SPRAYING IN YOUR DIRECTION SINCE BIRTH HAVE, THROUGH THE REMARKABLE DENSITY OF THE AVERAGE TEENAGER'S SKULL, BEEN RENDERED COMPLETELY INEFFECTIVE.

NO DOUBT, LEARNING HOW TO EFFECTIVELY TUNE OUT YOUR PARENTS IS A NECESSARY LIFE SKILL; HOWEVER, IT IS IMPORTANT TO REALIZE THAT THIS KIND OF TUNING OUT SHOULD NOT AND **DOES NOT** PERTAIN[9] TO THE ACT. THE WORDS IN INSTRUCTIONS, IN THE ITALICIZED INTROS TO READING COMPS, IN ANSWERS TO READING COMPS, AS WELL AS ALL THE WORDS IN WORD PROBLEMS ARE IMPORTANT. THEY ARE TRYING TO HELP YOU!

[CHANCES ARE YOUR PARENTS ARE TRYING TO HELP YOU TOO, BUT THAT'S ANOTHER MATTER.]

[9] relate, concern, involve

1st Ed. © ibidPREP llc

ACT FORMAT

The ACT is a test of basics and nothing can be more basic than three sections that comprise[10] the ACT: Reading Comprehension, English and Math—the old three R's—Readin', 'Ritin' and 'Rithmetic! The 4th section, Science, is its own beast, but it largely combines text and chart reading skills—it has only a little to do with basic science knowledge.

The best thing about the ACT is that it's always the same:
1. The sections always occur in the same order.
2. There are always the same number of questions in each section.
3. There are always the same number of passage in the reading comprehension.
4. The types of passages are always the same and in the same order.
5. There are always the same number of experiments in the science section.
6. The essay is always last.

ACT Format

Section 1—English   75 Questions   45 minutes
                               5 passages   15 questions per passage

75 Multiple Choice

Four Choices per Question

The ENGLISH section of the ACT is confusingly named. It should really should be called the "Grammar" section because that is what it tests. For some reason, however, "grammar" is a dirty word in American education—as if asking students to know the mechanics of their own language is somehow unseemly. Although it's thought to be unseemly to teach grammar or call things "grammar," it's somehow *not* unseemly to tests students' grammar. Weird huh?

Well, don't fret! We're here to teach you grammar, and we even dare to call it "Grammar" [p. 33]. Though our grammar sometimes gets a little tricky, we promise that we'll give you a strong foundation without too many esoteric[11] rules and exceptions. We also promise that learning our grammar won't hinder your creativity or turn you into a word fascist—or afflict you with whatever other evils we stopped teaching grammar in the U.S. to avoid.

Section 2—Math   60 Questions   60 minutes

60 Multiple Choice Questions

Five Choices per Question

The MATH section on the ACT is fairly straightforward. A strong grasp of **Arithmetic**, **Algebra**, and **Geometry** will cover 95% of the test. The rest is reserved for advanced topics such as functions, trigonometry and matrices. Master the main topics and then worry about filling in the rest.

The biggest concern almost ALL students have on this section is with time [as with most sections]. We will help you master time on the math and organize your time better, so as to make it much, much less of a concern.[12]

[10] make up, consist of...
[11] hard to understand, highly specialized
[12] Too many kids end up obsessing about time on the math and most sections. That definitely doesn't help!

Section 3—Reading   40 Questions   35 minutes

Four Reading Passages

40 Multiple Choice Questions—Ten questions per section

Four Choices per Question

The READING section is comprised of four reading passages. These passages always occur in the same order.
   a. Fiction
   b. Social Sciences
   c. Humanities
   d. Natural Sciences

Since there are four passages and 35 minutes, you should allot about nine minutes per passage! That does not seem like a lot of time, but if you read well and briskly, you will have enough time. Although moving quickly is important, it is still important to read each passage well enough to grasp the Three T's we'll be telling you about. We'll also show you ways to find what you need to find quickly and how best to answer the questions.

Section 4—Science   40 Questions   35 minutes

Seven Experiments

40 Multiple Choice Questions—5-7 questions per section

Four Choices per Question

1. The SCIENCE section is comprised of seven passages with five, six, or seven questions each. Breaking it down, you should allot yourself five minutes per passage. With so little time for each, you must be very efficient in reading and processing what's going on.

2. The SCIENCE section does not really require much knowledge of science. Knowledge of science doesn't usually hurt, but sometimes it can if you hit on a topic you have recently covered in school and feel as if:

   a. you should know all about it,

   b. or think you do know all about it.

This first feeling is dangerous because it can lead you to get down on yourself for not having studied more or whatever. The second feeling can be dangerous because it may lead you to ignore the text in front of you, impose your own thoughts or, worse, half-knowledge on the topic at hand. Nothing is worse than partial knowledge! It is far better to:

   i.   simply read each experiment as if the topic it takes up is completely new to you,
   ii.   absorb and process the information given to you,
   iii. and then figure things out from there.

3. The SCIENCE section **does** require an ability to read and comprehend descriptions of experiments and studies, and an ability to read and comprehend charts, figures and graphs.

1ˢᵗ Ed. © ibidPREP llc

Section 5—Essay [optional] 40 minutes

The principal function of the ACT essay is to give admission offices something to compare your personal statement with to make sure you didn't hire William Shakespeare to write your personal statement while you write more like Cookie Monster [no offense Cookie Monster].

The essay on the ACT is optional, so not everyone will take it. Because it is optional, YOUR SCORE ON THE ESSAY DOES NOT AFFECT YOUR OVERALL AVERAGE (This means that, if you do choose to write an essay, then you will get a score for the multiple choice portion of your English test [the first section], a score for your essay and a combined score for your English and Reading multiple choice questions and your essay.) When your overall ACT score is calculated, it is calculated as an average of your English, Math, Reading and Science scaled scores. The English scaled score that is used to calculate the average is only ever the multiple choice scaled score. The ELA score, if you have one, is listed separately.

The essay itself is pretty straightforward. You are given a topical question and three general perspectives on that question. You are then asked to consider and analyze the three perspectives, in your own. Once you know how to answer a question, basic essay structure and how to proofread for grammar and punctuation, you should be fine and dandy!

PRACTICE TESTS

When you're ready to take a practice test...

Once you worked through the book a bit, reviewed and learned topics you'll need, and practiced a bit, you'll be ready for a practice test. You're welcome to take one through us, or on your own.

After you have finished, corrected and scored your test [or gotten your results from us], focus on the questions you get wrong [remember to give yourself a pat on the back for the ones you get right]. Don't just look at the correct answer to your incorrect questions, say "Oh yeah," and move on. Really analyze your mistakes and try to figure out why you made them in terms of the things discussed in this book. Did you rush? Did you skim? Did you panic because it looked difficult? Was it a subject/topic you need to go back and review? Tackle every wrong question one by one, and really try to grasp your errors on each, so that you don't continue to make those same errors for the rest of your test-taking life!

THE MOST IMPORTANT THING TO REMEMBER WHEN SCORING AND WHEN TAKING THE ACT IS THAT THERE IS NO PENALTY FOR WRONG ANSWERS. SO PUT DOWN AND ANSWER FOR EVERY QUESTION!

Scoring the Test

In order to score the ACT, first you must get a RAW SCORE. To do this, simply count all the correct answers in each section. Once you have a raw score for each section, find its scaled score equivalent in the table below. Do this for each of the sections, but use the second table to find a scaled score for your ENGLISH with WRITING section.

The combined score for the ENGLISH with WRITING score is based on your raw score for the ENGLISH multiple choice section AND your essay score. Your essay score is determined by two readers each of whom rate your essay on a scale 6 of for a total of 12 possible points. If you use the essay scoring guide to approximate your essay score, you can then approximate your ENGLISH with WRITING score by cross-indexing your ENGLISH score with your ESSAY score.

Once you have a scaled score for each section, you may evaluate how you did and figure out how to manage your test the next time around in order to do even better!

1st Ed. © ibidPREP llc

Scale Score Conversion Table

Scale score	English	Mathematics	Reading	Science	Scale Score
		Raw Score			
36	75	60	39-40	40	36
35	74	58-59	38	39	35
34	73	57	37	-	34
33	72	56	36	38	33
32	71	55	35	-	32
31	70	53-54	34	37	31
30	69	52	33	-	30
29	67-68	50-51	32	36	29
28	66	48-49	31	35	28
27	64-65	46-47	30	33-34	27
26	63	44-45	28-29	32	26
25	61-62	41-43	27	30-31	25
24	59-60	39-40	26	29	24
23	57-58	37-38	25	27-28	23
22	54-56	35-36	23-24	26	22
21	52-53	33-34	22	24-25	21
20	49-51	30-32	21	22-23	20
19	46-48	27-29	20	21	19
18	43-45	24-26	19	18-20	18
17	40-42	20-23	18	17	17
16	38-39	17-19	17	15-16	16
15	35-37	14-16	15-16	14	15
14	33-34	12-13	14	12-13	14
13	31-32	9-11	12-13	11	13
12	29-30	8	9-11	10	12
11	26-28	6-7	8	8-9	11
10	24-25	5	6-7	7	10
9	21-23	4	-	6	9
8	17-20	3	5	5	8
7	14-16	-	4	4	7
6	11-13	2	-	3	6
5	9-10	-	3	2	5
4	6-8	-	2	-	4
3	5	1	-	1	3
2	3-4	-	1	-	2
1	0-2	0	0	0	1

How to Break—20/25/30 etc...

The ACT curve functions more like a "bowl" curve then a bell curve within each section. The idea of what I call a bowl curve is that it aims to get the bulk of students to fall into and around the middle of the curve, the 18-20 range.

That means, for any section, the first few questions you get right on the test drop you quickly into the soup.[13] As you can see from the table below for all sections except the ENGLISH section the first and last quarter of the total questions correct are worth more on the scale. That is, it takes fewer right to get into the middle and fewer wrong to fall out of the top scores.

What does all this mean for you? Mostly:

- On the low end of the scale to start:
    - Be bold—
        - Answer every question
        - Take chances
        - Don't bail!
- At the high end of the scale looking for those last few points:
    - Take the extra care to make sure you're answering the right question
    - Slow down where necessary
    - Don't fritter away points on careless errors or because you checked out on a question or two.

	English			
	Questions Correct	Scale	Increase	Questions Correct
Quartile 1	0-19	1-8	8	0-15
Quartile 2	20-37	9-16	8	16-30
Quartile 3	38-56	16-24	9	31-45
Quartile 4	57-75	24-36	13	46-60

	Reading			
	Questions Correct	Scale	Increase	Questions Correct
Quartile 1	0-10	1-12	12	0-10

---

[13] Do not confuse the value of the questions in the scale with their value in the raw score. All questions are worth the **same** in terms of raw score. It's just that in terms of AMOUNT of questions you answer correctly, the first few and the last few you get correct are worth the most.

1st Ed. © ibidPREP llc

Time and the ACT

If you've ever had lox you know a few things about it.
1. It tastes great.
2. If you slice it and lay it on a plate, it won't move. It just kind of lies there, well, like a piece of lox.

The ACT is like a plate of sliced nova. It just sort of lays there unmoving and unchanging. Getting through it is a bit of a grind. It's up to you to keep things lively, to keep from zoning out and to keep plowing through the material. Once you have mastered the topics on this test, handling the questions from ACT to ACT is not a hard thing. There's nothing really to "get." You just have to tuck in, get to work and NOT WASTE TIME.

Not wasting time **does not mean**:
1. Hurrying
2. Not thinking

Not wasting time **does mean**:

1. Reading and processing all the words the first time through, so you don't have to go back endlessly and don't misread questions

2. Reading and processing all the answers, so you don't overlook the right ones or fall for the wrong ones

3. Don't wrestle with whether or not doing work or reading something is "worth it." If you see a way to do something, do it.

4. Don't try to recall formulas or definitions that have clearly escaped you. If you can't recall something in 5 seconds or fewer, it's not there. Move on.

5. Don't wrestle over answer choices.

6. Have in mind an answer before you go sifting through the multiple choices.

7. Eliminate bad, clearly wrong answers if you can't find your answer.

8. Guess the least wrong answer.

9. Start to become aware of when you stare off into space or read without really processing the words. We ALL do this. The only/best way out of this is to become aware of when it's happening and STOP YOURSELF. Reset and then continue reading.

10. Don't stare off into space looking for answers. The answers are on the page, in your pencil and in your mind. There are no clues floating in space or out the window.

EXTENDED or DOUBLE TIME Management—

Time is a large issue on the ACT. If you have regular time, it may be a challenge to finish all your sections even if you have a strong grip on the material. Since everyone could benefit from more time on this exam, the ACT organization makes it difficult to receive extra time. If you are granted extra time, the ACT allots you **one** extended time period in which to execute the *entire* exam.

Since there are no imposed time divisions by section, it is important for the student to determine how to break up his time. When you are practicing, see how long it takes you to do a section at natural relaxed pace. Build around that.

If you don't need all the time, don't feel compelled to use it. With extended or double time, it can be a VERY long test, so budget your energy to make sure you have something left for the SCIENCE section and the ESSAY.

| **Extended Time—** | **Five Sections (including essay)** | **6 hours** |
| **Double Time—** | **Five Sections** | **7 hours 10 minutes over two days** |

1st Ed. © ibidPREP llc

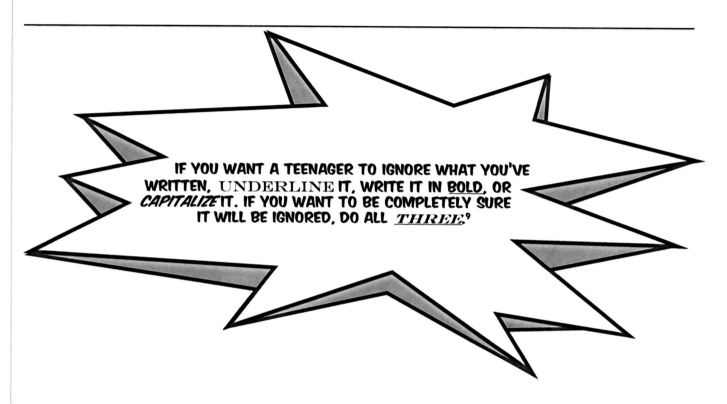

IF YOU WANT A TEENAGER TO IGNORE WHAT YOU'VE WRITTEN, UNDERLINE IT, WRITE IT IN <u>BOLD</u>, OR *CAPITALIZE* IT. IF YOU WANT TO BE COMPLETELY SURE IT WILL BE IGNORED, DO ALL *THREE*.[9]

Parents love this line because it's absolutely true. I have watched countless times as students get questions wrong and then discover that they had in effect answered the wrong question:

*Oh, they wanted the first number that was **NOT** a perfect square...*

*Damn, they wanted to know which was the **LEAST** like the author's main idea...*

*Oh, they wanted **PERIMETER** not **AREA**!*

Oops.

*Did they say **<u>EXCEPT</u>**?*

Oh.

HOW TO AVOID EXAMICIDE

PART I—CARTOON CATS & OTHER CREATURES!

1. THE CAT & THE RAKE

There is an old expression:
Fool me once, shame on you; fool me twice, shame on me.

For many of my students the rule seems to be:
Fool me a thousand times, and I'll keep coming back for more.

Some students make the same mistakes over and over and over again, which is why the makers of these tests are so fond of building the same pitfalls into every section. Think of those poor cartoon cats chasing the mouse through the yard. They've been around that backyard so many times that you'd think by now they would know there is going to be a rake lying in the grass just waiting for them to step on and thwack them in the head. Yet episode after episode, those cartoon cats step on the same darn rake. Don't be that cartoon cat.

2. WATER FLOWING DOWN A HILL

When contending with tests, think of yourself as water flowing down a hill [I swear this is as Zen as I'm gonna get]. When water hits a tree, it doesn't stop, head back up the hill or freak out; it merely finds a way around, under or over the tree. You should too. If your approach to a problem fails, try something else. If that doesn't work, find another hill.

I often ask my students what water flowing down a hill does when it hits a tree. Most answer the basic "Goes around," "Goes under," etc. When I asked one student, a broad-shouldered soccer player, what the water did when it encountered a tree, she told me: "It knocks the tree down." She did just fine on her tests.

1st Ed. © ibidPREP llc

HOW TO AVOID EXAMICIDE

3. ADRENALINE IS GOOD FOR ONLY THREE THINGS, NONE OF WHICH IS TEST—TAKING...

Adrenaline is a magical substance. In moments of danger, it can give us strength and energy unimaginable in ordinary circumstances. For teenagers who have so many other hormones raging in their system, adrenaline surges are fairly common occurrences. Only problem is adrenaline evolved to aid prehistoric man in peril, not 21st-century teens taking tests.

Adrenaline worked great in frightening situations when most of our frightening situations involved lions, tigers and bears or other dudes with spears. Now, however, most of our frightening situations involve accidentally posting those pics from spring break, forgetting to erase our texts or taking standardized tests. If a caveman left his cave in the morning and right outside the cave he saw a mountain lion, his brain would shut down and adrenaline would take over. Adrenaline would give his brain one of three simple commands for his body to execute: fight, flee or freeze. That means the dude could use the adrenaline to get mad strong, pick up a rock and bash the lion [Me Kill Test Before It Kill Me], use the adrenaline to power his legs and get the heck out of there [Me Rush Through Test Before It Kill Me] or stand very, very still in the hope that the lion would not notice him [Me Freeze and Completely Choke on Test, So Test Not Kill Me]. A little adrenaline bump will certainly perk you up and keep you going during test times, but a total surge is not good for most test situations because all your energy and strength is in your body and your mind is completely focused on fighting, fleeing or freezing, NOT solving complex problems.

SEE NEXT EXAMICIDE ON PAGE PAGE 296!

1st Ed. © ibidPREP llc

CHAPTER TWO

ENGLISH

1st Ed. © ibidPREP llc

Section 1—
English

75 Questions   45 minutes
5 passages   15 questions per passage

Four Choices per Question

MY DAD

MY DAD IS A VERY KIND AND LOVING MAN BUT NOT A NATURAL TEACHER. HE ALWAYS LOVED CARS AND WOULD TALK TO ME ABOUT THEM EVEN WHEN I WAS VERY LITTLE. HE WOULD TALK ABOUT MAKES AND MODELS AND ENGINES AND HORSEPOWER. I COULDN'T REALLY TALK TO HIM ABOUT CARS BECAUSE I HAD NO IDEA WHAT HE WAS TALKING ABOUT. I FELT LIKE I WAS LETTING LET HIM DOWN. IT ONLY OCCURRED TO ME YEARS LATER THAT I DIDN'T KNOW ANYTHING ABOUT CARS BECAUSE MOST 8 YEAR OLDS DON'T KNOW ANYTHING ABOUT CARS UNLESS SOMEONE TEACHES THEM. MY DAD FORGOT TO TEACH ME ABOUT CARS. IT'S THE SAME WITH GRAMMAR ON THE ACT. THE ONLY GRAMMAR MOST STUDENTS KNOW IS BY EAR, WHATEVER THEY SENSE IS RIGHT, BECAUSE NO ONE EVER TAUGHT THEM GRAMMAR!

How To Approach The English Section

1. **Don't read the passages first thing**. This is the one and only time I'll tell you NOT to read something fully or even at all. Reading word-for-word is vital for comprehending **ALL** forms of writing whether it be literature, history, social science, science or math. Word-for-word reading promotes a firmer grasp of the nuances[14] of content. **However**, the ENGLISH section is mostly <u>not</u> concerned with CONTENT. It is all about FORM. The form of a passage is HOW it is written, not what is being said [the CONTENT]. It is very important to begin to differentiate between FORM and CONTENT and to identify the way in which a piece is composed and its overall structure.

2. **Do read the passages when you have to!** Occasionally a question in the ENGLISH will ask you an EDIT-ING question regarding the ways in which the passage is written.

    Since these types of questions pertain to the CONTEXT and CONTENT, you will have to read for content

---

[14] subtle details

and context. If they ask for how they fit into the meaning of the overall passage, then you must read the passage for theme and thesis [see p. 258]. If they ask how a sentence fits into a paragraph, read the paragraph for theme and thesis. If they ask how two paragraphs fit together...read the paragraphs...you get the idea. Basically it means, that when I said don't read the passage, I was lying.

3. **Don't read the answers.** Many of the questions on the ENGLISH section focus on an underlined word or words and their attendant punctuation. The first thing to do here is look at the underlined part of the sentence and in the context of the sentence. Then determine:
    a. What, if anything, is wrong with it
    b. If NOTHING is wrong with it, Choose "A," NO CHANGE
    c. If something is wrong with the underlined selection, try to figure out the best way to fix it, THEN
    d. Look at the answers and see which choice is closest to your correction
    e. READ BACK

4. **Formal questions.** Not all questions are strictly grammatical. Some might ask you structural questions: ways to improve or reorder paragraphs. These questions often seem daunting, but are almost always asking basic questions about subject/predicate flow that is discussed in the grammar section. If you become aware of some simple rules of composition these questions become much more transparent. If not, they're great ones to skip!

    These questions might ask you about:
    a. The impact of deleting a particular sentence
    b. The impact of adding a particular sentence
    c. The function of a sentence in terms of the passage.
    d. How best to connect two paragraphs
    e. The best location for a sentence in a paragraph

    If the question asks you about placing a sentence in a new location, try it out in the new location, READ IT in its new place. The rule for connecting sentences is the same for connecting paragraphs, the front end or subject of a sentence or paragraph leads to its predicate or back end. This predicate usually becomes or ties into the the subject of the following sentence. Therefore, sentences need to connect back to front and back to front. It's the same for paragraphs: a paragraph starts with one topics that usually leads to a new one. Wherever the end of the paragraph gets to, that's the start of the following paragraph. And on and on! These are editing rules for the multiple choice, but they should also work well for your own writing [see The Essay, p. 309].

    YES or NO Questions—If you are asked to add or subtract text from the passage, you will probably then be asked if that change improved the content or made it less clear. You will almost be given two YES answers and two NO answers. Of course, if you think that the addition was a good thing, that doesn't mean you're going to pick the first YES answer does it? You know better than that. Don't you?? Once you've decided that your answer is YES, then read both YES answers very closely, or better yet, figure out for yourself why the new text [or deletion of text] improves the passage and then read the two YES answers.

5. **Vocab questions.** There are very few direct vocabulary questions on the ACT. Of course, the broader your vocabulary, the easier reading comprehension can be, etc. Also, the easier some ENGLISH questions will be! Occasionally, a passage will have a word or words underlined in it, and you will be asked which of the answer choice words would NOT be an apt[15] replacement for that word in context in the sentence. What the question is really asking, is which of the words in the choices is NOT a synonym.

---

[15] appropriate, suitable

1st Ed. © ibidPREP llc

For example:

Every time I <u>hail</u> a taxi, I feel like royalty!

Ex 1. Which of the words below is NOT a suitable substitute for "hail"?
    A. signal
    B. hire
    C. flag
    D. wave for

The key to these questions is being aware of alternate definitions and NOT forcing close meanings.

Alternate definitions: In this question, you might want to pick "flag" right away because at first glance it looks like it has nothing to do with hail. However, "flag" as a verb means "wave" or "signal!"

Even if you didn't know "flag" also meant "signal," you should be very rigorous[16] with the word "hire." "Hire" is close to what you want but it is not a true synonym. That is, we <u>hail</u> a cab in order to <u>hire</u> it for a ride, but <u>hailing</u> a cab is not the same thing as <u>hiring</u> a cab. One thing leads to another; they are related, but they are NOT the same. In this case, as with most all vocabulary type questions, close is wrong—pick B!

      WORDS WITH SNEAKY ALTERNATIVE DEFINITIONS.

6. **English Section; Timing**. As with ALL sections of ALL tests, you might feel that if you need to slow down and think then you're doing something wrong and WASTING TIME. This thought could not be further from the truth. If you determine your answer BEFORE sifting through the multiple choices, then YOU SAVE TIME. Also, if you stop to read the sentences you need to read in the FORMAL questions and read back any revised orders or newly added sentences in context, then you'll save time on those AND get a lot more correct. However, if you do find yourself consistently running out of time on the ENGLISH section and you often have trouble on the FORMAL questions, then those are the ones to skip.

Don't worry if you have trouble with the FORMAL questions because:

---

[16] exact, thorough

1st Ed. © ibidPREP llc

ENGLISH

AKA

GRAMMAR

1ˢᵗ Ed. © ibidPREP llc

When we teach reading, we teach the ABCs; when we teach math, we teach the 1, 2, 3s; but when we teach writing, for some reason, we do not teach nouns, verbs and adjectives, or spelling, or how to make sentences connect to each other. Instead, we teach students how to say ABSOLUTELY NOTHING over the pre-scribed length of an assignment [which is really the only thing most kids end up caring about when they write: how long does it have to be?] Yuck.

Imagine a world in which students are taught certain rules about the words they are meant to write with and certain rules about how to put those words together! Imagine a world in which students are taught to mine their thoughts and lay them out in an ordered fashion!! Imagine. It's easy if you try.

Below, I will give you the benefit of our brief but extremely clear grammar recipe. If you learn and follow it, not only will you do better on grammar questions, not only will you write better and with greater focus, not only will you learn to proofread your work for grammar and sense, but you will also end up having a better handle on English grammar than 92% of your fellow citizens, including the grown-ups [Stufact!].

How to Learn Grammar—It's WRITING, not SOUNDING

The thing to remember about grammar is that it is a measure of **WRITTEN** English, not **SPOKEN** English. Spoken English relies on a lot of implied meaning and, often, what *sounds* good or right. But since no one is around to explain what has just been said, **written** English needs to follow certain rules in order to be clear. As a result, what **sounds** right may be wrong, and what sounds weird or awkward may be 100% correct.

Which are correct?

- Beth is taller than her. / Beth is taller than she.
- I feel badly for you. / I feel bad for you.
- There is competition between the teams in the league. / There is competition among the teams in the league.
- Just between you and I, this test sucks. / Just between you and me, this test sucks.

If you go by how things sound on the questions above, you would probably be wrong every single time: the second option is the right one in each example! We explain below...

Before you learn the grammar of what is, for many of you, your *native* tongue [for heaven's sake!], you need to learn the basic building blocks of our grammar, the parts of speech.

Parts of Speech

Noun
- person, place, thing, idea:
    - chef, mall, bat, freedom

Proper Noun
- particular person, place, thing or idea:
    - George, Nevada, Coke, Communist

Verbs
- Action words [he **runs**, she **has**, they swam] **+**
    - Being verbs and the verb "to be" [I **am** short]

	To Be	
	Singular	Plural
1	am/was	are/were
2	are/were	are/were
3	is/was	are/were

Linking Verbs

- These are verbs that describe **how** we notice things through our senses or **how** things change from one way of being to another....
  - *appear, taste, smell, feel, look, sound, grow [when it means "become," not "get bigger"], seem, remain, become*
  - I **remained** still while the nurse removed the splinter from my foot.
  - The jester **seemed** crazy.
  - The jester's laugh **sounds** creepy.
  - I **grow** tired of your whining.

Verb Tenses

- The basic verb tenses are easy. You probably already knew that the verbs in the sentences below agree with their subjects.

The coat **hangs** in the closet.
The cats **played** with the mice.
The house of cards **shook**.

Passive Voice

- In English, we prefer to have our subjects be the **active** partners, the nouns that are performing the verbs. Passive constructions, in which the subject is being acted upon, are not technically ungrammatical, but they are less powerful

YES: John Guare wrote *Six Degrees of Separation*.
NO: *Six Degrees of Separation* was written by John Guare.

YES: The dog was wagging its tail.
NO: The tail was being wagged by the dog.

When it comes to active voice, try to avoid having too many "ing" words [aka "gerunds"] lead off your sentences. Especially "being."

YES: Being that we were hungry, we got pizza.
NO: We were hungry, so we got pizza.

Parallel Structure

- This is one of the main concepts of grammar. Any time you have consecutive actions in a list, all the verbs must be in the same form and tense. Parallel structure also holds true for lists of nouns, adjectives or anything else—all items must be in the same form.

NO: After school, I like to change my clothes, eat a snack and doing my homework.
YES: After school, I like to change my clothes, eat a snack and do my homework.

Adjectives

- Words that modify [describe] nouns:
  - The **blue** hat
  - The **delicious** burger
  - The **angry** leprechaun

Adverbs

- Words that modify verbs, adjectives AND other adverbs.
  - The boy ran **quickly.**

1ˢᵗ Ed. © ibidPREP llc

- She wore a **pale** blue hat. ["pale" modifies the adjective "blue"]
- He ate a **red** hot chili pepper. ["red" modifies the adverb "hot" which is itself an adverb modifying "chili" which is an adjective describing "pepper"—whew!]

How do you know when it's an adverb modifying an adjective and not just two adjectives strung together? If you see a comma between the modifiers, they are distinct [separate] adjectives. If there's no comma, then the first word is the adverb modifying the following word. E.g.,

- *The still, dark night* means the night was still AND dark.
- *The still dark night* means the night continues to be dark.

One of the reasons teachers became loath[17] to teach grammar was due to the weight of exceptions. Kids love rules/hate exceptions because they require thought. Ugh.

Luckily, there are far fewer exceptions of consequence in English grammar than there are in English spelling, which truly is bonkers and rule-resistant.

WHY WE HATE GRAMMAR

EXCEPTION #1: WHEN WE DON'T USE ADVERBS

There are times when we don't use adverbs. Pay attention to the following scenarios. **Linking verbs** [verbs dealing with the senses] **do not** take adverbs; they take adjectives instead.

Modifying the Five Senses [Especially Important for the Essays That Ask for *Sensory* Detail]

1. ***Feel:*** [emotions vs. touch] Mary feels **bad** about your pain.

   If Mary felt "badly," that would mean that there was something wrong with her fingers and she couldn't feel things properly when she touched them. In other words, "badly" used here would be referring to/modifying her ability to touch. If you're having trouble understanding this point, try replacing "badly" with another adverb. If you say, "I feel greatly," that doesn't really make sense, does it?

2. ***Smell:*** [scent vs. smelling] I just took a shower; I smell good. / The perfumer smells excellently; he can tell what kind of cologne you are wearing in an instant.

3. ***Look:*** [appearance vs. seeing] That piece of pizza sure looks good. / Make sure you look over the contract well.

4. ***Sounds/Hear:*** That song sounds good. / I haven't been able to hear well since touring with my band.

5. ***Taste:*** The rabbit stew tastes good. / The food critic accurately tastes all the spices in the dish

---

[17] resistant to, dread

ADVERB   ABUSE

SOME PEOPLE ... GROW UP ... NOT USING ... ADVERBS TOO OFTEN IN THEIR EVERYDAY SPEECH AND WRITING. THEY GET IN THE HABIT OF SAYING THINGS LIKE: "I DID GOOD," "HE EATS FAST," "SHE RAN SO QUICK..." SOMETIMES LATER IN LIFE [LIKE IN COLLEGE], THESE PEOPLE DISCOVER THE BEAUTY AND PURPOSE OF ADVERBS. OFTEN, LIKE A COOK WHO HAS JUST DISCOVERED SPICES, THEY THEN START SPRINKLING THEM ON EVERYTHING.

MY FAVORITE OVERUSE OF ADVERBS PERTAINS TO THE WORD "FEEL," AS IN ONE'S EMOTIONAL STATE. A LOT OF LATE ADVERB LEARNERS LOVE TO SAY, "I FEEL BADLY ABOUT THAT." I FEEL BAD THAT THEY FEEL COMPELLED TO DO THAT. PRESIDENT BILL CLINTON, WHO GREW UP IN RURAL ARKANSAS [PROBABLY NOT A HOTBED OF ADVERB USE], SAYS, "I FEEL BADLY." NO ONE HAS HAD THE TEMERITY[18] TO TELL HIM HE'S WRONG, SO PLEASE DON'T FEEL BAD [AND DEFINITELY DON'T FEEL BADLY] IF YOU MAKE THE SAME MISTAKE!

BEING/BECOMING EXCEPTION

The verb "to be" and other verbs of becoming **do not** take ad-verbs; it takes adjectives instead. That's because the modifiers correspond to the subject, not the verb.

- I am fast [not "I am quickly"].
- That song seemed slow.
- He is loud.
- Those potato chips are excellent.
- He became tired.

PRONOUNS—
The MOST IMPORTANT PART of ACT GRAMMAR

Pronouns are generic[19] words that take the place of specific nouns. The noun that a pronoun replaces is called its "antecedent." It is always important, as a reader, to be able to identify the antecedent of a pronoun; like-wise, as a writer, it is your job to make sure your writing is free of ambiguity and that antecedents are easily identified. ("The novel's plot is tedious, as is the writing style. It could definitely use some improvement." What does "it" refer to? The novel's plot, or its writing style? Or the novel as a whole? Don't confuse your readers!)

Types of Pronouns

There are many, many kinds of pronouns in the world of grammar, but the ones you most have to concern

18 nerve, chutzpah, boldness
19 universal, all-purpose

1st Ed. © ibidPREP llc

yourself with here are subject and object pronouns.

Subject Pronouns replace nouns that function as the subject.
Object Pronouns replace nouns that function as the object.

Here's a table of the subject and object pronouns for you to learn.

Subject Pronouns:		Object Pronouns:	
I	We	Me	Us
You	You	You	You
He/She/It/Who	They	Him/Her/It/Whom	Them

Now that you know which are subject pronouns and which are object pronouns, you should learn what the subjects and object of the sentence are.

Subjects & Objects And How To Find Them

Not all nouns are subjects but **all** subjects are nouns! A noun can be either a "subject" or an "object," depending on its relationship with the verb. The subject of a sentence [or a clause—more on that later] is the noun that is performing the action. Usually in English, the subject comes before its verb and is toward the beginning of the sentence.

> **Betty** eats cake for breakfast. /**Lou** likes toad-racing. /**We** are family.

Occasionally in English, however, the subject comes after its verb.

> There are three **things** that I like. /Here are **a key and a hat** for you. /[Weird, huh?]

Sentences can contain more than one verb and so can have more than one subject. Each verb gets a subject even if it's just implied:

> Get over here!

> [the subject is whoever is getting bossed around there]

When there's more than one verb in a sentence, get in the habit of determining the subject for each one [I was just bossing you around in that sentence!].

Objects

Objects are easy: whatever nouns aren't subjects are objects! Put another way: a noun that is not performing the action of the sentence [or clause] but is being affected by the action is an object.

> Betty eats **cake** for **breakfast**.

> Lou likes **toads**.

In the above sentences, "cake," "breakfast" and "toads" are objects.

<u>**SPOT THE SUBJECT/OBJECT**</u>
Underline the subject and object. Put an (s) next to the subject.

1. Billy ate a gyro.

2. The gyro was on whole wheat pita.

3. The gyro tasted like heaven.

4. There are few things that taste as good as a well-made gyro.

5. I like that Billy was willing to try this cool food.

6. Billy is a cool kid.

Special Singular Pronouns—Be on the Lookout!

Singular pronouns such as *everyone, no one, none* and *one* all take singular pronouns. That means if you want to write:

Everyone knows _____ must learn how to write better,

the pronoun in the blank must be *one, he, she* or *he or she*, NOT *they*. No matter how much sense *they* makes [it maintains gender neutrality for everyone and is so much less clumsy], *everyone* is singular, so the pronoun replacing it must also be singular. If you catch this in your writing, it will signal serious grammar chops!

Other Singular Pronouns

There is a whole boatload of what I call special singular pronouns which, when you write them, might make you want to pair them with plural pronouns, but they actually take singular pronouns. Most of them, helpfully, have singular words in them like "one," "body," and "thing." Here's a sampling of the most used ones, and since there is a whole boatload of them, we'll use the mnemonic device, ONSEA, to remember them.

O—one,
N—no body, no one, neither*, none
S—somebody, someone
E—everybody, everyone, either*, each
A—anybody, anyone

1ˢᵗ Ed. © ibidPREP llc

Exception #3—Subject Pronouns/Object Pronouns

Pronouns are especially difficult to use when we're making comparisons. Consider which of the following two sentences is right:

I am cooler than[20] he. OR I am cooler than him.

In normal speech, most people would say, "I am cooler than him." Again, if this were the **Sounding Section,** they'd be right. However, this is GRAMMAR, and according to the rules of WRITTEN grammar, in a comparison, both nouns [things being compared] are considered **subject** nouns, so both take **subject pronouns.**

So...the correct answer is: I am cooler than he!

Here's a trick for understanding this odd rule. Because both "I" and "he" are subjects, they must both have verbs. But, you say, there's only one verb here, "am," and it definitely does not go with "he." That's true. But that's just because we cut off the second verb.

What we're *really* saying is this: *I am cooler than he [is]!*

You would never say, "I am cooler than him is," so that's why you do NOT say "I am cooler than him." Just put in that missing verb yourself, and you'll see that the subject actually sounds better than the object.

Exception #4—Subject Pronouns/Object Pronouns

Another challenging application of the subject/object pronoun rule involves that "to be" verb.

Believe it or not, we do not write:

It is me!

We write:

It is I!

Sounds awful and pretentious, but that's English.

The Great ACT Neither*/Either** Trick

When *either* and *neither* are used alone in a sentence, they are always singular

Neither walks to school/*Either* is a good choice.

However, when *neither* and *either* are used in conjunction with the nouns to which they are referring, then the number[21] of the verb is determined by the second noun mentioned. That means:

Neither my mother nor my after **is** home.
But
Either my brother or my parents **are** at school.

However, on the ACT, the second noun WILL NEVER BE PLURAL!! Why? Because most kids think that when they see either or neither listed with their nouns that the verb should be plural, SO most kids would pick ARE for both sentence 1 **and** 2. So, in effect, if the test did have a sentence with a plural second choice, then students would be accidentally getting it right—or getting it right for the wrong reason. The test HATES that, Soooooo—anytime you see NEITHER and EITHER on the WRITING SECTION, they will ALWAYS take singular verbs!

---

[20] Whenever you see the word "than" you know you have a comparison.
[21] When we say a verb "agrees" with its subject, we mean that it has the right "number" and tense —i.e., the verb is singular or plural if the subject is singular or plural, and the verb takes place in the right time period (past, present, future, etc.)

Practice

PRONOUNS
Choose the correct pronoun.

1. Between you and me/I this is a terrible drill.

2. Suzie is taller than he/him.

3. A person who likes baloney should have his/their head examined.

4. Some people think they are better than we/us.

5. None of us/we went hungry.

6. Which are your favorites? These are they/them.

7. My mother is afraid of me/my[22] getting hurt playing football.

8. They gave the balls to them/they.

9. Ashton smells better than she/her.

10. Who is it? It is I/me!

11. To Carly and I/me, his story sounded fishy.

12. Give the burger to they're/their friends.

PRONOUNS & ANTECEDENTS
The ACT English Section is really into pronouns. One of the things it tests often is a student's ability to determine which pronouns go with which antecedents and whether or not they are the correct pronouns for the job. In the sentences below, circle the pronoun and underline its antecedent.

1. Maurita always forgets to do her homework.

2. If the fire department faces any more budget cuts, it will be seriously hampered.

3. Matthew and I wanted to go to the pool, but we had to stay and clean the house instead.

4. Ernesto thought his teacher would give him a B on the test, but she gave him an A instead.

5. The program helps citizens learn their rights.

6. Anyone who wants to look better on the beach should improve her diet and exercise now!

---

[22] This is tricky. Gerund ("ing" words) phrases take possessive pronouns because your mother is not afraid of <u>you</u> as you're getting hurt. Your mother is afraid your getting hit.

DON'T ABUSE THE "I"

ANOTHER COMMON ERROR PEOPLE MAKE WHEN THEY START WANTING TO USE GOOD GRAMMAR IS OVERUSING "I." PEOPLE WHO GROW UP SPEAKING WITH LESS THAN PERFECT GRAMMAR OFTEN UNDERUSE "I": ME AND MOM WENT TO THE MALL, MY FRIEND AND ME ATE PIE...YOU GET THE IDEA. ONCE THESE PEOPLE FIND OUT THAT IT'S "MY MOM AND I...," "MY FRIEND AND I...," ETC., THEY START STICKING "I" IN EVERYWHERE, INCLUDING INTO PREPOSITIONAL PHRASES AND THE OBJECTS OF THE SENTENCES WHERE THEY DON'T BELONG!

YES: HE GAVE THE BALL TO MY FRIEND AND ME.
NO: HE GAVE THE BALL TO MY FRIEND AND I.

YES: THERE ARE MANY DIFFERENCES BETWEEN MY TWIN AND ME.
NO: THERE ARE MANY DIFFERENCES BETWEEN MY TWIN AND I.

Prepositions

Prepositions are words that describe the relationship between a subject and an object. The relation generally refers to location, direction or time—or possession.

The dog is **under** the tree.

"Under" tells us where the dog is in relation to the tree.

The cat came **from** the house.

"From" tells us the direction in which the cat is moving.

After the party, the house was a mess.

"After" tells us when the house was a mess.

The friends **of** the cat and dog wrecked the house.

"Of" tells us the friend belonged to the cat and dog.

Grammar

There are many words that may be used as prepositions. Fortunately, only [only!] about 48 are in common use. The highlighted ones in the box below are words that at first do not seem like prepositions. [Learn to know them on sight.]

About	Among	Beneath	During	Into	Over	Until
Above	Around	Beside	Except	Like	Since	Up
Across	At	Between	For	Near	Through	Upon
After	Before	Beyond	From	Of	To	With
Against	Behind	By	In	Off	Toward	Within
Along	Below	Down	Inside	On	Under	Without

Prepositions always take **objects**, never subjects. So:

NEVER   *Between you and I*
ALWAYS   *Between you and me*

NEVER   *Math is the hardest subject for him and I*
ALWAYS   *Math is the hardest subject for him and me*

Conjunctions

There are a lot of different kinds of conjunctions out there. The main ones we are interested in are called *co-ordinating conjunctions*—these are your basic conjunctions:

For, And, Nor, But, Or, Yet, So—aka FANBOYS! But remember—

- ***And, Nor, Or*** are NOT conjunctions when they are part of a list or grouping—Jack ***and*** Jill / beer, wine ***and*** sangria / neither Jack ***nor*** Jill / either beer ***or*** wine.

- ***For*** is a conjunction when it means **because.** It is not a conjunction when it's acting like a preposition.

    Conjunction: I went to the store, for the books were on sale.

    Preposition: I went to the bookstore for the book sale.

- ***Yet*** is not a conjunction when it means, "now" or "at this time."

1ˢᵗ Ed. © ibidPREP llc

CONJUNCTION JUNCTION AND THE REST OF SCHOOLHOUSE ROCK

HERE'S ONE OF THOSE THINGS THAT MAKES MY BRAIN POP. ENTIRE GENERATIONS OF KIDS KNOW ABOUT CONJUNCTIONS BECAUSE OF THOSE SWEET, DELIGHTFUL SCHOOLHOUSE ROCK COMMERCIALS THAT RAN IN TANDEM WITH SATURDAY MORNING CARTOONS FOR YEARS. IMAGINE WHAT WE COULD TEACH CHILDREN [AND ADULTS ON THE SLY] IF WE HAD, YOU KNOW, SAY MORE THAN ONE SET OF CONSISTENTLY REPEATED ENTERTAINING EDUCATIONAL COMMERCIALS ON A CONTINUOUS BASIS! PEOPLE MIGHT FIND OUT HOW MANY SENATORS THEY HAVE, WHAT THE 3/5 COMPROMISE REALLY MEANT, WHERE CANADA IS, ETC.

Interrupters

What the heck is an *interrupter*? An interrupter interrupts!

All of you, *by all means*, eat more cheese!

Heck, we all want more cheese!

However, you stink!

When an interrupter interrupts, it is followed by or contained within commas.

Practice

CLASSIFY PARTS OF SPEECH
Part A: Please classify each of the following as a noun, proper noun, verb, adjective, or adverb.

1. Last week, I played my favorite <u>game</u>. _____

2. I really love playing <u>Apples to Apples</u> because it involves logical thinking. _____

3. The <u>whale</u> is an important character in Moby Dick. _____

4. You're a <u>funny</u> person, but your jokes don't always hit the mark. _____

5. Last week I went to a <u>play</u>, which included a section when a randomly chosen spectator gets to <u>play</u> a uku-lele _____ / _____

6. I <u>am</u> a jolly guy, who loves to bake flan. _____

7. If you're going to make the train, you'd better start moving <u>quickly</u>. _____

8. The plot of my favorite movie moves <u>slowly</u>, but it's an interesting four-hour film. _____

9. Koalas are <u>slow</u> creatures that can take over an hour to navigate a single tree branch. _____

10. Although that wasn't the <u>correct</u> answer, your effort is appreciated. _____

11. <u>Thomas</u> is planning a party that will be held at an old factory on the outskirts of the city. _____

12. I had a terrible cough, so I went to my <u>doctor</u>. _____

13. I always enjoy my visits to <u>Dr. McKay</u> because he always gives his patients lollipops. _____

14. Margo is a <u>much</u> better dancer than I am. _____

15. My favorite <u>number</u> is 20, and I always take the opportunity to use it when I <u>number</u> books at the library. _____ / _____

16. On <u>Saturday</u>, I plan to go to the movies and then to the museum. _____

17. I always get sad in <u>November</u> because I know winter is approaching. _____

18. I went to <u>France</u> when I was in high school, but I didn't speak the language well enough to communicate with the locals. _____

19. Mary <u>frantically</u> rifled thorough her purse to find the keys to her apartment. _____

20. <u>Yo Gabba Gabba</u> is a show that is popular among children. _____

Part B: Please list the conjunctions in FANBOYS:

F _____

A _____

N _____

B _____

O _____

Y _____

S _____

1ˢᵗ Ed. © ibidPREP llc

PARTS OF THE SENTENCE

Every sentence must contain a verb and a subject. That's it! In fact, in English sentences, the shorter the better. Some sentences may even have only one word. When the verb is a command, the subject is implied in the verb:

> Stop! [It is implied that someone should stop.]

If, in your writing, you find yourself tacking together clause upon clause with lots of phrases sprinkled in among your sentence, START ANOTHER SENTENCE. They're free!

Phrases

A phrase is a group of words that contains **neither** a subject **nor** a verb. Phrases provide additional information about the material in the sentence but have no overall impact on the rest of the sentence they live in.

My brother, by the way, is an idiot.

"By the way" is a phrase that tells you this is incidental[23] info about my brother. If you get rid of that phrase, you still have a grammatically fine [if troubling] sentence:

My brother is an idiot.

Prepositional Phrases

All prepositional phrases begin with prepositions. Prepositional phrases combine a preposition + an object of the preposition [since there are no *subjects* of the preposition]. **Since phrases do not contain either subjects or verbs, they have NO impact on the number or tense of the verbs in the sentence [subject / verb agreement].** Which of these is correct?

> Each of the boys **is** tired.
> OR
> Each of the boys **are** tired.

Here, "of the boys" is the prepositional phrase, so it **cannot** contain the subject. In fact, to avoid getting confused, whenever you see a prepositional phrase in a sentence, put parentheses around it and <u>then</u> look for the subject. In this case, "Each (of the boys) is/are tired," the only word left that could be the subject is the word "each." "Each," unlike "boys," is singular [a singular pronoun in thise case], sooo...the answer is:

> Each of the boys <u>**is**</u> tired.

Pronouns in Prepositional Phrases

Since the nouns in prepositional phrases are never the subject of the sentence, the pronouns inside prepositional phrases are NEVER subject pronouns.

> Between you and me, this test sucks.
> OR
> Between you and I, this test sucks.

---

[23] Less important

As we know from our chart, "between" is a preposition, so "between you and ___" is a prepositional phrase, *sooooo* you have to put an OBJECT pronoun in it, *sooooo* the correct answer is:

Between you and me, this test sucks.

SUBJECT, PREPOSITION & VERB—PART 1
Put parentheses around the prepositional phrase or phrases [if any] in each sentence.

1. Gerald lives above St. Nicholas.
2. Nina's desk is against the wall.
3. When Sylvia goes to class, she always sits between Shakima and me.
4. In the sand-covered parking lot, the tour bus idled as the group stopped to picnic on the beach.
5. I like all kinds of fruit except tomatoes.
6. I am now a health nut; I have not eaten a hot dog since I was a little kid.
7. In the 1950's, the United States of America made cars for the world.
8. Please do not talk during the movie.
9. My brother and I like to ride our bikes around the block.
10. It is hard to believe there is another state across the Hudson River.

SUBJECT, PREPOSITION & VERB—PART 2
For each sentence below,
   • Place parenthesis around all prepositional phrases.
   • Underline the verb or verbs in each sentence and connect each to its respective subject.

1. The pack of cards is on the table.
2. The basketball went through the window and under the couch.
3. Across the street from my apartment, there are a grocery store and a dry cleaners.
4. Julio, the ballet dancer from Montreal, has been studying Mandarin Chinese since 2010.
5. Because she did so well in high school, Liz has many colleges among which to choose.
6. Unfortunately, each of the movies that David wanted to see was playing during the test.
7. Off in the distance, three pigeons, speckled with coal dust, perched upon the roof.
8. After mowing the lawn, my mom drove Kevin and me to the mall in her pink Cadillac.
9. Darren amazed his friends and bet Betty that she also would not be able to figure out his magic trick.
10. The prize, a trip to Paris, a treat beyond my wildest dreams, dangled before my eyes.
11. All along the watchtower, princes kept the view.
12. Detailed study of the coverage of the event exposed a certain bias in the reporting.

1st Ed. © *ibidPREP llc*

Clauses

Clauses are groups of words that contain a subject AND a verb [the opposite of phrases, which contain neither]. There are two principal types of clauses:

TYPE 1: Dependent Clause—Contains a verb and a subject [stated or implied] but cannot stand alone as a sentence; it must be joined to an independent clause. When a sentence **begins** with a dependent clause it HAS TO BE set off by a comma:

Waking up this morning, I heard the telephone ring.

Immediately following the comma, the independent clause MUST start with the implied subject of the dependent clause. The subject must be in subject form, not possessive or anything else:

YES   *After seeing the movie, John did not like Jennifer Lawrence as much as he once did.*

NO   *After seeing the movie, Jennifer Lawrence was no longer John's favorite.*

YES   *While leaping a tall building in a single bound, Superman smiled at Lois.*

NO   *While leaping a tall building in a single bound, Superman's cape fluttered in the breeze as he smiled at Lois.*

TYPE 2: Independent Clause—These can stand alone as their own sentences, but they don't have to!

The monkey laughed.

Or:

When the dog barked, the monkey laughed.

• An independent clause must immediately restate the subject of the dependent clause (or modifying phrase) linked to the front of it.

*When he hit his keeper with poop, **the monkey** laughed.*

- If two independent clauses are joined together in a sentence, they must be connected either by a **comma with a conjunction** or the mysterious **semicolon** (without a conjunction).

*The monkey laughed, **and** the zookeeper cried.*

The monkey laughed; the zookeeper cried.

Building Sentences

As you combine clauses and phrases to make sentences, please be careful to use parallel structure and to avoid the passive voice. (p. 26)

Practice

PHRASES AND CLAUSES PRACTICE
Please give two examples of PHRASES.

1. _____

2. _____

Can these PHRASES stand alone as sentences?

_____

Please give two examples of DEPENDENT CLAUSES.

1._____

2._____

Can these DEPENDENT CLAUSES stand alone as sentences?

_____

Please give two examples of INDEPENDENT CLAUSES.

1._____

2._____

Can these INDEPENDENT CLAUSES stand alone as sentences?

_____

1st Ed. © ibidPREP llc

PUNCTUATION

Commas

At last the secrets are revealed!

Let's be honest. Besides using commas to separate items in a list, most of us have NO idea when to use them. Most students drop them into sentences whenever they feel it may have gone on too long or where they feel a breath should be taken or just 'cause! Wrong, wrong and wrong.

If you were marking a speech you were giving, you might put a comma in to remind yourself where to pause for breath. But again, reading isn't speaking, and you don't need to tell your reader when to breathe. She can figure that out all by herself.

HERE IS A LIST OF WHAT COMMAS <u>ARE</u> FOR:

1. To separate a dependent clause at the start of a sentence from the rest of the sentence:
     When I woke up this morning, I heard the phone ring.
2. To separate a long prepositional phrase or phrases at the start of sentence from the rest of the sentence:
     After a night of dancing, Cinderella needed a rest.
3. To separate items in a list of nouns, verbs, or adjectives:
     The hats, coats and scarves were in a pile on the bed.

     After school I like to change clothes, eat a snack and draw stuff.

     It was a cold, dark, stormy, scary, dread-filled night.

     You may also put a comma before the "and" in a list, but I prefer not to because that confuses things with:
4. To separate independent clauses linked by conjunctions:
     I like cake, and I like soda.

     I like cake, but I hate pudding.
5. To set off appositive [descriptive] phrases within or at the end of sentences:
     My brother, the one in Boulder, likes rocks.

     Genie, the devil, loves grammar.

     There's nothing better than sleep-away camp, which is usually a bug-infested swamp of adolescent and pre-ad-olescent angst[24].
6. To separate out interrupters or exclamations:
     ***<u>However,</u>** I disagree.*

     *There are, **<u>nevertheless,</u>** many things still to learn.*

     ***<u>Holy guacamole,</u>** Batman is in trouble!*
7. To set off a quotation:
     John said, "I do not want to go school today."

     "But you must, " answered his mother, "because an education is a wonderful thing.

HERE IS A LIST OF WHAT COMMAS ARE <u>NOT</u> FOR:

1. Don't add a comma before a conjunction when you are NOT adding a new subject or repeating the old one.

     Yes: I ate lunch with my friends and worked on my book all afternoon.
     No: I ate lunch with my friends, and worked on my book all afternoon.

---

[24] Anxiety; unease

Yes: I ate lunch with my friend, and I worked on my book all afternoon.

2. Don't add a comma just because you've been writing for a while and haven't used one.

3. Don't add a comma where you think the reader might want to pause or catch her breath.

4. Joining two independent clauses by themselves. This is called a **comma splice** and it is wrong.

   NO: I like to eat hoagies, you like to eat subs.

   YES: I like to eat hoagies, and you like to eat subs.

   YES: I like to eat hoagies. You like to eat subs.

   YES: I like hoagies; you like subs.

5. You don't have to add a comma before the "and" in a list. That's just what British people do.

   GOOD: Bobo likes to eat, run, and poop.

   BETTER: Bobo likes to eat, run and poop.

All of the commas in the following paragraph have been removed. Read through it and insert commas where they are needed based on the rules you just read.

Did you notice the title of this book? Did you notice what was wrong with it? Or did you think the title was **Remain Calm**? *Don't be embarrassed if you did. MANY people grown-ups and kids alike make the same mistake. Why? Well the brain wants the title to make sense. Remain Calm makes sense; Remain Clam doesn't. Also most of us only glance or skim things like titles instructions or epigraphs [which is what this paragraph is]. If we do read more closely we might read too quickly or too anxiously and flip letters automatically. This is what some dyslexic people do and when we're stressed we all become a little bit dyslexic: letters switch negatives and positives flip and up becomes down. So? Why does this matter? It matters because test makers on every level are all too aware of this tendency which is especially common in young minds. They know if you feel rushed stressed or distracted that you'll be prone to miss details get things backwards or answer the question you imagine rather than the one on the page. That means it is VERY important that you find a way to quiet your mind focus on ALL the words and by all means no matter what Remain Clam!*

Done? Check your commas against the epigraph on the first page of this book!

The Mysterious Semicolon

Semicolons are not so mysterious after all. Their main purpose is to allow you to connect two independent clauses WITHOUT using a conjunction, so you can write:

Studatuta likes hot dogs, so he's fat.
Studatuta likes hot dogs; he's fat.

Semicolons are great for linking two VERY closely related independent clauses—such as those pertaining to my love of hot dogs and my weight!

One more use of semicolons: if you have a list of items that start with:

The Mysterious Colon

Even less mysterious than the semicolon is its big, two-buttoned cousin, the colon. The colon does two closely related jobs.

1. Colons introduce lists and examples.

   These are my favorite things: dog bites, bee stings and pies.

2. Colons also provide a singular example, presenting it with a sort of ta-da! effect. Sort of like this:

   There is one thing I like best in the whole world: pizza!

1st Ed. © ibidPREP llc

COMMAS
Write each sentence correctly adding commas as needed.

1. Darrin likes to eat to drink and to fly kites.

2. The way Bobby my brother talks you would think he's from a different country.

3. Tomorrow will be July 4 2020.

4. My favorite date is Wednesday November 22 1961.

5. Mr. Getz my principal also teaches math science and gym.

6. Noah shine the light over here so I can see you better.

7. The kids were wearing fuzzy wool hats over their big round heads.

8. Even though you saved your money you still do not have enough for a bicycle.

9. Since you are late we had to start without you.

10. If you don't finish the project by tomorrow you won't get a good grade on it.

11. Before we moved to the city we had many animals on our farm.

12. Providing that you study for the test I am sure you will do well.

13. No there is not enough time to play a game of Monopoly before we leave.

14. Before we leave we need to turn off all the lights.

15. Well if you must choose the red dress I guess that is all right with me.

16. The light fluffy lemon cake was the hit of the party.

17. A new highway was built so motorists can move around the city more smoothly.

18. However we have tried to find our dog for two days.

19. Well do you want to be a squirrel instead?

20. The last time you told me a lie I believed you but not this time.

COMMA, SEMICOLON AND COLON PRACTICE
Write each sentence correctly, adding or subtracting commas, colons and/or semicolons.

1. She wanted organic fruit, and went to the other supermarket to get it.

2. Beyond the city limits; there is an abandoned chocolate factory.

3. This is what I like to take to the beach a good book sunblock and two towels.

4. As I walked down the street the strangest thing happened I lost my way.

5. Out of all the coffee shops you could walk into; why did you choose this one?

6. If you didn't want me to find out about the surprise party, you should not have put it on Facebook, I am on Facebook all the time.

7. My favorite musicians in no particular order are Jimi Hendrix, Nina Simone, and, Beyoncé.

8. There are so many good parts to that coffee shop free wifi great lattes and the best cookies and scones in town.

9. Jackson loved to surf rain or shine he was in the water.

10. When I listen to that song I feel like dancing it is very catchy.

11. Riley loved going to the country yet he seldom got to go.

12. I wanted to tell her one thing and one thing only don't go shark diving.

13. Summer is my favorite season; and I love the month of July the most.

COMMA, SEMICOLON & COLON
Part 1:
Write Each Sentence Correctly, Adding Commas As Needed.

1. Turning up the stereo I heard the speakers fill with static.

2. Before the race began he drank a cool glass of water.

3. The panel seemed to prefer films that were well-written funny and uplifting.

4. I hope you like this song but I also have other music.

5. Nina wore a big blue hat and a pale pink sweater.

 1st Ed. © ibidPREP llc

6. I loved the artist's funky color choices and how he mixed neon and pastels and I also loved the incorporation of writing and photography on the canvas.

7. No one thought the Ramones would like Lady Gaga's music because they were so punk but I guess everyone misjudged the situation.

8. During orientation most campers were wishing the big beautiful lake were open.

9. Will was normally up for any stunt yet he lost his nerve when asked to tightrope without a net.

10. While in England Anna called "soccer" her greatest passion "football" because that is what the English generally call it.

Part 2:
Write each sentence correctly, omitting commas as needed.

1. As the kicker got injured, right after the coin toss, the team had a rough start.

2. As usual, I had to go, around seven o'clock, but I didn't want to leave, this time.

3. It was such a long trip, not only because of the traffic and snow, but, also because he had to go to the bathroom every five minutes.

4. I wish the park had a swing set, some sprinklers, and more plants, and trees.

5. If you want a good seat at the movies, you should leave the house early, and buy tickets online.

6. Do you really like both sweet, and salty foods?

7. If you didn't know, that fact, now you know it.

8. Green farms is a great, health food store; however, it does not have many gluten-free options.

9. I like to run, and bike, but, because I don't stretch properly, I get injured often.

10. Although he had all his shots before he traveled, he still got sick, on the trip.

Practice

MORE COMMA REVIEW
Please put commas in the text where appropriate and eliminate commas that have been placed incorrectly.

Passage 1:

"Come back in fifteen months and I'll show you something special," said the doctor. When Paul Peters returned to his doctor friend in Maine. The doctor however was dead.

Peters found a drawing, on the doctor's table. When he picked up the drawing he knew it was a map. The map directed him to a hole. Peter found the hole and there a few feet down Peter saw a chain attached to the wall of the hole.

As Peters reached down for the chain he noted it was growing dark. The chain was very long and the "something special" felt heavy. A metal box appeared, below him. Peters reached for the treasure box but it was too far from his grasp. The weary man sadly admitted defeat and dropped the chain.

Before Peters died from his exhaustion he wrote this story in his diary. No treasure unfortunately has ever been found.

Passage 2:

As four men were walking around Pine Creek Island in 1796 they found a shallow hole. The hole was twenty feet wide and a branch was stuck in its center. The men unsurprisingly became curious. They returned with shovel to look for what they thought was pirate treasure. After they dug ten feet down they found a copper rod. A second marker appeared at twenty feet and a third was seen at 30 feet. At this depth however the digging became impossible.

When a different group dug in 1815 they also found markers, every ten feet. While they were shoveling someone hit a stone at 100 feet. The stone had strange markings but no one understood what the markings meant.

Other treasure seekers have tried their luck. One group finally met with some success. They discovered links of chain, and pieces of paper but nothing else was ever found. Pine Creek Island's secret like so many secrets is still a mystery. If the truth is discovered it will be of great interest, to the world.

1st Ed. © ibidPREP llc

Apostrophes

An **apostrophe** is a mark that has two main uses: to show **possession** [this belongs to...] and to make **contractions** [combine two words into one].

Contractions

We use contractions to combine two words. **Use an apostrophe to show where a letter or letters have been removed (a contraction).**

Examples:

it is	**it's**
does not	**doesn't**
they are	**they're**
were not	**weren't**
you are	**you're**
class of 1987	**class of '87**
who is	**who's**
cannot	**can't**
will not	**won't**
would have (not would of)	**would've**

Examples:

Why didn't you answer the phone?

She hasn't received her paycheck yet.

CONTRACTIONS 1
Add apostrophes where necessary.

1. Sam isnt coming to the library with us.

2. Dont you want something to eat?

3. Weve been working on this project all month.

4. Its starting to feel like spring.

CONTRACTIONS 2
Write the contraction form of the following words.

1. he would _____

2. would not _____

3. will not _____

4. he is _____

5. we would _____

6. I have _____

Possession

Use an apostrophe to indicate possession by adding ' or 's to the end of the word. But how we do this depends on if the word is singular, plural, ends in s or does not end in s!

Add **'s** to the singular form of a word (even if it ends in s)
>Jason's car
>James's cat
>The printing press's pages

Add **'s** to plural forms that do not end in s.
>The children's museum
>The geese's food

Add **'** to plural forms that end in s.
>Three friends' letters
>Two cats' toys

If something belongs to two nouns, just make the second one possessive.
>Tom and Jerry's apartment.
>Jim and Jess's cake.

Examples:

All the players' uniforms are blue.   (uniforms belonging to all the players)
The player's uniforms are blue.   (uniforms belonging to one player)
A child's ball was kicked in our yard.   (ball belonging to the child)
The men's department is on the second floor.   (department for men)

APOSTROPHES
Using what you have just learned about apostrophes, circle the correct choice(s) in the sentences below.

1. (Its / it's) time to go, so make sure the (suitcases / suitcase's) latch is closed.

2. The kitten should be able to find (its / it's) way home.

3. The TV was so loud that she did not hear her (children's / childrens) cries.

4. (Whose/ Who's) the (partys / party's) candidate for vice president this year?

5. The (dogs / dog's) bark was far worse than (its / it's) bite.

6. My dog is pretty old, but (theirs / their's) is young.

7. The (twins's / twins') bedroom was so disorganized that you could barely step into the room without step- ping on something.

8. She claimed the watch was (her's / hers) but was unable to correctly answer the question about the (man- ufacturers' / manufacturer's) name inscribed on the back.

9. The (principals / principal's) name was so long that, for everyone (else's / elses) sake, she shortened it to just the first syllable.

 1ˢᵗ Ed. © ibidPREP llc

POSSESSION 1
Please put in apostrophes as needed.

1. All the boys bicycles are gone.

2. The dancers dress was made of silk.

3. Did the cat eat the Smith familys food off of the table?

4. Marta plays on the girls basketball team.

5. Matthews and Marshas toys are all over the floor.

6. The heros arrows aimed for the villains heart.

7. The family of dragons breathed fire on the heroes shields.

8. The heroes horses heads were covered in flameproof armor.

9. The boys went to the girls party and danced with her friends.

10. Some of the girls friends danced while her other friends played Frisbee.

11. Unfortunately, it was the girls dogs Frisbee.

12. The girls dog chased its Frisbee, much to all her friends fear.

POSSESSION 2
Please put in the proper possessive noun or pronoun as needed.

Example: Charlie Brown kicked the football and missed. He landed on ___his___ back.

1. The team needed new uniforms. They were tired of _____ old uniforms.

2. You need to put the collar on _____dog. If it is not wearing _____ collar, it may get lost.

3. The workers went on strike. The boss hoped _____ strike wouldn't last long.

4. The girl wanted to do better and asked Mr. Willard how she could improve _____ grade.

5. As the bus was idling, the kids breathed in _____ toxic fumes.

6. The books were destroyed in a great fire, and we have lost _____contents forever.

Grammar

Quotation Marks

Quotation marks are used to indicate that words are:

- being spoken
  - "I really like clams!" said the clown.

- copied from somewhere else
  - My recipe says, "Add garlic and butter to your clams."

- being used as titles of stories, articles or poems.
  - "Death Be Not Proud" is a brilliant sonnet, but "Batter My Heart" is better.

- referring to words in order to define them or single them out
  - Some people think "disinterested" means "not interested," but it really means "impartial."

- to indicate that the words being used have different or opposite meanings from the ones intended
  - Congress is supposed to be a "working" part of government.

For a lot of us, quotations marks can be tricky to use. Mostly because there is often a lot of punctuation and capitalization to keep straight. Let us help you keep things straight!

Spoken Quotes

> *Bill's mom barged into his room and said, "Clean up this pigsty!"*

As is often the case with grammar, more than just quotation marks are involved here.

Capitalization In Quotes

Whatever is between the quotation marks is what Bill's mom said; everything else is what the narrator says. Because what Bill's mom says begins a new sentence, the first word in her quote is capitalized.

> *Bill's mom barged into his room and said, "**C**lean up this pigsty!"*

Commas In Quotes

Commas ALWAYS come after the last word the narrator said and before the quotation marks. Like so:

> *Bill's mom barged into his room and said, "Clean up this pigsty!"*

> *So I shouted back, "Well, I don't remember asking you to come in my room!"*

And so on. It doesn't matter what word comes before the first quotation mark; it is always followed by a comma.

Punctuation in Quotes

At the end of the quotes, we often have another punctuation mark. In the examples above, we have periods and exclamation points. If the punctuation is in the original quote, it always comes inside the quotation marks.

When We Don't Capitalize

If a sentence starts with a quotation, do NOT capitalize the first word **after** the quotation.

1ˢᵗ Ed. © ibidPREP llc

> *"I don't care. You must clean it up before you go out to play,"* **my** *mom said, angrier than ever.*

Or:

> *"Fine, ruin my life, why don't you?"* **s**obbed her sulky son.*

Don't let the question mark throw you: "sobbed" is still part of the sentence and therefore **not** capitalized.

But:

> *"Oh, it's hardly as bad as that." My mom examined the mess on my dresser and laughed at how thick the dust was.*

My is capitalized in this sentence because it has begun a new sentence that is separate from what has been said, and we *always* capitalize the beginnings of those. So, unless the first word after the quotation is a proper noun or the beginning of a new sentence, **DO NOT** capitalize it.

This same rule holds for a quote that has been broken up mid-statement:

> *"Oh, come on," I said, "this will take all afternoon."*

We do **not** capitalize *this* because it is a continuation of the quoted sentence that started with *Oh, come on.*

When you're trying to figure out whether or not to capitalize something, just ask yourself two questions:

- Is it the start of a new sentence [either the narrator's or the speaker's]?
- Is it a proper noun?

Unless the answer to one of those is "yes," don't capitalize it!

Practice

QUOTATION REVIEW
Choose the correctly punctuated sentence for each question.

1. Which of the following sentences is correctly written?
    A. "Do you want to go to the movies?" Asked the boy's dad.
    B. "Do you want to go to the movies," asked the boy's dad.
    C. "Do you want to go to the movies?" asked the boy's dad.
    D. "Do you want to go to the movies," Asked the boy's dad.

2. Which of the following sentences is correctly written?
    A. "Doctor Robert" is a great song by The Beatles.
    B. "Doctor Robert," is a great song by The Beatles.
    C. "Doctor Robert" Is a great song by The Beatles.
    D. "Doctor Robert," Is a great song by The Beatles.

3. Which of the following sentences is correctly written?
    A. "Go to your room!" Shouted the boy's mother.
    B. "Go to your room!" shouted the boy's mother.
    C. "Go to your room"! shouted the boy's mother.
    D. "Go to your room"! Shouted the boy's mother.

4. Which of the following sentences is correctly written?
    A. My friend said, "baseball is my favorite sport."
    B. My friend said, "Baseball is my favorite sport".
    C. My friend said, "baseball is my favorite sport".
    D. My friend said, "Baseball is my favorite sport."

If necessary, make changes to the following sentences so they are written correctly.

5. "Call your dad and tell him we'll be late", Said Tom's mother.

6. "Make sure that he understands why" she added, "Because I don't want him to get confused".

7. She switched off the radio, which was playing "Rolling in the Deep" by Adele.

8. I called, and my dad picked up after the first ring and said "hello".

1ˢᵗ Ed. © ibidPREP llc

USAGE

English is a mutt language; it is formed from a number of different languages, so not everything makes sense. Sometimes words that seem like they should be related to one another are not at all. Worse, words that seem like they should be spelled one way are really spelled another way—or are actually different words if spelled the other way! Therefore, it is very important to be aware of the confusing words and try to keep them straight!!

Fewer/Less[25]

When your teacher tells you to write a paper in "five pages or less," she's wrong! The "Ten Items or Less" aisle in the supermarket is also wrong.

When it comes to nouns that cannot be counted, "less" is more, er, better. With nouns that can be counted [have plurals], fewer is correct:

> My monkey has **fewer** French fries than your monkey.
> The monkey has **less** water in his cup than he did yesterday.

The same rule applies to choosing between "much" and "many." "Many," like "fewer," applies to countable things. For example:

> There are many ways to solve this problem.
> She holds much animosity towards her former best friend.

FEWER/LESS
Practice your knowledge by writing in the correct usage word in the blanks below (choose fewer / less):

1. The plants were nearly drowning in water; I wish I had given them _____ water.

2. This math problem requires _____ than ten steps to solve.

3. At the end of the night, she'd eaten _____ slices of pizza than anticipated.

4. These days there are _____ cars on the road.

5. I have _____ time these days.

6. At the party I ate _____ cake than Tim did.

---

[25] The same rule holds true for many/much.

Grammar

Superlatives

If you have only one sibling, you are the SMARTER child, not the SMARTEST child in your family. "Smartest" [and any of the "est" words] can only be used when comparing three or more things.

The same is true for

a. **Between/Among**

The competition is intense between the Yankees and the Red Sox, BUT

The competition is intense AMONG the teams in the NL East. (there are more than two teams)

b. **Better/Best**

George is better than Diane at Ping-Pong.

BUT

George is the best Ping-Pong player on the team.

c. **Er/est words in general**

Sarah is the prettier twin.

BUT

Sarah is the prettiest triplet.

SUPERLATIVES
Practice your knowledge of comparisons and superlatives by putting the word in parentheses in the correct form for the sentence:

1. The Four Seasons is the _____ (expensive) hotel I've ever stayed in.

2. He is _____ (tall) than I am.

3. Betsy is the _____ (fast) horse in the group.

4. Amy is the _____ (beautiful) girl I've ever seen.

5. When the group was caught trying to break into the store room, John had the _____ (red) face out of everyone.

6. She is _____ (better/best) at tennis than her twin.

BETWEEN/AMONG
Now practice between/among by writing either "between" or "among" in the blanks below:

1. _____ you and me, I don't think his claims can be believed.

2. There is a lot of competition _____ the teams in my travel league.

3. _____ math and English, I prefer to study English.

4. I study best when I am _____ people who have similar study habits.

5. Who _____ you is responsible for spilling the milk on the counter?

6. The Mets are _____ the worst three teams in the league

1st Ed. © ibidPREP llc

Misused Words

The power nerds at the College Board really steam up their glasses over these jewels. Misused words tend to be words that look very similar to other words but do not have similar meanings. Occasionally, though, there are words the meanings of which have, through common usage [the way most people talk], become weirdly different from their original meaning. Language does this; it is plastic[26] and evolving. Of course, the ACT would like to penalize you for being on the forward edge of evolution. So make like a dinosaur and learn these word meanings and distinctions. Then you can play power nerd and correct your friends when they misuse these common words[27]:

Because English spelling can be so weird, spell check can sometimes be more of a problem than a help. Let's say you wrote "than" when you meant "then". The spell check will NOT help you there!

a. Aggravated/Annoyed
   - To aggravate is to make worse ("She aggravated the situation"), not to annoy or irritate.

b. Stationary/Stationery
   - To remain stationary is to stay in place.
   - Stationery refers to writing materials like envelopes, greeting cards, etc. Papyrus, for example, is a stationery store.

c. Differed/Deferred
   - If you differ from someone, you are different from him/her in some way (often on an opinion.)
   - Deferred has two meanings: to put something off ("I deferred making the decision until I had more information.") or to submit humbly ("Since you are more knowledgeable in this area, I defer to your opinion.").

d. Indifferent/Not Different
   - Indifferent does not mean "not different." It means "unconcerned," or not having any particular feeling on the matter.

e. Disinterested/Not Interested
   - Disinterested usually means "unbiased," or "not having a personal stake in something." It can mean "not interested" or "indifferent," but because this is the more intuitive choice that people will gravitate to, the College Board will most likely be using "disinterested" in the first sense.

f. Affect/Effect
   - To affect something is to have an effect on it. Notice how "affect" is used as a verb, while "effect" is a noun. This is the most common usage.
   - However, "effect" can also be used as a verb meaning "to cause something to happen." The most common example of this usage is the phrase "to effect change."

g. Eminent/Imminent
   - Eminent means famous/respected.
   - Imminent means something is about to happen ("Her arrival is imminent.")

h. Drank/Drunk, shrank/shrunk, hang/hung, swam/swum
   - These words are only misused because it's hard to know which tense to use for which form. Is it I drank/drunk? I have drank/drunk? It's easier if you think of ran/run. I ran/drank. I have run/I have drunk, etc.

---

[26] shifting, malleable, moldable, flexible
[27] See Sppendix for definitions of these words and how to distinguish among them.

Grammar

MISUSED WORDS

Try your hand at identifying misused words in the following sentences:

1. An eminent / imminent scholar, he is widely known for his theory of postcolonial literature.

2. My sweater shrunk / shrank in the dryer.

3. The boy drowned because he had swam / swum too far and was unable to swim back to land due to his exhaustion.

4. She had drank / drunk all the milk in the fridge.

5. He needs to accept / except the fact that he is not the best basketball player on the team.

6. The CGI effects are incredible / incredulous in this movie.

7. The movie's tragic story affected / effected her more than she could say.

8. These stationary / stationery bicycles are good for exercise.

9. I felt so nauseous / nauseated watching that video that I had to leave the room.

10. The video was nauseous / nauseating to watch.

11. The Romanis were persecuted / prosecuted by the local government.

12. One brand of gasoline is indifferent from/not different from the next.

Comparisons

You can rest assured that you will see at least one comparison question in the ENGLISH section because it's easy to make grammatically incorrect comparisons in everyday speech. The ACT especially wants you to make truly parallel comparisons. That means if you compare two things to each other, it must be abundantly clear that you are comparing two things of the same kind [otherwise, grammatically, you are asking for trouble].

YES: My mother's cooking is better than your mother's cooking. [Comparing one type of cooking to another.]
NO: My mother's cooking is better than your mother. [You are comparing cooking to someone's mother.]

NO: The rules of chess are harder than checkers. [The rules of one game are being compared to another game as a whole.]
YES: The rules of chess are harder than the rules of checkers. [Now you are comparing rules to rules, which is okay.]

COMPARISONS

Rewrite the following sentences correctly:

1. Virginia Woolf's writing style is harder to read than Henry James.

2. I prefer eating at Jimmy's BBQ over eating at Roberta's because the food at Jimmy's is less greasy than Roberta's.

3. The new biology teacher says that this textbook is much more up-to-date than last year.

4. Greek artists were far more innovative than Romans.

5. The rules of Go are far simpler than Chess.

1ˢᵗ Ed. © ibidPREP llc

Department Of Redundancy Department

Redundancies are super fun for super nerds such as I. Once you become aware of them, you see or hear them everywhere, and they can be quite amusing [if you are a super nerd]. What the heck do I mean by redundancy? Basically, it means saying the same thing more than once—essentially, repeating yourself—more than once. And again.

At 7a.m. this morning, the phone rang ["a.m." = "morning"]
The taco was way too spicy for Clara ["way" = "too"]

The following is my favorite because it's a triple redundancy that actually occurs quite often in everyday speech:

The reason why I left was because it was late.

Wow! That's terrible because "reason" = "why" = "because"!

The following would be correct:
The reason I left was that it was late. [better]
or
I left because it was late. [best]

REDUNDANCY
Eliminate redundant words in the following sentences

1. The reason she wanted to go to the dance is because Tim will be there.

2. There's a good chance it'll probably rain tonight.

3. I prefer strawberry ice cream to vanilla ice cream because I like it better.

4. President John F. Kennedy was assassinated in the year of 1963.

5. Please meet me at the office this evening at 7pm.

Misplaced Modifiers

A modifier is a word or group of words that describe or qualify another piece of the sentence. A modifier is like a phrase in that it can be tossed out of the sentence without wrecking the grammatical integrity of the sentence.

A losing team forever, the Mets are still my favorite!

"A losing team forever" is the modifier in the sentence. Without it, "the Mets are still my favorite!" is still a valid sentence. The important thing to keep in mind about modifiers on the ACTs is that if they start a sentence, they need to butt right up against the noun or nouns they are modifying. If a modifier is stuck next to the wrong noun, it is called a **misplaced modifier**. Whenever you see a descriptive phrase [or dependent clause] at the start of a sentence, make absolutely sure that the first noun immediately after the comma is the subject of that clause.

Grammar

YES: After seeing *Hunger Games*, we decided our favorite actress was Jennifer Lawrence

NO: After seeing *Hunger Games*, Jennifer Lawrence was our favorite actress.

The second example is really saying:

> After **Jennifer Lawrence** saw *Hunger Games*, she became our favorite actress.

instead of what it probably tried to say which is:

> After **WE** saw *Hunger Games*, Jennifer Lawrence became our favorite actress.

MISPLACED MODIFIERS
Fix these [if they need fixing]:

1. While getting into bed, a horse galloped through Henry's room.

2. After hanging out on the beach all day, Henry's back was burnt.

3. Upon further analysis, the masterpiece was deemed to be a brilliant forgery.

4. To guarantee a spot on the team, workouts are mandatory for players.

5. As he was waking up, Henry heard the phone ringing.

6. After seeing the play, Shakespeare was our favorite playwright.

That/Which

That is used to point out an object or to signify which object is important.
> **That** hat is my favorite kind of hat.
> Please hand me **that** oxygen tank over there.

It is also used to add important information in restrictive clauses. For example:
> Clothing **that** is dark colored is harder to see at night.

If you take out "that is dark colored," the sentence becomes, "Clothing is harder to see at night," which changes the meaning completely. It's not that **all** clothing is hard to see at night, just dark colored clothing. In other words, "that" is used at the beginning of restrictive clauses (i.e., the phrase limits the scope of the preceding noun).

Which is used in a phrasal manner [that means: like a phrase] and is usually set off from the rest of the sentence to provide additional "good to know" information that doesn't change the sentence's meaning when removed.

> The hat, **which** I bought in Genoa, is full of rain.

1st Ed. © ibidPREP llc

The fact that the hat was bought in Genoa doesn't affect that it's full of rain, so using "that" in this case would not be appropriate.

Another Thing About *WHICH*:

Which is often used in sentences as a way to avoid ending a sentence with a preposition [an old timey no-no]. Often when kids see it, they think it "sounds" weird and want to pick it as wrong.

In other words:

WRONG: Please bring the bottles back to the store where they came from.

RIGHT: Please bring the bottles back to the store from which they came.

THAT/WHICH
Circle the correct answer in the sentences below:

1. As far as I'm aware, this is the only book (that / which) he's written.

2. This is just to say that I've eaten the plums (that / which) were in the icebox.

3. (That / which) of these is yours?

4. The car, (that / which) he had bought only a year ago, was completely totaled.

5. A bicycle (that / which) does not have air in its tires is essentially out of commission.

6. Font (that / which) is red or green colored will be difficult for the colorblind to distinguish.

Unconditional Adjectives

Most adjectives have degrees. You can be pretty, prettier or [if there are more than two of you] the prettiest girl in the room [I know I am]. However, some words cannot be made more than they already are—in other words, when it comes to these things, either you are or you aren't. For example:

- pregnant
- dead
- unique
- perfect
- different

Wrong: Today was the most perfect day ever.
Right: Today was perfect.
Wrong: Her voice is so unique.
Right: Her voice is unique.

"Different From" Not "Different Than"

"Different" is one of those words that doesn't really have degrees. "Than" is a word that is used to show comparisons between things by degrees: The boy is taller than that frog. Since there are not degrees of being different [you cannot be more different, you are either different or not], then something cannot be different

THAN something else, something is different FROM something else!

Idiotic Idioms

Idioms are often thought of as figures of speech. I often think of them this way, but on this test, you also must think of them as ways in which prepositions are combined with nouns and, more often, verbs. Unfortunately, these idioms are just something you have to know and be familiar with because there's no rhyme or reason to them. These kinds of idioms are why non-native English speakers have such a tough time perfecting their knowledge of our language.

For instance:

- Why do we put on our shirts, but we don't put off our shirts?
- Why do we take off our shirts, but we don't take on our shirts?
- Why do we live in a building and on a street, but at an address?

There are about a million more of these, which is why instead of whining about your taxi driver's English, think of how lucky we are that millions of people around the world even bother to try speaking and learning our language.

I hate to say it, but the best way to learn idioms is to read a lot. If you don't or haven't, remember: After you have checked the verbs and pronouns in a sentence, check the prepositions and make sure they work with their verbs.

PREPOSITIONAL PHRASES
Practice your knowledge of prepositional phrases by filling in the correct prepositions below:

1. We agreed _____ a theme for the party.

2. He lives _____ Windsor Street.

3. She used to live _____ 101 Corning Street.

4. They now live _____ the Park Plaza Hotel.

5. Her confidence _____ me is reassuring.

6. She is so different _____ me that I'm not sure how we ever became friends.

7. Her biting sarcasm puts _____ a lot of people.

8. Her attitude towards me is always condescending; I don't like it when she talks _____ to me.

9. _____ time, you will no longer feel the pangs of heartbreak.

10. Ever since she lied about the incident, she has been afflicted _____ guilt.

      1st Ed. © ibidPREP llc

HOMOPHONES, HOMOGRAPHS AND COMPOUND WORDS

Homophones

As if writing weren't hard enough already, now you've got to be on the lookout for something new: **homophones**! Homophones are words that *sound* the same but are spelled in different ways and mean different things.

You probably already know a few of them. The two most common sets of homophones are made up of three words that sound the same. They are *there, their* and *they're* and *to, too* and *two*. Here's how you use them:

- **There/they're/their:**

    ◦ **There:** this one is talking about a place. *Please take this book to the table over **there**.*

    ◦ **Their:** this one shows that people own something. *The family took **their** dog to the park to play.*

    ◦ **They're:** this one is a contraction that means "they are." If you can substitute "they are" and the sentence still makes sense, you need to use *they're*: *Many schools are in my hometown, but **they're** not all very good.*

    ◦ To/too/two:

    ◦ **To:** this one talks about direction or is used with verbs: *It is important **to** do your homework before you go **to** the park.*

    ◦ **Too:** this one means *also*, or it means excessively: ***Too** many people are in the stadium for me to enter, **too**.*

    ◦ **Two:** this one is simply the number 2. It's really simple: *There are **two** kinds of people: those who understand grammar and those who don't.*

These two sets of homophones are the most common, but there are many, many more. Unfortunately, there is no trick for knowing which one to use in a given situation; you just have to learn them by heart! Here are a few more common ones that you should know.

    ◦ **Which/witch:** A *witch* is a person who casts spells on you; use *which* for everything else! (*Which* book did you read? The book, *which* is 300 pages long, is on fire.)

    ◦ **Rose/rows:** A *rose* is a flower and the past tense of rise (I *rose* from my chair); *rows* are the lines of seats at the movie theater.

    ◦ **Right/write:** *Right* means to be correct, and it is also a direction (turn *right* up ahead); *write* is what you do with your pencil in class.

    ◦ **It's/its:** *It's* is a contraction that means "it is," so if you can substitute "it is," you know you need to use *it's*. On the other hand, *its* is a word that shows possession: a dog licks *its* tail. This pair is a big one, so make sure you get it straight!

    ◦ **Your/you're:** *Your* is used to show that you own something: you clean *your* room. *You're* is a contraction that means "you are," so you have to be able to substitute "you are" in order to use this one: *You're* going to get in trouble if you do that.

- **Our/Are:** These aren't strictly homophones, but kids (and grown-ups) still get them confused. *Our* is another word that shows ownership, and it means "belongs to us": *Our* house is in a nice part of town. *Are* is a verb that means "to be": Those men *are* all over six feet tall.

- **Weather/whether:** These are important ones to get right. *Weather* refers to what goes on outside—rain, wind, the sun, etc. *Whether* is the word we use to signal that there's a choice: I don't know *whether* or not I'll go to the beach today. It depends on the *weather*.

- **Addition/edition:** *Addition*, with an "a," is what you do in math class; that's why it has "add" in it. *Edition* with an "e," is a version of something: first-*edition* copies of the book are quite rare and therefore worth a lot of money.

- **Flower/flour:** *Flower*, with a "w," is something you pick from a plant to give to your valentine; *flour*, with a "u," is what you bake a cake with.

- **Soar/sore:** *Soar*, with an "a," is what an eagle does when it flies above you. *Sore*, with an "e," is how you might feel after an injury playing sports.

- **Then/than:** *Then* is used to talk about time: I went to the mall, and *then* I went home. *Than* is the word we use to compare things: My brother is much taller *than* I am.

- **Whole/hole:** *Whole* is used to talk about the entire something: I can't believe I ate the *whole* thing. *Hole* is what we use to talk about a big gap: the dog was walking along and suddenly fell in a big *hole* in the construction site.

HOMOPHONES

Choose the right homophones in each sentence.

1. Which/witch woman was accused of being a which/witch?

2. In New York City, there/their/they're are many museums that are world famous for the quality of there/their/they're collections. There/Their/They're an important part of New York's international appeal.

3. To/Too/Two many people these days struggle when they try to/too/two choose among homophones. But hey, if there are only to/too/two choices, at least the odds of getting it right are pretty good.

4. If it's important to you that you right/write well, you'll have to develop the right/write editing habits.

5. It's/Its always funny to watch a dog chase it's/its tail.

6. Do you know weather/whether or not the weather/whether is suitable for a ski trip?

1st Ed. © ibidPREP llc

Homographs

Now for another confusing set of words: **homographs**. Homographs are words that are spelled the same (though sometimes pronounced differently in different situations) and have different meanings. Huh? Here's an example.

*I **live** in a big house on Montague Street.*
*I went downtown to see my favorite band **live** in concert.*

Live is spelled the same way in these two sentences, but it is pronounced in two different ways and means two different things. In the first sentence, *live* means where you and your family spend all your time, but in the second *live* means that the music was not a recording.

There are many homographs in English, but the only way you can learn them is by hearing people speak and being a careful reader. Just be on the lookout for them.

Compound Words

The final kind of word to look out for is the **compound word**. As you might guess, a compound word is a word that is made up of two other words stuck together. *Lighthouse, doorknob* and *shoelace* are common compound words you probably already know.

However, there are some compound words that are not so straightforward (see? Another compound word). Here are two of them that might be confusing.

- **Someone.** This is a compound word. It is NOT two words. *Someone* is calling me on the phone. I need *someone* to help me with this.

- **Sometimes.** This is also a compound word. It is NOT two words. *Sometimes*, I feel like winter will last forever. I get to go visit my family in California, but only *sometimes*.

Here are some more:

- **A lot NOT Alot**
  "A lot" means "very much."—Thanks a lot, Goober!
  "Alot," is not a word. Don't use it. EVER.

- **All together v. Altogether**
  "All together" means "as a group."—We succeed or fail all together.
  "Altogether" means "completely" or "entirely."—I find lumpy oatmeal altogether revolting.

- **Every day v. Everyday**
  "Everyday" means "ordinary" or "usual."—These are my everyday kicks.
  "Every day" means a "period of time."—I like to eat food every day.

- **All right v. Alright**
  They both mean the same thing: "okay," "satisfactory," "certainty," or "safe."—
  Everything is all right, and that's alright by me!

- **Some Time v. Sometime**
  "Some time" means "a considerable period of time." For some time, the world has been turning.
  "Sometime" means "a vague time in the future."—I'll call you sometime.

- **Cannot NOT Can Not**
    "Cannot" means "unable."
    "Can not" means "this is not a can."

<u>COMPOUND WORDS</u>
Choose the right word to fit the sentence.

1. A lot/Alot of people like ice cream.

2. Some people would eat it every day/everyday.

3. Celery can not/cannot make people fat.

4. Altogether/All together, the team must decide if the sacrifice is worth the risk.

5. Booboo went some time/sometime without blinking his eyes.

6. Everyday/every day thoughts usually include imagining sometime/some time when everything will be perfect.

1st Ed. © ibidPREP llc

Chapter Three

Math

1st Ed. © ibidPREP llc

OVERVIEW/INTRO

Section 2—Math   60 Questions   60 minutes

60 Multiple Choice Questions

Five Choices per Question

How To Approach The Math Section

1. **Math on the ACT is fairly straightforward**—A strong grasp of **Arithmetic, Algebra,** and **Geometry** will cover 95% of the test. The rest is reserved for advanced topics such as functions, trigonometry and matrices. Master the main topics and then worry about filling in the rest.

2. **Math questions have five multiple choices**—whereas the questions for all the other sections have only four answers choices. More answer choices mean guessing is harder and that there are more false answers to tempt you. Because there are more false choices, it is even more important for you come up with an answer **on your own** if at all possible BEFORE you look at the choices given. It will also be VERY important for you to read the answers carefully as some choices might look VERY similar. For example, you do NOT want to pick -3<x<4 when you wanted $-3 \leq x < 4$.

3. **Math section is LONG**—Many students don't finish it. Do not worry. Remember, this section, like all the other sections, is curved, and you do not need to be perfect in order to score well. Pick a target number of questions to finish at a comfortable pace. Try to hit that number in less than an hour and then try to pick and choose from among the rest. Better to do 40 questions well than 60 questions carelessly and in a rush.

4. **Wordy Math Problems**—I will guarantee you that 90% of the time the longer word problems are CRAZY easy. Why? Because these questions look *soooo* long and hard that most students skip them or tune out on them. Hang in there and wait for the real easy question beneath the avalanche of words.

5. **Special Topics**—The math on the ACT covers the basics that most standardized tests do, namely: arithmetic, number knowledge, algebra and geometry. Like every other standardized test, the ACT has certain special topics it likes to drop in here and there. Please don't get too worried about these special topics. Don't freak out if you never covered *logarithms* or *matrices* or never got the gist of *trigonometry*. If you ground yourself on the basics and learn how to avoid careless errors and the rest, that will serve you very well on 90% of the MATH section. The rest is in the Special ACT Math Section, p. 225.

6. **Math Section Timing [60 min]**—Depending on your goals for this section, you may want to break your times into splits if that helps. That is, you might want to give yourself 15 minutes for 15 questions if you're shooting to do them all. If you think getting to 45 questions is a more realistic goal, give yourself 20 minutes for each set of 15, etc. If you have trouble figuring out the time break, or if you don't want to waste time figuring it out, there are devices out there such as the ACT Pacing Watch, which will break each section down for you.

http://www.testingtimers.com/product/act-pacing-watch/

READING WITH 13 LETTERS

IT'S HARD TO UNDERSTAND WHY MATH IS TAUGHT THE WAY IT IS TO MOST STUDENTS. THERE IS THIS MYTH THAT EITHER YOU'RE A "MATH" PERSON OR ELSE YOU'RE OUT OF LUCK. TEACHERS TRY TO TEACH YOU A LITTLE ARITHMETIC, SOME FRACTIONS MAYBE, AND IF YOU DON'T GET IT RIGHT AWAY, THEY HAND YOU A CALCULATOR AND OFF YOU GO TO ALGEBRA, GEOMETRY AND TRIG.

GUESS WHAT? IF YOU'RE NOT COMFORTABLE WITH ARITHMETIC AND BASIC NUMBER RULES, THEN LEARNING ALGEBRA, GEOMETRY AND TRIG IS GOING TO BE A NIGHTMARE, AND YOU WILL NEVER BECOME A "MATH" PERSON, JUST ANOTHER CONFUSED MATH PERSON. FOR MATH TEACHERS TO MOVE STUDENTS ON TO ALGEBRA, GEOMETRY AND TRIG WITHOUT HAVING TAUGHT ARITHMETIC PROPERLY IS A LITTLE LIKE ENGLISH TEACHERS TEACHING STUDENTS HALF THE ALPHABET AND THEN SENDING THEM OFF TO READ.

THE RESULTS WOULD LOOK SOMETHING LIKE THIS:

I*** A *E** *I*** *A* *O *** *O *EACH *A*H, AND *H* ** *A** **UDEN** A*E *E**IBLE IN *A** *HO DO** * HA*E *O BE.

TRANSLATION: IT'S A VERY SILLY WAY TO TRY TO TEACH MATH, AND WHY SO MANY STUDENTS ARE TERRIBLE IN MATH WHO DON'T HAVE TO BE.

1st Ed. © ibidPREP llc

How to Do
the Math

1ˢᵗ Ed. © ibidPREP llc

One thing many students want when they come to us is a sure fire method to conquer ALL the math. That is not possible. Try as you might, and in spite of whatever claims other tutors and companies may make, at certain times you're just going to have to THINK FOR YOURSELF. As with reading comprehension, learning how to process **every** word is going to be the biggest key.

MENTAL MATH IS MENTAL

MOST EVERY STUDENT MISINTERPRETS MENTAL MATH AS ABOUT BEING ABLE TO DO MATH IN YOUR HEAD. THAT'S MENTAL. KNOWING CERTAIN MATH FACTS AND PATTERNS BY HEART [AND HEAD] IS ONE THING AND VERY HELPFUL [$4^2=16$], BUT DOING MATH OPERATIONS IN YOUR HEAD IS WORSE THAN USELESS—IT'S DESTRUCTIVE. IT LEADS TO CARELESS, RIDICULOUS ERRORS AND WASTED TIME. I CAN'T TELL YOU HOW MANY TIMES I'VE SAT AND WATCHED STUDENTS STARE OFF INTO THE AIR TRYING TO FIGURE OUT 8×18 INSTEAD OF JUST GRABBING A PENCIL AND GETTING TO WORK. YES, THERE ARE WAYS TO DO LARGER MULTIPLICATION PROBLEMS IN YOUR HEAD IF YOU KNOW CERTAIN PATTERNS AND RELATIONSHIPS, BUT LET'S SAVE THAT FOR CLASS OR WHEN YOU'RE TRAPPED ON A LIFEBOAT WITHOUT PAPER OR PENCIL AND YOUR HANDS ARE TIED BEHIND YOUR BACK.

WHEN YOU SEE PICTURES OF ALBERT EINSTEIN SOLVING THE THEORY OF RELATIVITY, IS HE STANDING IN FRONT OF A BLANK BLACKBOARD?

How to Read **MATH** Questions

1. Remain Clam!
2. Break It Down.
3. Reread the Last Part of the Question.

First, **REMAIN CLAM!** Nothing on Your Test Is Impossible!!

You open to the first question of the math section, you start to read the question, and you have **NO IDEA** what they're asking! This is definitely a good time to *Remain Clam!*

Remind yourself that you are never going to be asked to solve an impossible question. It will only ever *seem* impossible or nonsensical.

In other words, in spite of what you may think, these tests are never going to ask you anything that is impossible. It may *sound* like the question is asking,

Q. If there are 400 miles to Spooneggyville and Ansel is carrying Ponto Juice Boxes at 58 kilos per pound, what is the velocitude of the Mushroom Charger to the 5th power?

Trust me, if you chill out and read the questions clause by clause, you're going to realize that they are really just asking you,

Q. If there are 400 miles to Spooneggyville and Ansel is traveling 50mph, how long will the trip take him if he makes a one-hour stop for lunch and takes a 10 minute break at a rest stop?

It is still a long, multi-step question, but each step makes sense and can be worked out using step two:

BREAK IT DOWN

Now that the words don't throw you, let's make sure the phrasing doesn't. Here's something radical to try. DO NOT read the whole question first [this does NOT mean "do not read the whole problem ever"]. For most word problems you would be better off rubbing the test on your face than reading the whole question first. Reading the whole question first, besides wasting time, might also cause you to believe some mistaken notions, latch onto some misleading directions or just plain get confused and dispirited. Instead of reading the whole question, getting to the end and saying, "HUH?", and then starting all over [a COLOSSAL waste of time and confidence], break every question down clause by clause [basically just stop at each comma or period]. Breaking it down in this way means that as you get to the end of each clause or sentence, stop and take stock of what you're being given and start setting up whatever equations you can.

If there are 400 miles to Spooneggyville and Ansel is traveling 50mph,

$$\text{Distance} = 400 \text{ miles}$$
$$\text{Rate} = 50 \text{mph}$$

Then if I remember Distance = Rate × Time, I know:

$$400 = 50 \times \text{time } \textbf{so } \text{Time} = 8 \text{ hours}$$

NOW WE CAN CONTINUE BREAKING IT DOWN: how long will the trip take him if he makes a one-hour stop for lunch and takes a ten-minute break at a rest stop?

We already know that the trip is going to take 8 hours of driving, so now we add in the new information:

$$8 \text{ hours} + 1 \text{ hour} + 10 \text{ minutes} =$$

Be *careful* here: you may only add units of the **same** measure to each other, so either change minutes to hours or hours to minutes, and then add!

$$480 \text{ minutes} + 60 \text{ minutes} + 10 \text{ minutes} = 550 \text{ minutes}$$

1st Ed. © ibidPREP llc

Therefore, it took Ansel 550 minutes to get to Spooneggyville!

If you set up as you go, more often than not you will have the information you're solving for before you get to the end anyway! There are only so many things you can be asked in any case. They are not going to tell you all about Ansel going to Spooneggyville and then ask you what his favorite fruit is!

Try reading this sentence all at once:

> *The man from Sheboygan had four daughters, each of whom had three sons, who each had one daughter and two sons who each also had two sons. How many sons did the man from Sheboygan have?*

If you read it all at once, chances are you're thinking, "Boy, that's a lot of sons, I better get my calculator, but wait, do they mean....oh never mind." However, if you stopped reading at the first comma, you would see it's really a very easy question: the man from Sheboygan only had daughters!

Reread the Last Part of the Question [the Part That Tells You What the Question Is Truly Asking For]

Here's a great test maker's ploy: they lay out some humongously long word problem or some multi-step geo + algebra problem for you to solve, you put your head down, get to work, and darn if you don't solve it! You get down to the last line of the problem and determine that, say, x = 2. You're excited and hurrying [as always], so you look right to the multiple choice answers and, sitting there waiting for you, is 2! You pick it and move on. Unfortunately, you're wrong.

Upon rereading the LAST CLAUSE of the question, which you may never have read or have forgotten while you were busy solving the long problem, you discover that the last phrase is not asking for what **x equals** but what **2x equals,** or if there was a **y** somewhere in the problem, they may want **y**, etc.

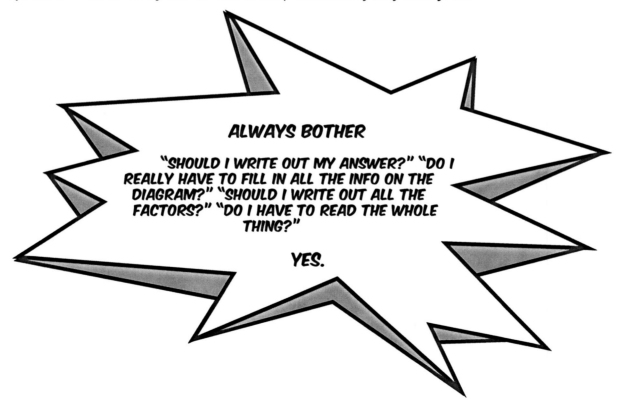

ALWAYS BOTHER

"SHOULD I WRITE OUT MY ANSWER?" "DO I REALLY HAVE TO FILL IN ALL THE INFO ON THE DIAGRAM?" "SHOULD I WRITE OUT ALL THE FACTORS?" "DO I HAVE TO READ THE WHOLE THING?"

YES.

How to Answer

Come Up with an Approach [See Also HOW to SOLVE Later]

Once you've correctly read and broken down your question, you will be able to choose from several ways to solve the problem before you. Once you decide on an approach, it is up to you to execute that approach. If you execute that approach correctly and commit to following it through and it doesn't work, check your work [by redoing everything, not just running your eyes over what you've already done], and if you're still wrong, COME UP WITH ANOTHER APPROACH!

In Math, Close Is Wrong. Really, Really Wrong.

A lot of times while doing a problem, a student makes a careless error or misunderstands something and ends up with an answer that is not among the answer choices. Correct procedure here would be to start again and redo the problem—preferably in a new way, if possible. Normal procedure for most is to panic and start picking through the answers for something "close."

One of the beautiful things about math is its clarity and simplicity. In the arts, as in life, it is often hard to know when something is right. Or complete. In math there are right answers, which means of course there are wrong answers [boohoo, kid]. However, if you've had dealings in life or in the arts, you don't worry so much about being wrong, but you might take great joy, comfort and relief in once in a while being right. Since there are right answers, you can take joy, comfort and relief in knowing there are no gray areas. If you get .5 for an answer and .5 is not an answer choice, it's because .5 is wrong. Not because you were supposed to pick .55, which is close. Or .3 when you get $\frac{1}{3}$ for an answer. Or –8 when you got 8. No, instead of freaking out in these moments, embrace the clarity and joy of knowing that at the very least you know one answer it isn't.

The Answers Are in Your Pencil

I can't tell you how often I have asked kids questions only to watch them stare up at the ceiling. Often kids try to do math that way, as if there were some sort of invisible LED screen hovering in the air. Or they'll roll their eyes into the backs of their heads and try to recall something from a passage they've just read. Of course if they just looked down at their tests and reread the passage in front of them, they'd have a far better chance of getting the right answer. Sometimes, even when students are writing things out in the math, they'll stop when it comes to doing a simple calculation and look up in the air instead of scribbling it out on the side. Dunno why. You do not score extra points for doing math in your head. You'll just waste time, energy and probably points. Don't do this. Use your paper. Use your text. Use your pencil. The answer is in it.

OH, SO I CAN JUST...?

NO!

If a tiny voice starts chirping up while you're reading a problem and says, "Oh, I can just add this!" or "Oh, I just have to pick the biggest number," etc., IGNORE IT. Most of the time, you can't JUST do anything.* That's sort of the point of the questions.

*The only possible time you might be able to "just" add or multiply [for example] is when the problem looks really hard and you would never think, "Oh, so I can just..."

1st Ed. © *ibidPREP llc*

THE RAKES—MATH EDITION!

Careless Errors

Careless errors are a fact of our mathematical lives. You have to be very precise to avoid them, and still it's so easy to stumble into one or two. However, there are several ways to, at the very least, reduce them:

1. ***Slow down.***

2. As we've said before and will continue to say: read the question clause by clause, translating each part of the question from *words to math* as you go. If there's a diagram, fill in the diagram with all you know about it as you go.

3. **FINISH YOUR DARN PROBLEMS**[27] Even though the math questions are multiple choice, pretend they're not. Be sure to get into the habit of **finishing** solving your equation all the way down to *x = ANSWER*. Why? Most students work toward an answer and when it looks like they're getting close, they cheat and peek at the multiple choice selections. If you do this, you might:

   a. be in the midst of making a careless error and not get the right answer for *x*;

   b. not see your answer immediately, freak out and end up doing something dopey like picking the "close" answer;

   c. get the right answer for *x*, but not realize that they really want you to solve for *2x* or *y* or something else entirely. To be able to give them the right answer, you must complete your equation all the way, and then...

4. **Reread the last part of the question** to make sure you **answer the question the test is asking.** As discussed above, so often kids decide what a question is asking without really reading the question. When they invariably get those questions wrong, they are shocked and hard-pressed to figure out why. When we review it, they rework the problem step by step for me and prove that they are right. I agree and tell them, "Yes, you are right: **for your problem.**" Then I point out to them that the problem they were meant to answer was entirely different from what they imagined and executed.

5. **Know your and everyone else's RAKES.** When there is a question involving, for example:

   a. parentheses, you must remember to **distribute**;

   b. when there are negative numbers, BE EXTRA CAREFUL AND SLOW WITH THEM.

   c. do you flip x and y in graphics problems? So does everyone else.

   d. be extra careful when using radius and diameter.

   e. bake sure your units (inches, feet, pounds, cm, k, etc.) all match up.

   f. remember you can reduce across multiplication signs, NOT ADDITION, EQUAL SIGNS, etc.

6. If you go through all these steps and the answer still isn't there, you are still not allowed to FREAK OUT. *Reread* the question: Chances are VERY good that you've misread one teeny-weeny, tiny-whiny portion of the question. Clear your mind. See the problem anew, and you'll find the glitch. Then fixing it will be a breeze. If you don't find your flaw, look at the answers, get rid of any that make absolutely no sense [if possible], and then GUESS AND GO ON!

---

[27] I am at a loss to express just how vital this point is or how many thousands of points students lose each year because they don't follow through on their problems.

OMG—IT'S NOT THERE!!

IT HAPPENS TO ALL OF US. OK, MAINLY JUST TO YOU, BUT IT HAPPENS. YOU WORK HARD ON A PROBLEM, YOU SET IT UP, DO IT OUT AND SOLVE THE THING. THEN YOU STROLL OVER TO THE ANSWER CHOICES, AND IT'S NOT THERE!!!!

THE FIRST THING TO DO IS NOT FREAK OUT! NUMBERS ARE LIKE WORDS IN THAT MOST HAVE MANY EXACT SYNONYMS. 1 IS THE SAME AS: 1.00, $\frac{9}{9}$, ETC, SO IF THE YOU DON'T SEE THE NUMBER YOU GOT AMONG THE ANSWER CHOICES, DON'T WORRY; IT MIGHT ACTUALLY BE THERE, IT JUST MAY LOOK DIFFERENT FROM WHAT YOU HAVE. IF YOUR SOLUTION IS $\frac{3}{2}$ THEN IT WOULD BE COMPLETELY FINE FOR YOU TO PICK 1.5. JUST DON'T PANIC AND PICK $\frac{2}{3}$!

THIS IS WHERE KNOWING FRACTIONAL AND DECIMAL EQUIVALENTS AND KNOWING HOW TO TRANSLATE MIXED NUMBERS COMES IN REALLY HANDY.

WRITE IT RIGHT:

GIVE YOURSELF ROOM. DON'T WRITE OVER TEXT OR TRAIL OFF THE END OF YOUR PAP

Among the many things I have learned from my students over the years:

1. Chances are, the straighter you write, the straighter and more organized your thoughts. I'll go one step further:
   a. Writing out steps of equations clearly and in a direct line helps you think better and more clearly. When you're solving for x as you move down the page, keep your equal signs aligned vertically. If you start solving for x with x on the right side of the equal sign, FINISH with it on the right side of the equal sign. Often kids just for the hell of it switch it to the left and in the process forget to move a negative sign with it or some other genius move that guarantees a careless error. SO:
   b. If you find yourself jamming your writing into a margin, over printed text or on staples, or if it starts trailing off into the breeze, stop and realign yourself [that takes another nanosecond], and get back on the right track!
   c. If you run out of space by your current problem, you can always use empty space beneath problems you've already finished!

2. If you are setting up equations, start them at the **top left** of the available space, then use your equal sign as a guiding line—i.e., place the equal sign for the next line of the equation directly below the first equal sign and work down from there. Once your equal signs start trailing off or, even worse, disappearing, it's a one-way ticket to *CrazyLand*!

3. All your info should be listed in linear fashion either across or down your work space, and all info should be complete. Don't leave numbers or variables hanging in space. Make them be equal to *something*!

1st Ed. © ibidPREP llc

Do I Have to Do It Out?

I am not so great at listening to my own mind. Over the years, I have gotten better. I realize now that if I start thinking a lot about going to the corner to get a cup of coffee, it probably means I want a cup of coffee, and I should go get it.

If the tiny voice in your brain is starting to debate whether or not to do something, stop wasting time and DO IT! No one has ever suffered ill effects from writing out an equation. And if you think it might be a waste of precious time to do it, rest assured that it takes five times longer to debate with yourself whether or not to do it—and then you still probably have to do it anyway!

And please: even if you can't see how to solve a problem straight through from beginning to end, start with what you know how to do. Do the first couple of steps and see where that gets you. You'll be amazed at how often the next step becomes obvious when you do this. So just try!

NINE BLOCKS

WHEN MY MOTHER LEARNED TO DRIVE SHE WAS DEATHLY AFRAID OF MAKING LEFT TURNS, SO SHE ONLY MADE RIGHT TURNS. THE ONLY PROBLEM WAS THAT SHE LIVED ON A ONE-WAY STREET AMONG A GRID OF OTHER ONE-WAY STREETS. THIS MEANT THAT WHEN SHE WAS ONE LEFT TURN AWAY FROM HER HOUSE, SHE HAD TO DRIVE NINE BLOCKS OUT OF HER WAY TO GET HOME!

I HAVE SAT AND WATCHED BOATLOADS OF STUDENTS WORK THROUGH PROBLEMS ONLY TO COME TO A DEAD HALT WHEN THEY NEEDED TO DO SOMETHING UNPLEASANT OR ANNOYING LIKE LONG DIVISION OR REWRITE NUMBERS IN ORDER OR PLOT POINTS ON A GRAPH OR DIVIDE BY π. INSTEAD OF PLOWING AHEAD, THEY TRY GUESSING, PLUGGING IN, WORKING BACKWARD, EYEBALLING THE NUMBERS OR IMAGINING STUFF IN THEIR HEADS. IN SHORT, THEY GO NINE BLOCKS OUT OF THEIR WAY INSTEAD OF MAKING ONE SLIGHTLY SCARY LEFT-HAND TURN.

It Doesn't Matter That It Doesn't Matter. It Matters.

For some reason many students do mental triage[28] on their math problems. They automatically decide what to bother reading and what not to bother doing. They decide which pieces of info or points of math "don't matter." Trust me, until you get to the very end of a problem and process everything in a question, YOU DO NOT GET TO DECIDE WHAT IS IMPORTANT.

Nuts & Bolts of Doing the MATH

1. Do NOT read the question all at once.
2. Read the question to the first comma or period—whichever comes first.
3. Translate each clause or sentence into math terms and equations as you read.
4. Draw any figures or write out any formulas as they are mentioned.
5. Make a plan of How to Solve and follow through by:
   a. Writing out all your work fully and neatly
   b. Labeling all terms
   c. FINISHING YOUR PROBLEMS [don't peek at answer choices halfway through]
6. Once you completely execute your approach, RE-READ the last part of the question. Be sure you're giving the answer that is called for!

---

[28] a process of prioritizing which problems get dealt with first and which get dealt with later or not at all.

1st Ed. © ibidPREP llc

Must Know

Arithmetic

1ˢᵗ Ed. © ibidPREP llc

Must Know Math—Arithmetic

Must Know Terms

It's easy to speak any language if you know a few key basics. Learn these essential terms in order to start speaking better math:

- **Sum:**   The result of addition.
- **Difference:**   The result of subtraction.
- **Product:**   The result of multiplication.
- **Quotient:**   The result of division.
- **Integer:**   A whole number, positive or negative.
- **Even Numbers:**
    - Any whole number that can be divided by 2 without a remainder.
    - NOTE—When an odd number is divided by 2, the whole number remainder can only ever be 1.
- **Zero:** Zero is an integer and it's even [when zero is divided by two the remainder is zero!] However, it is neither positive nor negative, and although you may divide zero by any number, you CANNOT divide any number by zero.
- **Prime Numbers:**
    - Positive numbers that have only two distinct [different] factors: 1 and itself.
        2, 3, 5, 7, 11, 13, 17, 19, 23, 29, 31, etc....
    - 1 is NOT a prime number. [It only has one distinct factor (itself), not two.]
    - All primes are odd numbers except 2, which for obvious reasons can be divided only by itself and 1 [there are no other numbers between them].
- **Multiples**
    The whole number products of a number.
        E.g., the multiples of 12 are: 12, 24, 36, 48, 60, 72, 84, 96, etc.
        NOTE—The first multiple of every number is itself.
- **Factors**
    The factors of a number are those integers that can be multiplied with other integers to form that number.
        E.g., the FACTORS of 6 are 1, 2, 3 and 6.
- **Distinct**
    This simply means "different." As in, in the set {1, 2, 3, 3, 4}, there are five terms but only four DISTINCT numbers.
- **Consecutive**
    This simply means "in a row" or "one after the other." As in, the first five consecutive positive numbers are 1, 2, 3, 4, 5. Be careful, though; sometimes "one after the other" could mean different things. As in, the first five consecutive even numbers are 2, 4, 6, 8, 10.
- **Coefficient:**
    A number that comes before a variable, or a set of terms in parentheses. As in, the coefficient of $3x$ is 3, and the coefficient of $5(x + 8)$ is 5.
    - If a variable has no coefficient, then its coefficient is 1.
    - As in, $x + x = 2x$ because it's really $1x + 1x = 2x$!
- **Inclusive:**   Including. 1 to 10 inclusive includes both 1 and 10 in the set.
- **Between:**   Not including the numbers listed. Between 1 and 10 means 2 through 9, not including 1 and 10. Exclusive (the opposite of inclusive) has the same meaning.

MULTIPLICATION TABLES

MULTIPLICATION TABLES

It is vital that you know your multiplication tables by rote. Besides, needing a calculator to do simple multiplication and division is like needing a table saw to cut a sandwich in half. It's a waste of time and keeps you from recognizing vital relationships among numbers, like when you need to reduce fractions by finding factors.

There are ways to make the multiplication tables easier. First, it helps to have a solid grip on addition. I can't tell you how many times I've seen high school students use their fingers to add 9 + 4. Don't get me wrong, using your fingers is far superior to saying "12." However, better still is KNOWING that 9 + 4 = 13. Once you're comfortable with adding, let's go the multiplication tables and start with the ONES [always start *everything* at ONE].

In the glossary of this book are some fun [yay!] tips for learning your math tables. If you don't instantly know 12 × 7 or 9 × 7, then you must look below and LEARN YOUR TABLES—especially your 9's and 12's!!

	1	2	3	4	5	6	7	8	9	10	11	12
1	1	2	3	4	5	6	7	8	9	10	11	12
2	2	4	6	8	10	12	14	16	18	20	22	24
3	3	6	9	12	15	18	21	24	27	30	33	36
4	4	8	12	16	20	24	28	32	36	40	44	48
5	5	10	15	20	25	30	35	40	45	50	55	60
6	6	12	18	24	30	36	42	48	54	60	66	72
7	7	14	21	28	35	42	49	56	63	70	77	84
8	8	16	24	32	40	48	56	64	72	80	88	96
9	9	18	27	36	45	54	63	72	81	90	99	108
10	10	20	30	40	50	60	70	80	90	100	110	120
11	11	22	33	44	55	66	77	88	99	110	121	132
12	12	24	36	48	60	72	84	96	108	120	132	144

Know—Multiples That Pop Up All The Time:

15×1=15,	15×2=30,	15×3=45,	15×4=60
16×1=16,	16×2=32,	16×3=48,	16×4 =64
18×1=18,	18×2=36,	18×3=54,	18×4=72
75×1=75,	75×2=150,	75×3=225,	75×4=300

1ˢᵗ Ed. © ibidPREP llc

Make Friends with Tens

Multiplying and dividing by factors of ten is super easy. Just ignore the zeros! Most students get scared when they see 12,000 × 4,000. Of course, most of those same students wouldn't have any trouble with 12 × 4. In reality, it's the same problem!

$$12{,}000 \times 4{,}000 = 12 \times 4 \times 1{,}000 \times 1{,}000 = 48 \times 1{,}000{,}000 = 48{,}000{,}000$$

How did I know that 1,000 × 1,000 =1,000,000? That's easy! Anytime you multiply a multiple of ten times a multiple of ten, just count the zeros to find out what your new place value will be! In this case, 1,000 × 1,000 *yields six zeros, so it equals* 1,000,000.

The easiest and neatest way to multiply multiples of 10 is to separate out any integers besides zero and multiply them, and then add the number of zeros involved to the end of that problem.

E.g.   25,000 × 30 = 25 × 3 *and four zeros* = 750,000

Tens Places

100,000	10,000	1,000	100	10	1
one hundred thousand	ten thousand	thousand	hundred	ten	one

Each tens places is ten times greater than the one to its immediate right.

DECIMAL PLACES

1	.1	.01	.001	.0001	.00001
one	tenth	hundredth	thousandth	ten-thousandth	hundred-thousandth

Each decimal place is ten times greater than the one to its immediate right.

MAKE FRIENDS WITH 10s

1. 24,000 x 400 =

2. 16,000 x 90 =

3. 120,000 x 11,000 =

4. 60 x 20,000 =

5. 0.003 x 0.04 =

6. 0.13 × 0.3 =

7. 0.00005 × 0.0007 =

8. 2.2 × 0.009 =

9. 1,000 × 0.001

10. 42,000 × 0.02

11. 0.27 × 200 =

12. 0.11 × 3,300 =

Decimals—Follow the Bouncing Ball

Believe it or not, decimals, like fractions [their close cousins], were invented to make things *easier*, yet many students are as confused by decimals as they are by fractions. Decimals are really just a specific kind of fraction [just as percents are], i.e., fractions with a power of ten in their denominator.

$$E.g., .08 = \frac{8}{100}, \quad \frac{75}{500} = \frac{150}{1000} = .150$$

When we only call values less than 1 "decimals," we're not being entirely accurate. Every number really has a decimal, you just don't always see it. The decimal, whether you see it or not, is VERY important because it controls the values of the digits.

When you see the number 12, it is the same as the number 12 or 12.0 or 12.00, etc. The decimal is important because if we move the decimal in the number left or right, we can multiply its value by ten times, a hundred times, a thousand times, etc., or we can divide it by ten times, a hundred times, a thousand times, etc. Each place represents a zero. To move the decimal one place is to multiply or divide the number by 10, to move it two places is to multiply or divide by 100, to move three places is to multiply or divide the number by 1,000, etc.

12.0 × 1,000 moves the decimal place three places

[one for each zero in 1,000] to the right, so 12.0 0 0. =12,000

12.0 ÷ 1,000 moves the decimal place three places to the left, so .0 1 2. = .01

Please do the problems below WITHOUT your calculator. After you are finished you may check your work with your calculator.

> **DECIMALS TO FRACTIONS**
> Convert the decimals below to fractions:
>
> 1. .08 = _____
>
> 2. .9 = _____
>
> 3. .006 = _____
>
> 4. .17 = _____
>
> 5. .095 = _____
>
> 6. .32 = _____

Fractions to Decimals

To convert fractions to decimals, remember that a fraction is a division problem and divide!

1st Ed. © ibidPREP llc

$\frac{1}{8} = 1 \div 8$ [*It's always TOP divided by BOTTOM*] =

```
        .125
    8)1.000
      -.8
       .2
      -.16
       .04
      -.040
       .000
```

> **FRACTIONS TO DECIMALS**
> Convert the fractions below to decimals:
>
> 1. $\frac{2}{10}$ = _____
>
> 2. $\frac{3}{100}$ = _____
>
> 3. $\frac{70}{1,000}$ = _____
>
> 4. $\frac{15}{50}$ = _____
>
> 5. $\frac{22}{100}$ = _____
>
> 6. $\frac{22}{10}$ = _____

Multiply the Meat

Decimals and zeros in numbers confuse everyone's multiplication. The easiest way to perform these operations—ones that use numbers with zeros and decimals in them—is to ignore the zeros and decimal points and just multiply the meat, i.e., the non-zero integers! Then, when you're done, put a decimal at the end of your number and move it as needed by putting the zeros and the decimals back in. How?

- Count the number of zeros in the two numbers you multiplied and add them onto your answer [moving the decimal to the right one place for each zero].
- Count the number of decimal places in the two numbers you multiplied and move the decimal point to the left for each one. If the decimal ends up moving beyond your number, add a zero between the outermost digit and the decimal. E.g., 2,400 × .003

Step 1: disregard the zeros and decimal places— 24 × 3 = 72.

Step 2: add back in two zeros [taken off 2,400]—72+2 *zeros* = 7,200.

Step 3: move decimal point three places to the left.

[*Originally the decimal in .003 was moved three places to the right to make it* 3.0]—7.200

So: 2,400 × .003 = 7.200

Remainders

Reminders are the whole number amount left over when one number is divided by another.

Remainders are one of the first stops on the math highway. The point at which many students stop and say, "No thanks. I'm out." When you throw most kids 17 ÷ 4 the math gears grind to a halt and they look blankly at you and say, "You can't. It doesn't go in evenly."

While it is true that 17 ÷ 4 does not have an integer solution, 17 can absolutely be divided by 4. In fact, any number can be divided by any other number.[29] The answer may not be pretty, but there will be an answer!

When we first started dividing, numbers stopped at the decimal place. So when we got to the decimal place and there was still a part of the number left to divide, we were said to have a ***remainder, and that's perfectly acceptable!***

Once we learned how to go beyond the decimal, we were able to continue dividing to get a complete number value for our answer.

* **Note**: The remainder in this equation is **NOT** .25. That is merely the non-integer part of the answer. Also, remember, if you do not want to continue dividing out past the decimal, you may put the whole number remainder over the divisor and express it as a fraction, so 17 ÷ 4 = 4 $\frac{1}{4}$, 4.25 or 4 r 1!

$$
\begin{array}{r}
4.25 \\
4\overline{)17.00} \\
-16.00 \\
\hline
1.00 \\
-0.80 \\
\hline
0.20 \\
-0.20 \\
\hline
0
\end{array}
$$

Fun Facts About Remainders

- If a number goes evenly into another, the remainder is zero.
- The remainder can never be equal to or greater than the divisor.
- If the number being divided is less than the divisor, the remainder is equal to the number being divided.

$$5 \div 7 = 0 \text{ r } 5$$

KNOW:

$\frac{1}{2} = .50 = 50\%$ $\frac{1}{6} = .1\overline{66} = 16.\overline{66}\%$

$\frac{1}{3} = .\overline{33} = 33.\overline{33}\%$ $\frac{1}{8} = .125 = 12.5\%$

$\frac{1}{4} = .25 = 25\%$ $\frac{1}{9} = .\overline{11} = 11.\overline{11}\%$

$\frac{1}{5} = .20 = 20\%$ $\frac{1}{10} = .10 = 10\%$

---

[29] Except, of course, zero. No number may be divided by zero because zero cannot multiply with any number to get a value other than zero. That is why a fraction [which is a mini-division problem] with zero in its denominator is **UNDEFINED**.

     1ˢᵗ Ed. © ibidPREP llc

Factors

Factoring is an incredibly important skill for doing simple AND complex math [like factoring polynomials!], learning inverse variations, dividing and simplifying fractions, to name just a few things. In school you may have been taught prime factorization, but that does not give you all the distinct [different] factors of an integer. The best way to go about that [and to learn inverse variation] is to play bouncy-bouncy.

Place the number you want to factor [let's say 24] in the middle of the page or area you are writing in. Directly below that, on the left margin, write the number one [1]. On the right margin, write the number you are factoring [24]. Then think of the next number after one that could go into your number. In this case TWO works. As in a list, write a comma after 1 and write 2. Then, on the other side of the line, place a comma to the left of 24 and write 2's complement. In this case it's 12. Then you go up from 2 and keep seeing if each consecutive number is a factor of your number or not. By the time you get to the middle you will have covered all the numbers!

24

1,   2,   3,   4,   6,   8,   12,   24

FACTORING
Please factor these numbers, as demonstrated below [play bouncy-bouncy]:

54
1,   2,   3,   6,   9,   18,   27,   54

1. 18

2. 144

3. 64

4. 28

5. 132

---

6. What is the greatest common factor [GCF] of 35 and 91?

7. What is the greatest common factor [GCF] of 72 and 96?

8. What is the least common multiple [LCM] of 18 and 24?

9. What is the least common multiple [LCM] of 12 and 15?

10. What are the greatest common factors [GCF] and least common multiples [LCM] of 36 and 54?

FRACTIONS

DON'T BE AFRAID OF FRACTIONS. YOU ARE NOT IN 4TH GRADE ANYMORE.

Studatuta's Two Rules of Fractions

Everyone hates fractions. Except me. I see them as beautiful little units designed to make multiplication and division easier. The top of the fraction is the numerator and the bottom is the denominator, but the really important part of the fraction is the little line between the numerator and the denominator. That line means: DIVIDED BY. So the fraction 3/4 can be read as three fourths *or* three divided by four. Now here's where kids lose it: "But four doesn't go into three!" Of course it does. Any number can be divided by any other number [except zero]. What freaks kids out starting in fourth grade [and leaves them there] is when numbers don't divide *evenly* into one another. Don't be one of those kids. Push through the decimal barrier. *Bravely soldier forth*!!

1st Ed. © *ibidPREP llc*

When it comes to fractions in general, there are two things you must do to them automatically and on first sight. These are "Studatuta's Two Rules of Fractions." Do them and your arithmetic and algebraic fraction work will be that much better.

1. **Reduce** [where possible]—First and always reduce. One of the beauties of fractions is that they allow you to simplify your numbers and thereby make your arithmetic easier, thus reducing your chance of making careless errors.

2. **Eliminate Denominators** [cross-multiply where possible]—This is huge. Once you are able to recognize on sight and without hesitation that a/b = c/d is the same as ad = bc, algebra becomes that much easier, and it's not hard to do at all once you grasp the concept. What you are really doing with the denominators on each side of the equation is getting rid of them by **multiplying** each by its **reciprocal**. So if the denominator is b you multiply both sides by b. The b on the side with the denominator of b becomes b/b which is **1** [hence they cancel out]. The best way to eliminate denominators in fractions on opposing sides of an equation is to bring them up to their opposing numerators.

$$\frac{a}{b} = \frac{c}{d}$$

$$\frac{b}{1} \times \frac{a}{b} = \frac{c}{d} \times \frac{b}{1}$$

$$\frac{d}{1} \times a = \frac{cb}{d} \times \frac{d}{1}$$

$$ad = bc$$

Reducing

Now that you know how important it is to reduce, perhaps this is a good time to actually learn the proper way to do it.

How to Reduce #1

You may reduce the numerator and denominator [top & bottom of a fraction] within one fraction. We reduce by finding the GREATEST common factor of the numerator and denominator and then dividing the numerator and denominator by that factor.

$$\frac{5}{10} = \frac{5 \text{ divided by } 5}{10 \text{ divided by } 5} = \frac{1}{2}$$

Why? Because five is the greatest common factor of five and ten. It goes into five one time, and that leaves one as the numerator. It goes into ten two times, and that leaves two as the denominator.

Reducing makes it so much easier to multiply fractions. Once you've reduced your fractions, it's simple! You just multiply the numerators and the denominators!

So:

$$\frac{12}{48} \times \frac{9}{27} = \frac{\cancel{12}}{\cancel{48}} \times \frac{\cancel{9}}{\cancel{27}} = \frac{1}{4} \times \frac{1}{3} = \frac{1}{12}$$

Easy, right?

How To Reduce #2

You may reduce across the multiplication sign among two or more fractions.

$$\frac{3}{16} \times \frac{4}{15} = \frac{\cancel{3}}{\cancel{16}} \times \frac{\cancel{4}}{\cancel{15}} = \frac{1}{4} \times \frac{1}{5}$$

How Not To Reduce

You may **NOT** reduce across an equal sign or plus sign:

$\dfrac{4}{7} = \dfrac{x}{12}$ is **NOT** reducible to $\dfrac{1}{7} = \dfrac{x}{3}$, and:

$\dfrac{4+x}{12}$ is **NOT** reducible to $\dfrac{1+x}{3}$.

To reduce one fraction with a plus sign in the numerator, break the fraction out into two or more separate fractions and THEN reduce:

$\dfrac{4+x}{12} = \dfrac{4}{12} + \dfrac{x}{12}$ **is** reducible to $\dfrac{1}{3} + \dfrac{x}{12}$.

A fraction is a part of a whole. To get a part of a whole you must divide the whole. Therefore, a fraction is a divided whole.

A fraction is made of three parts: the numerator, the denominator and the dividing line.

REDUCING
Please reduce the following fractions

1. $\dfrac{18}{72} =$

2. $\dfrac{121}{44} \times \dfrac{4}{11} =$

3. $\dfrac{22}{42} \times \dfrac{14}{11} =$

4. $\dfrac{9}{32} \times \dfrac{8}{81} =$

5. $\dfrac{33}{84} \times \dfrac{49}{77} =$

6. $\dfrac{12}{30} \times \dfrac{15}{48} =$

7. $\dfrac{16}{20} \times \dfrac{50}{56} =$

8. $\dfrac{682}{3} \times \dfrac{78}{44} =$

9. Solve for x: $\dfrac{4x}{18} = \dfrac{6}{28}$

10. $\dfrac{4}{24} = \dfrac{6x}{32}$

11. $\dfrac{9x}{117} = \dfrac{5}{65}$

12. $\dfrac{56}{7x} = \dfrac{8}{72}$

1st Ed. © ibidPREP llc

Percents

Percents act as a bridge between fractions and decimals. If you translate the word "percent" into math, you realize it means "divided by 100." So, 50 percent really means 50 ÷100, which we know to write as $\frac{50}{100}$.

Many percent problems are expressed as word problems. If you remember that certain words can be replaced with math signs, you're in business.

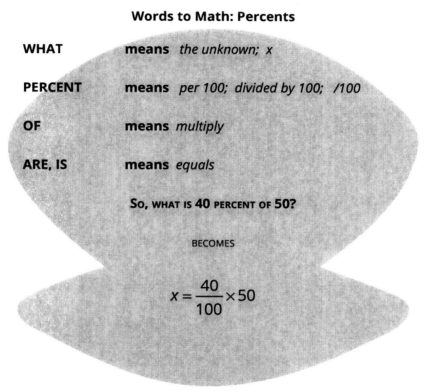

Words to Math: Percents

WHAT   means *the unknown; x*

PERCENT   means *per 100; divided by 100; /100*

OF   means *multiply*

ARE, IS   means *equals*

So, what is **40** percent of **50**?

BECOMES

$$x = \frac{40}{100} \times 50$$

E.g.:   80% of a class of 200 are nose pickers. How many are nose pickers?

80%: $\frac{80}{100}$ [PER means Divided By & CENT means 100—change all percents to fractions over 100]

To solve this problem, REDUCE FIRST!

$\frac{80}{100}$ × 200 = 160

E.g.,   What is 30% of 90?

Translate words to math and you get:

[What] x [is] = [30%] $\frac{30}{100}$ [of] × [90] 90 = $\frac{3}{1}$ × 9=27

Although there are many ways to solve percent problems, please try the following using the fractional, words-to-math approach!

<u>PERCENT WORDS TO MATH</u>

1. 20 is what percent of 20?

2. What is 48 percent of 25?

3. 15 percent of what is 180?

4. What is 150 percent of 150?

5. 45 is what percent of 225?

6. 16 is 80 percent of what?

7. What is 25 percent of 144?

8. 20 percent of 20 percent of what is 40?

9. 25 percent of 48 is what percent of 60?

10. 40 percent of 25 is 5 percent of what?

11. 12 is 30 percent of 25 percent of what?

Percent and Amount

A big issue with students and percent questions seems to revolve around percent increase and percent decrease. What often confuses students here is that amount and percent are very different things.

Amount is a fixed number: Julia ordered 12 loaves of bread yesterday and 3 more than that today.

Percent is a fraction based on the ratio of the parts to a whole. 3 is what percent of 12?

$$3 = \frac{x}{100} \cdot 12$$

$$\frac{3}{12} = \frac{x}{100};$$

$$\frac{1}{4} = \frac{x}{100};$$

$$25 = x$$

so 3 is 25% of 12

1st Ed. © ibidPREP llc

Still, we are often sorely tempted to confuse the two...

EXAMPLE 1. Manuel wanted to buy a jacket that he saw in the store for $100. He waited and a week later the price of the jacket had increased 10%. He waited another week and this time when he returned to the store there was a sale and the jacket was 10% off the latest price.

How much was the jacket now?

If you said "$100," congratulations! You are absolutely normal. But wrong!

Remember: 10 percent of 100 [the original price that was raised] is going to be equal to a different [and smaller] amount than 10 percent of the later price, so you will actually be paying less than the original amount for the jacket after it has been raised and then goes on sale!

> Original price: $100
>
> 10% of $100 = $10
>
> Price after first week [+10%] = $110
>
> 10% of $110 = 11 (not 10!)
>
> So, the sale price will equal: $110 – $11= $99!

Percent Rate of Change

To determine the rate [percent] of increase or decrease if you're given the original and final amounts, just work backward.

A car originally sold for $24,000. At the end of the year, the car went on sale for $20,400. What percent off was the sale?

First, determine the **amount** of change.

$$24,000 - 20,400 = 3,600$$

Then determine what percent of the **ORIGINAL**[30] the amount of the change equals.

> $$3,600 = \frac{x}{100} \cdot 24,000$$
>
> $$3,600 = \frac{x}{1} \cdot 240$$
>
> $$\frac{3,600}{240} = x$$
>
> $$15 = x$$

---

[30] Percent increase and decrease are ALWAYS based on the original or starting amount you are given.

Must Know Arithmetic

Here's a handy formula for figuring out percent change!

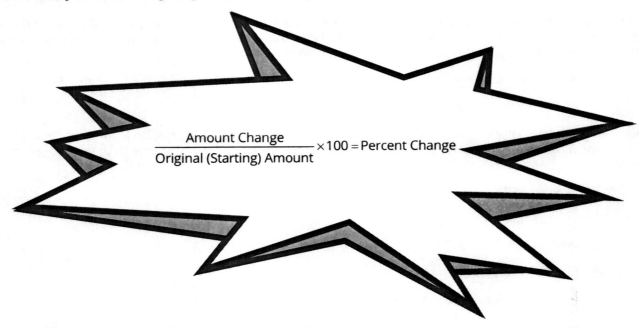

$$\frac{\text{Amount Change}}{\text{Original (Starting) Amount}} \times 100 = \text{Percent Change}$$

For example, Marge left 12 donuts on the counter. Homer ate three of them in two seconds. By what percent did the number of donuts decrease?

$$\frac{\text{Amount Change}}{\text{Original (Starting) Amount}} \times 100 = \text{Percent Change}$$

$$\frac{3}{12} \times 100 = \frac{1}{4} \times 100 = 25\%$$

You can also rework the formula in order to figure out the amount of change or even the original amount:

$$\frac{\text{Percent Change}}{100} \times \text{Original (Starting) Amount} = \text{Amount Change}$$

$$\frac{\text{Amount Change}}{\text{Percent Change}} \times 100 = \text{Original (Starting) Amount}$$

For example—

Bart ate 15% of the donuts Marge bought. If Marge bought 40 donuts, how many donuts did Bart eat?

$$\frac{\text{Percent Change}}{100} \times \text{Original (Starting) Amount} = \text{Amount Change}$$

$$\frac{15}{100} \times 40 = 6$$

1st Ed. © ibidPREP llc

PERCENT WORD PROBLEMS

1. If 80% of Steve's DVDs cost $25 each and if 20% of his DVDs cost $15 each, what is the average (arithmetic mean) cost per disc?
   A. $17.00
   B. $18.00
   C. $20.00
   D. $22.00
   E. $23.00

2. At Jefferson Middle School 40 percent of the students are boys. If there are 300 girls, what is the total number of students at Jefferson Middle School?
   A. 200
   B. 300
   C. 450
   D. 500
   E. 750

3. Bill and Ted shared a bucket of ice cream. If they ate all the ice cream in the bucket and Bill ate four times as much ice cream as Ted, what percent of the ice cream did Bill eat?
   A. 20%
   B. 25%
   C. $66\frac{2}{3}$ %
   D. 75%
   E. 80%

4. In a certain store, the regular price of a microwave is $750. How much more money is saved buying this microwave at 40 percent off the regular price rather than buying it on sale at 20 percent off the regular price with an additional discount of 20 percent off the sale price?
   A. $15
   B. $20
   C. $25
   D. $30
   E. $35

5. State Law School plans on accepting 2,000 students for next year's class. Of the 1,500 students accepted so far, 55 percent are male and 45 percent are female. How many of the remaining students to be accepted must be female in order for half of the total number of students accepted to be female?
   A. 100
   B. 175
   C. 250
   D. 325
   E. 400

1st Ed. © ibidPREP llc　　　　　　　　　ACT—105

6. If x > 0 and 25 percent of x is equal to 15 percent of y, then 40 percent of x equals what percent of y?
    A. 20%
    B. 24%
    C. 28%
    D. 30%
    E. 32%

7. Which of the following is equivalent to $\frac{1}{4}$ of 18 percent of 548?
    A. 18% of 137

    B. 18% of $\frac{137}{4}$

    C. $17\frac{3}{4}$% of 548

    D. $\frac{18}{4}$% of 137

    E. $\frac{18}{4}$ × 548

8. If 60 percent of p is equal to q percent of 40, where q > 0, what is the value of $\frac{p}{q}$?
    A. $\frac{1}{3}$

    B. $\frac{1}{2}$

    C. $\frac{2}{3}$

    D. 1

    E. $\frac{4}{3}$

1st Ed. © ibidPREP llc

PERCENT/AMOUNT

1. Find the percentage increase:
    From $2,000 to $3,000

2. Find the percentage decrease:
    From $75 to $60

3. Find the percentage increase:
    From $48,000 to $60,000

4. Find the **amount** of increase:
    Original amount: 240, Percent increase: 25%

5. Find the **amount** of decrease:
    Original amount: 90, Percent decrease: 35%

6. Find the **final amount**:
    Original amount: 6,000, Percent Decrease: 90%

7. Find the **final amount**:
    Original amount: 380, Percent increase: 32%

8. Find the **original amount**:
    Final amount: $690, Percent increase: 20%

KNOW: MEAN, MEDIAN, MODE

AVERAGE [MEAN]:

<u>Sum of all numbers in a group divided by number of terms.</u>

Any average problem can [and **MUST**] be written out as the formula:

$$AVG = \frac{\text{Sum of the Terms}}{\text{Number of Terms}}$$

Most average [mean] problems will give you two out of the three variables in the formula above. Fill the variables into their proper places in the formula **FIRST**. Then you'll be able to find the third variable. Then proceed to the rest of the problem as given and as necessary.

E.g., the average of Davis's five test scores is 82. After he takes one more test, his average goes up to 85. What did he get on his 6th test?

The average of Davis's five test scores is 82.

$$AVG = \frac{\text{Sum of the Terms}}{\text{Number of Terms}}$$

$$82 = \frac{\text{Sum of the Terms}}{5}$$

Using the second rule of fractions we know:

$$5 \times 82 = \text{Sum of Terms}$$
$$410 = \text{Sum of Terms}$$

Now we know he scored a **TOTAL of 410** on his first five tests.

After he takes one more test, his average goes up to 85. What did he get on his 6th test?

If we let x = the score he got on his 6th test, then:

$$85 = \frac{410 + x}{6}$$

Notice now that the number of terms has changed to six!

$$6 \times 85 = 410 + x$$
$$510 = 410 + x$$
$$x = 100!$$

1st Ed. © ibidPREP llc

MEDIAN:

Number that is the middle term of a set of numbers that have been put in ascending or descending order:*

The median of the set {3, 2, 4, 5, 7, 4, 5} is 4 because the set in order is:
{2, 3, 4, 4, 5, 5, 7} and the number in the exact middle of that set is 4.

If there is an even number of terms in the set, choose the **TWO** middle terms and average them [find their mean]. E.g., the median of the set {3, 4, 4, 5, 6, 7} = 4.5 [4.5 is the average of 4 & 5, the two middle terms of the set.]

*Whenever you have a MEDIAN problem, be sure to write out or rewrite all numbers in ascending or descending order.

MODE:

Number in a group that appears most often.

9, 12, 13, 13, 13, 14, 15, 18, 29 = ?

Practice

MEAN, MEDIAN AND MODE

1. The average of x, y, and 3x is 10. What is y?
   A. 4x − 30
   B. 30 − 4x
   C. 4x + 30
   D. 30 + 4x
   E. 4x

2. If x = y + 10 and y = 2x, what is the average of x and y?
   A. −30
   B. −15
   C. 0
   D. 15
   E. 30

3. Hayden receives the following scores on her math tests: 75, 78, 85, and 83. If she takes one more test and ends up with an average of 82, what is the median of her five scores?
   A. 78
   B. 80.25
   C. 82
   D. 83
   E. 89

4. The average of a list of 5 numbers is 15. If one of the numbers is removed, the average of the remaining numbers is 19. What number was removed?
   A. 4
   B. 2
   C. 0
   D. −1
   E. −4

5. There are 5 numbers in a set of positive integers. The mean of the set is equal to twice the median, and the number of numbers in the mode is equal to the mode. If the mode is 2 and mean is 6, what is the average of the two highest numbers in the set?
   A. 3
   B. 5
   C. 11.5
   D. 23
   E. 24

1st Ed. © *ibidPREP llc*

Exponents

One of the great [not] things about math is that as soon as you get multiplication slightly sorted out [3 × 2 =6], they change things and introduce exponents. Then, all of a sudden something that looks like 3 × 2, namely 3^2, doesn't equal 6; now it equals 9! Even though 2 × 2 and 2^2 both equal 4?? A lot of students, understandably, bow out at this point and simply decide to bail on exponent questions whenever they arise.

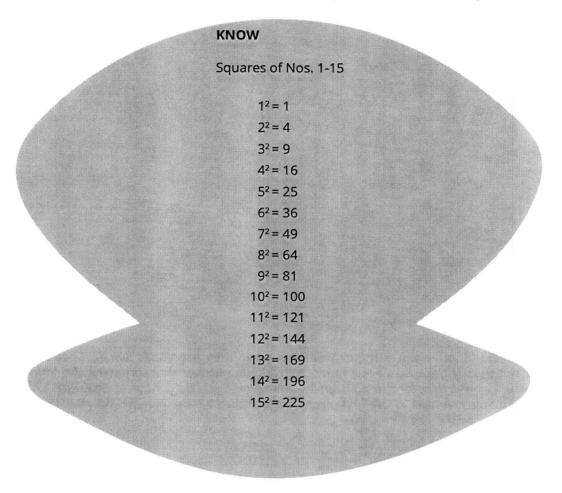

KNOW

Squares of Nos. 1-15

$1^2 = 1$
$2^2 = 4$
$3^2 = 9$
$4^2 = 16$
$5^2 = 25$
$6^2 = 36$
$7^2 = 49$
$8^2 = 64$
$9^2 = 81$
$10^2 = 100$
$11^2 = 121$
$12^2 = 144$
$13^2 = 169$
$14^2 = 196$
$15^2 = 225$

However, the good thing about exponents on standardized tests is they fall under that heading of SCARY TOPICS/ EASY QUESTIONS.

So, if you just hang in and remember a few basic rules about exponents, then you should be rewarded with a not too difficult question to get right.

The basic rules of exponents are listed below, but the most important thing to remember is that taking a number to a power simply means multiplying it by itself that number of times.

$4^3 = 4 \times 4 \times 4 = 64$

A square root is the number that, times itself, equals the number you are taking the root of. In better words, if you multiply the square root of a number by itself [square the square root], you will get the original number. Put an even better way: $\sqrt{x} \times \sqrt{x} = x$.

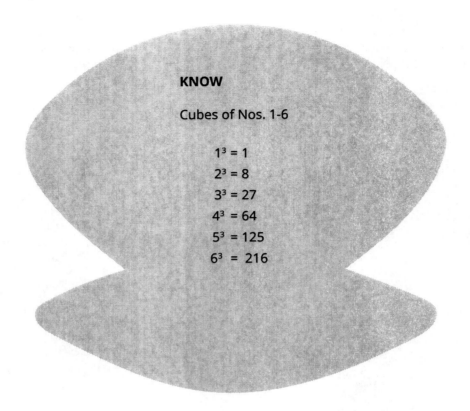

KNOW

Cubes of Nos. 1-6

$1^3 = 1$

$2^3 = 8$

$3^3 = 27$

$4^3 = 64$

$5^3 = 125$

$6^3 = 216$

Everyone knows that $\sqrt{9} = 3$, but most students freak out when they see things like $\sqrt{2}$. They freak out for a couple of reasons, but mostly because $\sqrt{2}$ is a hideous irrational number that threatens the fabric of human existence. [OK, maybe I went a little far there.] Happily, on this test, you don't have to deal with 1.414213562..., just $\sqrt{2}$, which is why it was invented in the first place: to symbolize a long, hideous number that no one else wants to deal with either. Treat it like a variable.

 1st Ed. © *ibidPREP llc*

Exponent Rules

NUMBER TO A POWER TIMES A NUMBER TO A POWER

To solve a number to a power times a number to a power, ADD the exponents:

$5^3 \times 5^4 = 5^{3+4} = 5^7$

NUMBER TO A POWER DIVIDED BY A NUMBER TO A POWER

To determine a number to a power divided by a number to a power, SUBTRACT the exponents:

$$\frac{7^9}{7^4} = 7^{9-4} = 7^5$$

NUMBER TO A POWER TAKEN TO A POWER

To determine a number to a power taken to a power, MULTIPLY the powers:

$$(5^3)^4 = 5^{3\times4} = 5^{12}$$

A NUMBER TO A POWER TIMES A DIFFERENT NUMBER TO THE SAME POWER

To determine a number to a power times a different number to the same power, MULTIPLY THE BASES and LEAVE THE EXPONENTS ALONE:

$$4^3 \times 5^3 = (4 \times 5)^3 = 20^3$$

A FRACTION TO A POWER

When you take a fraction to a power, remember to take the numerator and the denominator to that power:

$$\left(\frac{2}{3}\right)^4 = \frac{2^4}{3^4} = \frac{16}{81}$$

NEGATIVE EXPONENTS

This is REALLY confusing. Negative exponents have NOTHING to do with negative numbers. A number taken to a negative exponent equals the inverse of that number. [Flip it and put it under one.]

$$5^{-3} = \frac{1}{5^3} = \frac{1}{125}$$

A NUMBER TO A POWER PLUS THAT SAME NUMBER TO THE SAME POWER, PLUS ITSELF AGAIN, PLUS ITSELF...

Is just equal to the amount of times you are adding that number times itself:

$$4^3 + 4^3 + 4^3 + 4^3 = 4(4^3) = 4^1(4^3) = 4^{1+3} = 4^4$$

The Square Root Of A Fraction

Is equal to the square root of the top and the bottom:

$$\sqrt{\frac{9}{25}} = \frac{\sqrt{9}}{\sqrt{25}} = \frac{3}{5}$$

When a line of terms has an exponent at the end of them, ONLY THE LAST TERM GETS TAKEN TO THAT POWER....UNLESS THE TERMS ARE GROUPED IN PARENTHESIS.

$-3x^2 = -3x^2$ NOT $9x^2$ but $(-3x)^2 = 9x^2$,

AND [Believe it or not]:

$-4^2 = -16$ {because it's really: -1×4^2 } = 16*

* This is why you have to be VERY careful when using your calculator. In your calculator if you plug in -4^2, your answer will be -16. That is why, to be on the safe side, ALWAYS use parentheses: $(-4)^2 = 16$.

"Fun" Facts About Squares And Cubes The Uberdweeb Test Makers Love

There are few things the geeks who make these tests get more excited about than the fact that negative numbers squared become positive. The second thing they love, love, love is that a number between zero and one gets SMALLER when it gets squared. Here are some other annoying, er, amazing facts they like to exploit.[31]

"FUN" FACTS

- NEGATIVE NUMBERS SQUARED become POSITIVE.
- A number between zero and one gets SMALLER when it gets squared or cubed.
- $\frac{1}{2}^2 = \frac{1}{4}$ and $\frac{1}{4}^3 = \frac{1}{64}$
- A number less than -1 gets SMALLER when it's cubed.
- $-2^3 = -8$; $-2 > -8$
- A number between -1 and 0 gets BIGGER when it gets cubed.
- $-\frac{1}{4}^3 = -\frac{1}{64}$ [no matter how it may seem, $-\frac{1}{4}$ is LESS THAN $-\frac{1}{64}$]

---

[31] make use of, take advantage of

1st Ed. © ibidPREP llc

EXPONENTS

1. $5^3 \times 5^4 =$

2. $(3^4)^2 =$

3. $5^4 + 5^4 + 5^4 + 5^4 + 5^4 =$

4. $3^3 \times 5^3 =$

5. $(6^3)^4 \times 6^5 =$

6. $\dfrac{4^4 \times 4^{-6}}{4^{-4}} =$

PEMDAS—PARENTHESES, E**XPONENTS [**ROOTS**], M**ULTIPLICATION, D**IVISION, A**DDITION, S**UBTRACTION**

ADDITION IS THE SAME AS SUBTRACTION, MULTIPLICATION IS THE SAME AS DIVISION, & ROOTS ARE THE SAME AS EXPONENTS.

SUBTRACTING IS REALLY JUST ADDING A NEGATIVE.

$$8 - 5 = 8 + (-5) = 3$$

DIVIDING A NUMBER BY A DIVISOR IS THE SAME AS MULTIPLYING A NUMBER BY THE INVERSE OF THE DIVISOR.

$$16 \div 4 = 16 \times \frac{1}{4} = \frac{16}{4} = 4$$

TAKING THE ROOT OF A NUMBER IS THE SAME AS TAKING A NUMBER TO A FRACTIONAL POWER.

$$\sqrt[3]{125} = 125^{\frac{1}{3}}; \quad 7^{\frac{1}{4}} = \sqrt[4]{7}; \text{ ETC.}$$

THE ONLY THING "WRONG" WITH PEMDAS IS THAT ADDITION DOESN'T NECESSARILY HAVE TO GO BEFORE SUBTRACTION BECAUSE THEY'RE THE SAME THING! THEREFORE, JUST DO WHICHEVER OF THE TWO COMES FIRST. THE SAME IS TRUE FOR MULTIPLICATION/DIVISION AND EXPONENTS/ROOTS.

1st Ed. © ibidPREP llc

PEMDAS

1. $9 - 1 \times 4 =$

2. $(8 - 5) + 3.8 =$

3. $(2 \times 2)^2 \div 2(22 - 14) =$

4. $7 + 8 \times 7 \div 2 =$

5. $8 - 9 \times (6 - 9)^2 =$

6. $6 \times (6 \div 3)^2 =$

7. $3 \times 3 + 3 \div 3 - 3 \times 3 =$

8. $(49 \div 7^2) \times 5 =$

9. $(85 \div (7 - 2)) \times 4 =$

10. $(18 \div 6 + 2) \times \dfrac{7+3}{5} =$

11. $(9^2 + 7) \left(\dfrac{1}{11}\right) + 8 =$

12. $((8 \times 2)^2 + 5) \div (9 \div 2 + 4.5) =$

Practice

NUMBER KNOWLEDGE

1. In lowest terms, the product of $\frac{5}{6}$, $\frac{3}{10}$, and $\frac{8}{9}$ is:

    A. $\frac{2}{9}$

    B. $\frac{4}{9}$

    C. $\frac{12}{27}$

    D. $\frac{240}{540}$

    E. $\frac{23}{18}$

2. Please evaluate the following expression:

    $$\frac{\frac{5}{3} - \frac{3}{8}}{\frac{3}{4} - \frac{3}{8}} =$$

    A. $\frac{23}{18}$

    B. $\frac{40}{9}$

    C. $\frac{8}{3}$

    D. $\frac{31}{9}$

    E. $\frac{33}{5}$

3. How many positive two-digit numbers increase by 27 when you reverse their digits?
    A. 4
    B. 5
    C. 6
    D. 7
    E. 8

4. What four-digit number can ABCD represent if:
    • The four digits are 3, 5, 7 and 8.
    • The number formed by the digits AB is divisible by 2 without remainder.
    • The number formed by the digits ABC is divisible by 11 without remainder.
    A. 7,853
    B. 3,857
    C. 3,578
    D. 5,873
    E. 7,583

1st Ed. © ibidPREP llc

5. When the 58th odd natural number is subtracted from the 108th even natural number, what is the result?
    [Natural numbers are counting numbers: 1, 2, 3, 4...]
    A. 50
    B. 54
    C. 97
    D. 101
    E. 115

6. If a is an odd integer and b is an even integer, which of the following is an odd integer:
    A. 3b
    B. a + 3
    C. 2 (a+b)
    D. a + 2b
    E. b + 3

7. Each of the following is a factor of 90 EXCEPT:
    A. 5
    B. 6
    C. 15
    D. 16
    E. 25

8. If A is the set of prime numbers and B is the set of two-digit positive integers whose units digit is 7, how many numbers are common to both sets?
    A. none
    B. two
    C. four
    D. five
    E. six

9. Each of the following inequalities is true for some values of x except:
    A. $x < x^2 < x^3$
    B. $x < x^3 < x^2$
    C. $x^2 < x^3 < x$
    D. $x^3 < x < x^2$
    E. $x^3 < x^2 < x$

10. Let an IBID number be defined as one in which the sum of the distinct factors of the number not including the number itself is greater than the number. Which of the following is an IBID number?
    A. 15
    B. 16
    C. 18
    D. 21
    E. 23

11. The sum of nine different integers is zero. What is the smallest amount of these integers that MUST be positive?
    A. none
    B. one
    C. two
    D. four
    E. five

12. If k is a one-digit integer, which of the following is NOT a possible value of 1 – k?
    A. –9
    B. –5
    C. –2
    D. 0
    E. 2

1st Ed. © ibidPREP llc

Must Know

Algebra

1st Ed. © ibidPREP llc

How To Solve For X [One Variable] In All Situations:
All You Have To Do Is...

The goal in single-variable algebra is to get x [or whatever single variable you're solving for] alone on one side of the equal sign—everything that gets put onto the other side ends up being the value of x. To do this:

1. Combine Like Terms

Although you've heard this phrase before, you may not have entirely grasped precisely what it means. It means:

    a. Move all the x's to one side and all the numbers to the other. Add, subtract, multiply and divide all the x's with each other and all the numbers with themselves. Then:

    b. Put all the x's on one side of the equal sign and all the variables on the other.

        Putting the variables and numbers together with one another is not that hard, but moving terms across the equal sign may be. The reason we move terms and variables is so that we may get x [or whatever we're solving for] alone on one side of the equation. If we do that, then naturally everything on the other side of the equal sign will be what x is equal to! In order to avoid making the same mistakes most kids make again and again, we're going to peel away to the x following a little process called SADMEP.

2. SADMEP

SADMEP is PEMDAS in reverse, and you use it to keep in mind the process by which you move terms across the equal sign to peel away to x. So, first if there's anything attached to x by addition or subtraction, do the reverse to it to move it. Then divide away coefficients, take roots to powers or take the root of powers, and, lastly, undo parentheses!

$$e.g.\ 2(4+x)^2 - 3 = 47$$

$+3 = +3$	Subtraction! (Same as Addition)
$2(4+x)^2 = 50$	
$\dfrac{2(4+x)^2}{2} = \dfrac{50}{2}$	Division! (Same as Multiplication)
$(4+x)^2 = 25$	
$\sqrt{(4+x)^2} = \sqrt{25}$	Roots! (Same as Exponents)
$(4+x) = 5$	
$4+x = 5$	Parentheses!
$-4\ \ \ \ = -4$	Addition!
$x = 1$	

3. Yes, Backsies

The only way this whole algebra shebob works is if you remember that if you do it to one side of the equation you have to do it to the other. [If you give your brother a piece of Halloween candy, he damn well better give you one, no?] Once you have moved all the numbers to one side, you can go ahead and do the same with any x terms [remembering, of course, that just plain x means 1x]. Once all the x terms have been combined into one fat x term, then you can start peeling off the other doodads like exponents and roots.

REMEMBER!

$$2 + x = 7$$

When a number starts an equation, like the 2 in 2+x=7, that number is attached to the x by addition. So, in order to move it, you subtract it from both sides of the equation.

$$2 + x = 7$$

$$+ 2 + x = 7$$

$$\underline{- 2 \qquad -2}$$

$$x = 5$$

4. AGAIN, DON'T BE AFRAID OF EXPONENTS/ROOTS

Many students freeze like deer in the headlights when there is an algebraic equation with a root or power in it. Instantly, like moths drawn headlong into a deadly burning bulb, students try to root or square away the powers and roots. If you remember SADMEP, you might realize that dealing with exponents and powers must come LAST and should be only after x has been isolated. Then it's A LOT easier.

REMAIN CLAM! ROOTS

When most students see the square root sign, all heck breaks out in their brains, and whatever grasp they have on algebra [or their own middle names] seems to fly out the window. Having a root sign around a number does not change anything about how the number behaves in the algebraic expression:

* Technically you should rationalize your denominators, meaning NOT have roots in your denominator. The way you get rid of roots in your denominator is to multiply the numerator and denominator by the root:

$$x = \frac{6}{\sqrt{3}} \times \frac{\sqrt{3}}{\sqrt{3}} = \frac{6\sqrt{3}}{3} = 2\sqrt{3}$$

1ˢᵗ Ed. © ibidPREP llc

Once you have become aware of the process involved in solving algebraic equations, the best thing to do is to practice solving for x over and over in every way imaginable. Even more than most other math problems, writing out your steps here, clearly and neatly aligned, is vital. It's amazing how often students who have routine difficulties doing basic arithmetic try to do complete algebra steps in their heads. This is a GREAT way to make careless mistakes. [Adding when you should be subtracting a term is also an enduring classic careless error!]

RESIST YOUR ROOTS & POWERS [TIL LAST]

$$3\sqrt{x^2-9}=12$$

$$\frac{3\sqrt{x^2-9}=12}{3}$$

$$\sqrt{x^2-9}=4$$

NOW that you've combined like terms you may start to deal:

$$\left(\sqrt{x^2-9}\right)^2 = 4^2$$

$$x^2-9=16$$

$$\frac{+9\quad+9}{x^2\quad\ =25}$$

NOW YOU CAN ROOT IT UP

$$\sqrt{x^2}=\sqrt{25}$$

$$x=5\ *$$

* TECHNICALLY THE SQUARE ROOT OF A NUMBER IS THE POSITIVE OR NEGATIVE VERSION OF THAT NUMBER [X = ±5]. HOWEVER, EXCEPT FOR THE SAT2 TESTS, MOST OTHER TESTS ARE HAPPY TO ACCEPT THE POSITIVE ANSWER ONLY.

$-(6 - 3s) = -6 + 3s$

$(4x - 3) - (-2 + 3x) = 4x - 3 + 2 - 3x = x-1$

AND DON'T FORGET: DISTRIBUTE THE NEGATIVE.

SOLVE FOR X

Solve each of the equations below for x:

1. $x - 4 = 10$

6. $2(2x - 7) + 4(3x + 2) = 6(5x + 9) + 3$

2. $2x - 4 = 10$

7. $\sqrt{2}x - \sqrt{2} = 4\sqrt{2}$

3. $5x - 6 = 3x - 8$

8. $4x + 3 = 2 - 6(x + 4)$

4. $\dfrac{3}{4}x + \dfrac{5}{6} = 3x - \dfrac{2}{3}$

9. $\dfrac{4x-3}{9} = \dfrac{4-2x}{12}$

5. $\dfrac{5x-6}{7} = \dfrac{5x+3}{4}$

10. $\sqrt{x+3} = 25$

1ˢᵗ Ed. © ibidPREP llc

Solving for Other Than x

Sometimes, a problem requires that you solve for something other than a lone variable: a combination of variables or a variable with a coefficient. Fear not, the same principles apply. All you need to do is:
- Get the variables you want alone on one side of the equation,
- See what you have, and then
- Do what you need to do to get it to look like what the question required. For example:
  - if you are asked for 2a it might be easier to solve for a first and then double your results, or
  - if you're asked for $\frac{a}{b}$, it might be easier to solve for $\frac{b}{a}$ first and then flip your results.

MIXED VARIABLES

1. Solve for a in terms of b and x; solve for b in terms of a and x; solve for x in terms of a and b.

    i. $\dfrac{bx}{a-x}=1$

    ii. $\dfrac{2b}{ax-a}=1$

2. Solve for $\dfrac{a}{x}$: $5a = x$

3. Solve for $\dfrac{a}{b}$: $3a = 7b$

4. Solve for $\dfrac{b}{a}$: $\dfrac{2a}{5}=\dfrac{6b}{8}$

5. Solve for xy:

    i. $\dfrac{4}{y}=3x$

    ii. $\dfrac{4}{x}+7=3y$

6. Solve for 2a in terms of b

    i. $3b+\dfrac{3}{4}=4a$

    ii. $6b\,(a-2)=4b+20$

Practice

THE WORST OF ALL: ALGEBRA WITH FRACTIONS

1. If x is a positive integer which of the following CANNOT be equal to $\frac{2}{5x}$?
   A. 0
   B. 0.08
   C. 0.1
   D. 0.2
   E. 0.4

2. If a and b are each positive integers less than 16, and $\frac{a}{b}$ is equivalent to $\frac{3}{4}$, how many values of a are possible?
   A. One
   B. Two
   C. Three
   D. Four
   E. Five

3. In Springfield, $\frac{5}{9}$ of registered voters voted in the last election. If 1,000 votes were cast, what was the number of registered voters in Springfield at the last election?

4. If $\frac{x}{y} = k$ and k > 0, what is $\frac{2y + 3x}{y}$ in terms of k ?
   A. $\frac{2 + 3k}{k}$
   B. 2 + 3k
   C. 2k + 3
   D. 6k
   E. $\frac{2}{3}k$

1st Ed. © ibidPREP llc

5. If $\dfrac{x+y}{a-b} = \dfrac{5}{6}$, then $\dfrac{3x+3y}{5a-5b} =$

    A. $\dfrac{3}{5}$

    B. $\dfrac{1}{6}$

    C. $\dfrac{1}{2}$

    D. 1

    E. $\dfrac{5}{2}$

6. If $\dfrac{9}{b} = 45$ what is the value of $\left(\dfrac{2}{b}\right)^2$?

    A. $\dfrac{1}{25}$

    B. $\dfrac{4}{81}$

    C. $\dfrac{4}{25}$

    D. 25

    E. 100

7. A container is $\dfrac{5}{6}$ full of water. If 3 gallons of the water were removed from the container, it would be $\dfrac{1}{2}$ full. How many gallons of water does this container hold when completely full?
    A. 4.5
    B. 6
    C. 9
    D. 12
    E. 15

8. George is selling two different kinds of Candy: Candy A costs 1 dollar, and Candy B costs 1 dollar and 50 cents. George sells 30 pieces of Candy A and 40 pieces of Candy B. What fraction of his profits comes from selling Candy A?

WORDS TO MATH [AGAIN] & EQUATION CREATION

Now that you are able to isolate phrases, what is the best way to deal with all the screwy verbiage[32]? The best way to deal with the words is to turn them into math as quickly as possible. Here are some words translated into math. Learn this handy lexicon[33], so you won't get as easily thrown by their weird terminology:

SPECIAL *WORDS TO MATH* WORDS

- *What*—represents the unknown in the problem, can be replaced with *x*
- *Of*—when placed between numbers, it means to multiply; $\frac{1}{3}$ of 12 is the same as $\frac{1}{3} \times 12$
- *Is, Was, Are*—equals
- *Per*—divide
- *Less than [younger than, fewer than]* —subtract
  Note—When less than is written in a word problem, the order of the terms in the equation is reversed:
  Four <u>less than</u> eight translates to 8-4
- *In terms of x*— i.e., your answer must contain x [or whatever variable they are asking for]

Let's do an example:
If George [G] is three times Martha's [M] age and Martha is 4 years younger than Bill [B], then, in terms of B, how old will George be when Bill is 10 years old?

Breaking it down and translating words to math:
If George [G] is three times Martha's [M] age,

STOP!   G = 3M

and Martha is 4 years younger than Bill,

STOP!   M = B – 4

then, in terms of B, how old will George be when Bill is 10 years old?

B = 10

In this problem we are trying to get to George [G] from Bill [B].

---

[32] wording
[33] dictionary, word list

1st Ed. © ibidPREP llc

!!Often with word problems, it works best to start with the last piece of info and work backwards!!

$$M = B - 4,$$

Then, since B = 10:

$$M = 10 - 4 = 6$$

$$M = 6$$

Now we can use our first piece of knowledge and solve for G!

$$G = 3M \text{ and } M = 6, \text{ so}$$

$$3M = 3(6)$$

$$\underline{\textbf{G = 18}}$$

There are A LOT of words to math questions and equation creation in algebra. In fact, most of algebra comes down to converting words and abstract concepts into equations. Then wait until you get to try equation creation and words to math for GEOMETRY!

Fifth—Re-Read The Last Phrase [The Part That Tells You What The Question Is Truly Asking For]

Here's a great test makers' ploy: They lay out some humongously long word problem or some multi-step geo + algebra problem for you to solve, you put your head down, get to work, and darn if you don't solve it! You get down to the last line of the problem and determine that, say, x = 22.5. You're excited and hurrying [as always], so you look right to the multiple choice answers and, sitting there waiting for you, is (B) x = 22.5 ! You pick it and move on. Unfortunately, you're wrong.

Upon re-reading the LAST PHRASE of the question, which you may never have read, or have forgotten while you were busy solving the long problem, it turns out that the last phrase is not asking for what **x equals**, but what **2x equals**, or if there were a **y** somewhere in the problem, the equation may have set up as **x = ?**, but then they go ahead and ask for **y**.

EVEN MORE WORDS TO MATH

1. If five times a number x is 20 more than x, what is x?
   A. 2
   B. 3
   C. 4
   D. 5
   E. 6

2. Eight times a number is equal to the number added to eight. What is the number?

3. If $\frac{7}{8}$ of a number is 28, what is $\frac{1}{4}$ of the number?
   A. 7
   B. 8
   C. 10
   D. 12
   E. 32

4. The result when a number is divided by 3 is equal to the result when the number is divided by 3^2. What is the number?
   A. -9
   B. -3
   C. 0
   D. 3
   E. 9

5. If t is a number greater than one, then t^3 is how much greater than t^2?
   A. 1
   B. t
   C. t^2
   D. $t^2(t-1)$
   E. $t(t+1)(t-1)$

1st Ed. © ibidPREP llc

6. A large plain cheese pizza at Caesar's Pizza costs $12.00 and additional toppings cost $2.00 per topping. If the function P(t) represents the cost in dollars of a cheese pizza with (t) toppings, which of the following is correct?
   A. P(t) = 12.00 + 2.00
   B. P(t) = 12.00 + 2.00(t)
   C. P(t) = 12.00 + 2.00t²
   D. P(t) = 12.00(t) + 2.00
   E. t = 12.00 + 2.00P(t)

7. One number is 9 more than 3 times another number. If the sum of the two numbers is 45, what is the value of the greater number?
   A. 5

   B. 9

   C. $\dfrac{27}{2}$

   D. $\dfrac{63}{2}$

   E. 36

8. Buddy danced for 2 weeks on Broadway. During the second week he danced 2.5 times the number of hours he danced during the first week. If Buddy danced a total of 35 hours, how many hours did he dance during the second week?
   A. 10
   B. 15
   C. 20
   D. 25
   E. 30

Algebra

Absolute Value

One of the worst things ever to tell students is that anything is ALWAYS something, especially if that ALWAYS makes things easier for them. Case in point: Absolute Value! When most students see the absolute value goal-posts they start wiping out negative signs right and left and hope for the best. Sometimes this works; sometimes it doesn't. What do you want to bet that the test makers usually have questions of the "sometimes it doesn't" variety?

What you really need to remember about absolute value is:
THE ABSOLUTE VALUE OF A NUMBER = ITS **DISTANCE** FROM ZERO.

Since distance can only be positive, the absolute value of a number is positive, so: THERE ARE TWO NUMBERS FOR EVERY ABSOLUTE VALUE[34]. In other words:

$$\text{For } |x| = 5, x \text{ could be 5 or -5.}$$

Every number has one absolute value, but every absolute value has two possible real values: one positive and one negative. Another way to remember it is that whatever is inside the absolute value sign could be either positive or negative, so...

$$|x| = 5: x = 5 \text{ or } -5$$
$$|x - 2| = 5: x - 2 = 5 \text{ or } x - 2 = -5$$

Notice that the stuff inside the absolute value signs DOESN'T CHANGE—only its possible value. Once you figure out its possible values, then just solve for x:

$$|x - 2| = 5:$$

x - 2 = 5	or	x - 2 = -5, so
x = 7	or	x = -3

---

[34] exception: in $|x| = 0$, x can only be 0.

1st Ed. © *ibidPREP llc*

ABSOLUTE VALUE ALGEBRA WORD PROBLEMS

$$|a + 7| = 16$$
$$|b - 5| = 3$$

1. If a and b satisfy the inequalities above, then a + b could be any of the following EXCEPT
   A. −25
   B. −21
   C. −15
   D. 11
   E. 17

2. If $|3y - 8| < 4$, what is one possible value of y?

3. If $|3 + 4x| > 20$, which of the following is a possible value of x?
   A. −5
   B. −1
   C. 0
   D. 1
   E. 5

4. If $3 < |n + 2| < 4$ and $n < 0$, what is one possible value of $|n|$?

5. On a number line, a is a halfway between 4 and 9. What is the value of $|4 - a|$?

6. If Henry estimates a pole to be H meters high and it is actually T meters high, then his error, in meters, would be given as $|T - H|$. Which of the following could be the actual height, in meters, of a flagpole which Henry estimates to be 15 meters high if his error is less than .09 meters?
   A. 14
   B. 14.1
   C. 14.35
   D. 14.95
   E. 15.91

MULTI-VARIABLES

The thing to remember about solving equations with multi variables is: YOU CAN'T! No one, not even the illegitimate love child of Stephen Hawking and Albert Einstein can solve an algebraic equation for multi variables. Since you can't solve a problem for multi variables, this test is full of questions with multi variables.

2 Variables Are Really 1

Whenever a question asks you to solve for more than one variable, you must realize that you must think of those two variables as one. E.g., when a question asks you for s + t, it doesn't want to know two values, one for s and one for t. The questions is asking for **one** value, the value of s AND t combined.

Of course there is a better way to attack these problems. Most have to do with GETTING RID OF THE EXTRA VARIABLES or SEEING THEM AS ONE VARIABLE – in both cases the goal is to make it so you're dealing with only one variable.

How To Get Rid Of Extra Variables

Substitution—

When you are given more than one set of values for a variable, you may substitute the extra variable with one variable.

E.g. If $a = 2b$, $b = 3c$ and $c = 4d$, then what is the value of a in terms of d?

To begin to solve this one, keep in mind a few things:

> It usually works best if you begin with the last variable introduced. In this case d.

> Don't forget that, when substituting, the original variable equals itself! In this case a = a.

First substitute d for c = 4d then b = 3(4d) = 6c, so b = 12d, then a = 2(12d), so a = 24d!

Stack & Subtract [Or Add]—

When you are given two equations stacked on top of each other, you may usually simply add or subtract one equation from the other [be sure to add or subtract all terms from each other and on both sides!] to get rid of the extra variable.

$$3x - y = 11$$
$$\underline{2x + y = 14}$$

The variable that we can get rid of the easiest here would be y. The best way to get rid of y would simply be to ADD the second equation to the first:

$$
\begin{array}{r}
3x - y = 11 \\
+\,[\,2x + y = 14\,] \\
\hline
5x = 25 \\
x = 5
\end{array}
$$

Seeing Two Variables As One—

Sometimes a problem will seem to be asking for you to solve for two variables, but, upon further inspection, you will realize that the problem does not require that you solve for one or the other variable, but for both together as one.

> **E.g.,**   if 9(a + b) = 7a + 7b – 42, what is the value of a + b ?
> *In this problem, do not worry about the value of a or b just a+b. All you need to do is do your algebra until you get one side of the equation to look like a+b.*

$$
\begin{array}{l}
9(a + b) = 7a + 7b - 42 \\
9a + 9b = 7a + 7b - 42 \\
2a + 2b = -42 \\
a + b = 42
\end{array}
$$

Mulit-Variables From A Small Set Of Numbers—

The last piece of the multivariable puzzle regards multivariables from a small set of numbers.

90% of the time we recommend that students DON'T resort to plugging in numbers.[35] However, when you have multivariables and you cannot set them all in terms of one, or you cannot see two as one, etc., then algebra does not apply [remember, no one can solve for more than one variable!], so you must plug and chug... Fortunately, despite what you may think, the ACT does not want you working for two hours on one problem, so their multivariable plug and chugs are VERY manageable. What do I mean?

Example: The numbers p and n are positive integers and 3p + 2n = 12. What is the value of pn?

At first glance, it would look impossible to solve this problem because you can't solve for two variables.

At second glance, you might be really tempted to say p = 4 and s = 0 and make your life really simple, but that would be a BIG careless error, and <u>we don't make those anymore</u> [note: the beginning of the question tells us p and n are POSITIVE INTEGERS, so s can't be 0].

---

[35] Think of it this way: Humankind developed algebra because ultimately it's easier and far more efficient than pre-algebra. Plugging in numbers, that [not] great ACT prep strategy, is pre-algebra. Solving for a variable in an equation is algebra and works great once you learn it. Learn it!

Algebra

On third glance, we realize that p [always attack the larger value first – fewer options] can only be 1, 2, or 3. If you don't realize at first that it has to be even, then just try a few:

$$(3 \times 1) + 2(1) \neq 12, \qquad (3 \times 2) + 2(1) \neq 12, \qquad (3 \times 3) + 2(1) \neq 12,$$
$$(3 \times 1) + 2(2) \neq 12, \qquad (3 \times 2) + 2(2) \neq 12, \qquad (3 \times 3) + 2(2) \neq 12,$$
$$(3 \times 1) + 2(3) \neq 12, \qquad (3 \times 2) + 2(3) = 12, \qquad (3 \times 3) + 2(3) \neq 12!$$

Soon you will see that p must equal 2 and q must equal **3**! Even if you don't realize on your own that p must be an odd number less than 4, by plugging and chugging in this one situation, you find yourself having to do at most nine separate VERY simple arithmetic operations!

Example: If $x^y = 3$ and $x^z = 27$, what does x^{z+y} equal?

$$x^y = 3, \text{ so how about } 3^1 = 3! \text{ So } x = 3 \text{ and } y = 1.$$

If x = 3, then we can put that into the next equation and take a shot at solving that.

$$x^z = 27 \text{ become } 3^z = 27$$

If you remember that the ACT loves friendly numbers, then you can just start trying friendly numbers for z to see what fits:

$$3^z = 27: 3^1 \neq 27, 3^2 \neq 27, 3^3 = 27!$$

$$\text{So } x = 3, y = 1 \text{ and } z = 3.$$

$$\text{---SO: } x^{z+y} = 3^{3+1} = 3^4 = 81!$$

1st Ed. © ibidPREP llc

Practice

MULTIVARIABLES

$$a = 2b$$
$$b = 4c$$
$$c = \frac{b}{a}$$

1. For the system of equations above, what is the value of bc?
   A. ½
   B. 1
   C. 2
   D. 3
   E. 4

2. A cellphone service provider charges y for the first 20 gigabytes (GB) of data used and charges for any additional data at the rate of x dollars per GB. If the bill for this month is $25, and more than 20 GB of data were used, which of the following expressions represents the total amount of data used this month in GB?

   A. $\dfrac{25+y}{x}$

   B. $\dfrac{25-y}{x}$

   C. $\dfrac{25-y}{x}-20$

   D. $\dfrac{25-y}{x}+20$

   E. $\dfrac{5-y}{x}$

3. For positive integers x and y, $x - y = 4$ and $xy = 21$. What is the value of $\dfrac{x-y}{x+y}$?
   A. 84
   B. 17
   C. 5.25
   D. 2.5
   E. .4

4. If a – b = 4 and c + d = 5, what is the value of ac – bd + ad – bc?
   A. 10
   B. 15
   C. 20
   D. 25
   E. 30

5. If 2x + y = –3, z – y = 1, and 3z – 2x = 10, what is the value of y?
   A. -2
   B. 0
   C. 1
   D. 2
   E. 3

6. If –x – y + 3x + 4 – 2y = –y, what does x – y equal?
   A. –4
   B. –3
   C. –2
   D. –1
   E. 0

1st Ed. © ibidPREP llc

ACT—139

Algebra

Polynomials

Polynomials are classic Remain Clam! bait. The minute most students see anything remotely like polynomials, they panic and immediately start to drag out factors, roots, Pascal's triangle, and the eternally dreaded Quadratic Equation [few remember it, and the ones who do usually do so by singing it to the tune of "Yankee Doodle Dandy." Not cool in the middle of a test.].

The good news: the hardest thing about polynomials you'll ever have to do is factor them. Mostly, the College Board wants you to know on the ACTs comes down to knowing how to factor, but before you even get into that, you might just have to do simple algebraic substitutions or, most importantly, recognize certain quadratic identities.

KNOW These Three Quadratic Identities On Sight!

$$(x + y)^2 = x^2 + 2xy + y^2$$

$$(x - y)^2 = x^2 - 2xy + y^2$$

$$(x + y)(x - y) = x^2 - y^2$$

The trick here is that if you see the equation one way in a question, rewrite it the other way. Of course the only way you can do that is if you KNOW what their equivalents are.

1ˢᵗ Ed. © ibidPREP llc

POLYNOMIALS

1. If $(a - 2)(c - 5) = 0$ and $a < 0$, what is the value of c?
   A. -5
   B. -2
   C. 2
   D. 5
   E. 7

2. $8 - x^2 = 3$. What is x^2 equal to?
   A. 3
   B. $\sqrt{5}$
   C. 5
   D. 8
   E. $2\sqrt{2}$

3. If $x^2 = y^2 + 49$, which of the following expressions must equal 49?
   A. $2(x - y)$
   B. $2(x + y)$
   C. $(x - y)(x - y)$
   D. $(x + y)(x - y)$
   E. $(x + y)(x + y)$

4. If $x^2 + kx + 24 = (x + t)(x + 6)$ for all values of x, and if k and t are constants, what is the value of k?
   A. 2
   B. 4
   C. 6
   D. 10
   E. 12

5. If $a^2 + 4ab + b^2 = 5ab$, which of the following is equivalent to $a^2 + b^2$?
   A. $-9ab$

   B. $-ab$

   C. ab

   D. $\dfrac{5}{4}ab$

   E. $9ab$

6. If $(x^2 - y^2) = 63$ and $(x - y) = 7$, what is the value of y?

Practice

7. If $5x - 4 = 16$, what is the value of $x^2 + 6x - 10$?

   A. $\dfrac{12}{5}$

   B. 4

   C. 5

   D. $\dfrac{144}{25}$

   E. 30

8. The equation $x^2 + 5x - 36 = 0$ is equivalent to which of the following?
   A. $(x - 4)(x + 9) = 0$
   B. $(x + 4)(x - 9) = 0$
   C. $(x + 4)(x + 9) = 0$
   D. $(x - 4)(x - 9) = 0$
   E. $-(x + 4)(x + 9) = 0$

9. If $a > 0$, $x^2 + y^2 = a^2$ and $xy = 2a - 15$, what is the value of $(x + y)^2$?
   A. $a^2 + 2a - 15$
   B. $(a + 5)(a - 3)$
   C. $a^2 + 4a - 30$
   D. a^2
   E. $(2a - 15)^2$

   $a = x^2 + 2$ $b = (x + 2)(x - 2)$ $c = (x + 2)^2$

10. If $x > 0$ in the three equations above, what is the ordering of a, b, and c?
    A. $a < b < c$
    B. $b < c < a$
    C. $b < a < c$
    D. $c < a < b$
    E. $c < b < a$

11. In the xy-coordinate plane, P and Q are different points that have the same y-coordinate and lie on the parabola whose equation is $y = x^2 + 4x - 21$. What is the x-coordinate of the mid-point of $\overline{PQ}$?
    A. -7
    B. -2
    C. 0
    D. 2
    E. 3

1st Ed. © ibidPREP llc

12. If $x^2 + 12x = -32$, what is one possible value of x^2?
    A. 4
    B. 8
    C. 12
    D. 16
    E. 32

ALGEBRAIC EXPONENTS

1. If $9.27 \times 10^{t+3}$ is an integer between 900,000 and 1,000,000, and t is an integer, what is the value of t?
    A. 1
    B. 2
    C. 3
    D. 4
    E. 5

2. If $a^7 = 300$ and $z^3 = 27$, what is the value of $a^7 \cdot z^{-3}$?
    A. -327
    B. $-\dfrac{100}{3}$
    C. $\dfrac{3}{100}$
    D. $\dfrac{100}{9}$
    E. 273

3. If $x^{2Y} = 64$, what does x^y equal?
    A. 2
    B. 4
    C. 8
    D. 16
    E. 32

4. If x is a positive real number, which of the following is equal to $(x^5 \cdot x^3)^4$?
    A. x^{12}
    B. x^{17}
    C. $x^{20} + x^{12}$
    D. x^{32}
    E. x^{60}

5. If y is a positive integer satisfying $y^5 = n$ and $y^9 = k$, which of the following must be equal to y^{11}?
   A. $n^2 - k$

   B. $k + 2$

   C. $n + 6$

   D. $\dfrac{k^2}{n}$

   E. $\dfrac{n^4}{k}$

6. If $n \geq 0$, which of the following CANNOT be equal to $\dfrac{3}{4^n}$?
   A. 0
   B. 0.1875
   C. 0.75
   D. 4
   E. 5

7. If $3^n \times 3^{-9} = 81$, what is the value of n?
   A. 2
   B. 4
   C. 5
   D. 9
   E. 13

8. x is a positive integer and $x^2 y^6 = 1$. If y is equal to 2, what is the value of x^{-y}?
   A. 1/16
   B. 1/8
   C. 1/4
   D. 16
   E. 64

9. The expression $\sqrt[3]{\dfrac{-1}{x}}$, where x > 0, can also be represented as which of the following:
   A. $(-x)^{-1/3}$
   B. $(-x)^{1/3}$
   C. $3x^{-1/2}$
   D. $x^{1/3}$
   E. $-x^{-3}$

1st Ed. © ibidPREP llc

10. If B and C are positive integers and $2^B = 16^C$, what is the value of $\dfrac{C}{B}$?

A. $\dfrac{1}{8}$

B. $\dfrac{1}{4}$

C. $\dfrac{1}{3}$

D. 4

E. 8

11. If a > 1 in the equations $\dfrac{a^{2x}}{a^y} = a^{-8}$, and $a^{2x} \cdot a^y = a^{16}$, what is the value of y?

12. If x and y are positive integers greater than 1, and $x^y = 729$, what is the greatest possible value of $x - y$?

HOW TO CHECK YOUR WORK

• Find a different way to solve the same problem. This is a great way to ensure that you don't repeat the same errors.

• Redo the entire problem and don't just eyeball what you've already done, so that you're not just rubber stamping your same careless errors.

• Do everything backwards, working from your answer back to the question.

FONZP

Some questions require that you test out a number. In those questions make sure you test out ALL types of numbers.

Most of us reflexively put in a nice easy number like 2, and then maybe a slightly bigger number. The thing to remember here is to test DIFFERENT KINDS of numbers. For the purposes of this test there are five different kinds of numbers to concern yourself with [though of course there are many, many more kinds of numbers]. Those are best remembered as FONZP [ask your parents who the FONZ was].

- **F**–ractions–something between zero and one
- **O**–ne–always weird and worth testing...and easy too
- **N**-egative
- **Z**-ero—also weird and easy to test
- **P**-ositive—try both big and small positives

IF YOU ARE LOOKING FOR WHAT THE *GREATEST* QUANTITY IN A GROUP COULD BE, MAKE ALL THE OTHER VALUES THE *LEAST* THEY CAN BE.

These kinds of questions often pop up toward the end of the Grid-Ins. The question discusses a list of numbers with certain conditions and then asks what the greatest number in that list could be. The way to answer this is to try to figure out what the least amount all the other numbers could be. Be careful when you are doing this to note the conditions on the other numbers...are they distinct or different from each other? And are they all even, odd, positive, integers?

If a question asks you to find the **biggest** possible value for one variable out of a group of variables, the best way to figure out what it could be is to make all the other variables the **smallest** they can be.

If a question asks you to find the **smallest** possible value for one variable out of a group of variables, the best way to figure out what it could be is to make all the other variables the **biggest** they can be.

Question: If the sum of three odd numbers is 63, what is the *greatest* one of those numbers could be?

The key here is:

a. In order to find what the greatest of the three numbers could be, we make the other two AS SMALL AS they can be. **N.B.** Read this and all questions carefully. Note that the problems never says the two lower numbers have to be different from one another. That means if we want to make each of the smaller

1st Ed. © ibidPREP llc

numbers as SMALL AS THEY CAN BE, we can choose ONE for each.

b.   Then create an equation.

If the first two numbers are one, then: 1 + 1 + x = 63

$$2 + x = 63$$
$$\underline{-2 \qquad = -2}$$

SO:
$$x = 61$$

GREATEST/LEAST

1.   At a certain pizzeria, 51 pepperoni pizzas were sold in the month of April. If more pepperoni pizzas were sold on the sixth of April than on any other day in April what is the **least** number of pepperoni pizzas that could have been sold on the sixth of April?

2.   The sum of five positive integers is 41. What is the greatest possible value for one of the integers?

3.   In 2012, Bob ate 137 burritos. If he ate more burritos in the month of July than in any other month in the year, what is the greatest number of burritos that he could have eaten in June?

4.   The product of 3 integers is 330. If all of the integers are greater than 3, what is the greatest possible value for one of the integers?

Algebra

Real Ratios

Whenever you have a ratio problem that involves real things like eggs or students or ounces of tequila, use the ratio box. In the first line put the basic ratio, which you're usually given. Imagine that that ratio given represents real amounts. Instead of thinking that the ratio of brown eggs to white eggs is 3 to 4, imagine that you have 3 brown eggs and 4 white eggs. If you have three brown eggs and four white eggs, then you also know how many eggs you have total: 7. Now you can set up your box:

	Brown		White		Total
Given	3	+	4	=	7
Multiplier		+		=	
Actual Amount		+	12	=	

If you are told that you actually have one dozen [1 dozen = 12] white eggs, then you can figure out both how many brown eggs you have AND how many total eggs you have. Put the 12 in the WHITE column in the ACTUAL row. Then figure out how many times 4 goes into 12 [3!]. That's your multiplier. Then multiply all the GIVENS by 3!!

	Brown		White		Total
Given	3	+	4	=	7
Multiplier	3	+	3	=	3
Actual Amount	9	+	12	=	21

Now you can answer any question that comes your way!

1st Ed. © ibidPREP llc

RATIOS

1. In a student election, Tyler defeated Julia by a ratio of 7 to 6. If there are 221 students in the grade and all of them voted, how many votes did Julia receive?
   A. 119
   B. 107
   C. 102
   D. 89
   E. 42

2. A certain automobile company manufactured a total of 150 cars and trucks. If the number of cars made exceeds the number of trucks by a ratio of 5 to 1, how many more cars were made than trucks?
   A. 125
   B. 100
   C. 75
   D. 25
   E. 5

3. In a certain school, girls outnumber boys by a ratio of 9 to 7. If the school has 581 boys, how many girls does it have?

Questions 4 and 5 refer to the table below, which presents data collected by the Audubon Society. Over the course of two months, bird-watchers tabulated the number of birds spotted in New York parks and in wild habitats in surrounding areas.

SPECIES	PARK	WILD
Oriole	25	15
Robin	45	75
Sparrow	50	100
Egret	10	5
Hawk	5	15

4. What is the ratio of park birds to wild birds?
   A. 9 to 14
   B. 2 to 3
   C. 19 to 25
   D. 23 to 30
   E. 3 to 2

Practice

5. Which species has the highest ratio of wild birds to park birds?
    A. Oriole
    B. Robin
    C. Sparrow
    D. Egret
    E. Hawk

6. After the first term in a sequence of positive numbers, each term is half of the number immediately preceding it. What is the ratio of the third term to the seventh term?
    A. 32 to 1
    B. 16 to 1
    C. 8 to 1
    D. 3 to 7
    E. 1 to 32

7. Point C is the midpoint on the line segment $\overline{AE}$, point B is the midpoint on the line segment $\overline{AC}$ and point D is the midpoint on the line segment $\overline{CE}$. What is the ratio of the length of $\overline{CD}$ to length $\overline{BE}$?
    A. 5 to 1
    B. 4 to 1
    C. 3 to 1
    D. 1 to 3
    E. 1 to 4

1st Ed. © ibidPREP llc

INEQUALITIES

Solve for inequalities the same way you solve for equalities.

- Move the x [or whatever variable or combination of variables you're solving for] according to SADMEP until you isolate[36] it.
- The **ONLY** thing that is different—and the part that freaks most kids out—is the switching the sign part. THAT HAPPENS ONLY IF YOU **MULTIPLY** [OR **DIVIDE**] BY A NEGATIVE NUMBER [*negative* means **change** *direction*].
- In two-sided inequalities [e.g., 4 < x + 2 ≤ 7], simply solve by breaking the inequality into two problems [e.g., 4 < x + 2 and x + 2 ≤ 7]. Then combine your two solutions into one statement [e.g., 2 < x ≤ 5].

You may have been told a lot of tricks to remember your greater than and less than signs. Please don't bother with them. The simplest and best way to remember which sign means what is to look at the signs themselves. The bigger, wider, open side of the sign faces the bigger number, and the pointy small end of the sign faces the smaller number. It's as simple as that!

ENOUGH WITH THE ALLIGATORS

Bigger Number > Smaller Number

Smaller Number < Bigger Number

We use inequalities in everyday situations when we have limits on certain amounts in relation to other.

E.g. Buster has $6.50 and slices of pizza cost $2.25. How many slices can Buster buy?

The trouble most students have with these problems is knowing which way to point the inequality sign. The trick comes in knowing to make everything less than or equal to the limited quantity. In other words if you have a fixed amount of money or seats or votes, everything else should be less than or equal to that value in your equation:

In other words:

$$\text{NUMBER OF SLICES} \times \text{PRICE} \leq \$6.50$$
$$[P = \text{NUMBER OF SLICES: } \$6.50 = \text{LIMITED VALUE}]$$
$$\$2.50\,P \leq \$6.50$$
$$P \leq \$6.50/\$2.50$$
$$P \leq 2.6$$

Since they're probably not selling partial pieces of pizza at the pizza parlor, Buster can buy 2 slices, and maybe have enough left over for a soda.

[40] get it alone, put by itself

Practice

INEQUALITIES

1. x is a positive integer. If $x^2 - 3 \geq 0$ and $x^2 + 3 < 28$, what is the smallest possible value of x?

2. In order to be flown in a local competition, model airplanes must meet strict requirements regarding weight and length. For a plane that is c centimeters long and d ounces in weight, the difference between d and $\frac{3}{4}c$ can be a maximum of 10 but must be at least 4. If a plane weighing 40 ounces qualifies for the competition, what is the shortest possible length of the plane?

3. If x is a real number and $3 \leq 3x - 6 \leq 30$, then which of the following describes the range of possible values of x?
    A. $0 \leq x < 9$
    B. $3 < x < 12$
    C. $3 \leq x \leq 12$
    D. $3 \leq x < 18$
    E. $1 \leq x \leq 12$

4. If $t(x) \leq 0$ for all real values of x, which of the following could be the function t?
    A. $t(x) = -x^2 - 4x - 1$
    B. $t(x) = x^2 - 3x - 5$
    C. $t(x) = -x - 2$
    D. $t(x) = -|x| - 2x$
    E. $t(x) = -x^2 + 2x - 8$

Use the following equations to answer question 5.
$$a = -x^2 + 1$$
$$b = (x + 2)(x - 3)$$
$$c = x - 3$$

5. If $x \geq 4$, which of the following orderings is correct?
    A. $a < b < c$
    B. $c < b < a$
    C. $c < a < b$
    D. $a < c < b$
    E. $b < c < a$

Use the following inequality to answer question 6.
$$ab \leq a - b$$

6. If $0 \leq a \leq 3$, which of the following inequalities describes the possible values of b?
    A. $\frac{3}{4} \geq b \geq 0$
    B. $b \leq \frac{3}{4}$
    C. $b \geq 0$
    D. $-3 \leq b \leq \frac{4}{3}$
    E. $6 \geq b \geq \frac{3}{4}$

1st Ed. © ibidPREP llc

(t − 1) Questions

At least once a test or so, you'll see what I like to call a "(t − 1) question." The (t − 1) questions are generally word problems that pertain to real world situations in which you are paying for something, whether it be clothing, dvd's, miles in a cab or minutes on a phone. What all these questions have in common is that the **first** of these items you are purchasing [clothes, dvd's, miles, minutes] are all at one price while the remaining items are at another price. The key to figuring out the total price of these items [or total items, depending on what they want you to solve for] is putting (t − 1) into the equation you create. Here's what I mean:

Q. John took a taxi from his home to the airport. The taxi driver charged John $1.50 for the first mile, and then $.45 for every mile thereafter. If the ride to the airport cost John $10.05 [without tip or tax], how far was the airport from John's home?

Most kids would try pushing around a few numbers like peas on a plate, then get the bright idea to PLUG IN! or BACKSOLVE! or whatever else they couldn't remember to do from what they're friends told them about test prep, but you have a better idea: (t − 1)!

In (t − 1) problems, let t equal the **total** number of items being purchased. If you have a question like we do above in which you pay one price for the first item and a different price for every item after, you already paid the different price for the first item! So now it's easy to set up the problem:

Ben took a taxi from his home to the airport. The taxi driver charged John $1.50 for the first mile,

Let (t) = the total number of miles:

Let (t − 1) = the total number of miles John has to pay for at the multiple rate.

1st mile = $1.50 and then $.45 for every mile thereafter, and so:

$$\$1.50 + \$.45 (t - 1)$$

If the ride to the airport cost John $10.05 [without tip or tax],

$$\$1.50 + \$.45(t - 1) = \$10.05,$$

how far was the airport from John's home?

$$\$1.50 + \$.45 (t - 1) = \$10.05$$
$$\underline{-\$1.50 \qquad\qquad\qquad -\$1.50}$$
$$\frac{\$.45 (t - 1)}{\$.45} = \frac{\$8.55}{\$.45}$$

$$t - 1 = \frac{\$8.55}{\$.45} \quad \leftarrow \text{This is a fine time to use your calculator}$$

$$(8.55 \div .45 = 19)$$

$$t - 1 = 19$$

$$t = 20$$

John's trip was 20 miles!

Practice

(t – 1)

1. Ken offers Martial Arts classes in the park. He charges $195 for the first three classes and $43 dollars for each additional class. What is the amount in dollars that it costs to attend 10 of Ken's classes?

2. Emma bought d dozen cookies for her class. The bakery charged her $9 for the first dozen cookies and $6 for each dozen after that. If Emma bought more than one dozen cookies and spent q dollars total, which equation below represents the total dollars Emma will spend on cookies.
   A. $d + (d – 1) = q$
   B. $9 + (d – 1) 6 = q$
   C. $q(d – 1) = 9 \cdot 6$
   D. $9 – (d – 1) = 6q$
   E. $9d + 6(d – 1) = q$

3. Mark bought sneakers in bulk from Cheetah Footwear. Cheetah charged Mark $150 for the first shipment of sneakers, and then $64 for every subsequent shipment. If Mark spent $982 dollars, how many shipments of sneakers did he buy?
   A. 11
   B. 12
   C. 13
   D. 14
   E. 15

4. Emma's Phone Store sells calling cards from $5 to $35 in increments of $3. Calls using the calling card cost $1.15 for the first minute and $0.65 for each minute after that. What is the least expensive calling card that Travis can buy if he wants to make a call that will last 27 minutes?
   A. $15
   B. $17
   C. $18
   D. $19
   E. $20

5. Drew and Justin rented bicycles from Paul during the summer. Paul charged them $15 for the first 5 days, and then $1.75 for each day thereafter. If Drew returned his bike after 24 days and Justin spent $36.00 on his bike rental, then how many days earlier did Justin return his bike than Drew did?

6. Jon buys kale at his local co-op. The co-op is having a special holiday sale. The first three pounds he buys are k dollars per pound, and every pound after that is 30% off the original price k. If Jon buys z pounds of kale and z > 3, which equation below represents the amount of money Jon will spend?
   A. $3k + z(k – .30k)$
   B. $3k + (z – 3)(.30k)$
   C. $k + (z – 3)(.70k)$
   D. $k + (z)(.70k)$
   E. $3k + (z – 3)(.70k)$

1st Ed. © ibidPREP llc

Series, Sequences & Patterns

These are the problems in which you are asked to find what date something will fall on, the order of beads in a necklace, letters in a code, numbers in a sequence, etc. There are a few things to remember with these problems:

1. They are made to seem as if you'll have to do a lot of calculations in order to figure them out—wrong!
2. If the pattern is not given, and if you get going from the beginning long enough to see a pattern [see box below], you won't have to do a hundred calculations.

Example: if Eddy makes a necklace with beads colored blue, yellow, red in that order and he needs 100 beads to complete the necklace, what color will the final bead be?

1, 3, 9...

Example: every term in the sequence above is determined by multiplying the preceding term by three. Based on the sequence, what will the units digit of the 51st term be?

THE LONGEST JOURNEY STARTS WITH THE FIRST STEP[37]

WHAT WORKS FOR CHINESE PHILOSOPHY WORKS FOR MATH—EVERY SEQUENCE STARTS WITH THE FIRST TERM AND EVERY TRIAL STARTS AT ONE. WHEN YOU'RE FACTORING, START WITH ONE; EVEN THOUGH YOU KNOW WHAT IT IS, IT STILL COUNTS!

THIS PRINCIPLE WORKS ON MANY LEVELS:

1. YOU CANNOT GET TO THE FINAL TERM UNLESS YOU GO THROUGH THE FIRST TERM.

2. YOU CANNOT BEGIN TO SEE A PATTERN UNLESS YOU LAY IT OUT FROM THE BEGINNING.

3. WHAT WORKS FOR SMALL NUMBERS WORKS FOR BIGGER NUMBERS, AND SMALLER NUMBERS ARE EASIER TO WORK WITH.

[37] Attributed to Lao-Tzu, founder of Taoism, a great Chinese religious philosophy

Practice

SERIES, SEQUENCES & PATTERNS

648, 108, ...

1. In the sequence above, each term after the first term is $\frac{1}{6}$ of the term preceding it. What is the fifth term in this sequence?

   A. $\frac{1}{3}$

   B. $\frac{1}{2}$

   C. 3

   D. 6

   E. 12

2. The first term of a sequence is 24. The second term is 16. The third term and each term thereafter is the average (arithmetic mean) of the two terms immediately preceding it. What is the value of the first term in the sequence that is not an integer?

3. The first two terms of a sequence are 1 and 2, and all the following terms in the sequence are produced by subtracting the next to last term from the last term in the series. What is the 50th term in the sequence?

x, 13, 43, y, z, 1213

4. In the above sequence, each term after the first term, x, is 4 more than 3 times the previous term. What is the sum of $x + z$?

−3, 6, 3...

5. In the sequence above, each odd term (e.g., −3) is multiplied by −2 to find the next term. Each even term (e.g., 6) is subtracted by 3 to find the next term. What is the *absolute* value of the 12th term?
   A. -33
   B. -30
   C. 63
   D. 126
   E. 129

6. Paulina is making a Legos tower. She starts with 2 whites, 3 reds and 5 blues, in that order, and repeats that pattern until she runs out of Legos. If the last piece is red, which of the following could be the number of Legos in the tower?
   A. 42
   B. 44
   C. 46
   D. 48
   E. 50

1st Ed. © ibidPREP llc

COMBINATIONS AND PERMUTATIONS

These topics are great examples of partial knowledge being a dangerous thing. Chances are, when you see the words combination and permutation you start trying to remember which is which and what are those formulas you were taught.

The good news is that you don't need to remember any of that. Most combination and permutation questions are not called that. Usually you are asked to figure out how many *arrangements* or *permutations* of a number of items or events you can have.

Possibility × Possibility × Possibility: Arrangement problems usually come down to possibility times possibility, with limited possibilities going first. What the heck does that mean? Here we go:

a. Find the number of possible combinations of outfits you can wear over a three-day weekend if you have five different outfits.

   i. Figure how many possible outfits you have to choose from on Saturday (5). Now that you've chosen one outfit for Saturday, how many outfits do you have to choose from for Sunday? (4), and how many do you have to choose from for Monday? (3)

   ii. Take your possibilities for each day and multiply them together. That is your total number of possibilities:

$$5 \times 4 \times 3 = 60$$

b. If there are *limits* to the possibilities, **begin with the limited selections first**. If there are 5 people in a car but only 2 of them can drive, how many different seating arrangements can there be?

   i. Figure out how many possible drivers there are to choose from, since that is the limited role (2). Now that one slot has been filled, how many people are there to choose from for the passenger seat? (4); how many for the first back seat? (3); how many for the middle back seat (2); and how many for the last back seat? (1).

   ii. Your total number of possibilities is:

$$2 \times 4 \times 3 \times 2 \times 1 = 48$$

COMBINATIONS, PERMUTATIONS & ARRANGEMENTS

1. How many different positive three-digit integers can be formed if the hundreds digit must be 7, the tens digit must be greater than 1, and the integer is even?
   A. 32
   B. 35
   C. 40
   D. 175
   E. 409

2. There are 7 girls and 5 boys in a group. One boy and one girl are the leaders. How many different pairs of leaders are possible?
   A. 2
   B. 7
   C. 12
   D. 35
   E. 70

3. In how many different ways can five people stand in line if the tallest person stands in the middle of the line?

4. The digits 1,2,5,7 and 9 will be used without repetition to form different four-digit numbers. Of all such numbers, how many are less than 5,000?
   A. 24
   B. 36
   C. 48
   D. 120
   E. 240

5. A man walks across the park each day. Each day he enters the park at the West Gate, and goes first to the lake along one of four paths. When he leaves the lake, he goes to the zoo, choosing from five possible paths. He then goes to the East Gate along one of eight different routes. After how many days will it be until the man has to repeat a route across the park?

   1ˢᵗ Ed. © ibidPREP llc

6. Six different bands are playing at a music festival, bands A, B, C, D, E, and F. Bands E and F are the most popular and must be the last two bands to perform. In how many different orders can the bands perform?

7. A starting team in the new sport of Cartlop consists of a forward, a defender and a goalie. If there are 5 forwards on the team, 4 defensemen and 2 goalies, how many different starting lineups can the coach make?

8. Wilbur still needs to choose 1 wide receiver and 1 running back for his fantasy football team. He has 8 wide receivers and 3 running backs to choose from. How many different selections of a WR and RB are possible?
    A. 3
    B. 8
    C. 11
    D. 24
    E. 48

Algebra

Probability

Probability is one of those scary-looking topics that turns out to be redunkulously simple. Remember:

$$Probability = \frac{Number\ of\ Your\ Event}{Number\ of\ All\ Events}$$

As with all things we're trying to figure out, let's try understanding this with the simplest example first. A coin toss works perfectly.

What are the chances of getting a heads on a coin toss?

$$Probability\ of\ Tossing\ a\ Heads = \frac{Number\ of\ heads}{Number\ of\ sides} = \frac{1}{2}$$

NOTE—If multiple parties are working toward a single goal, the sum of the probabilities of all parties must equal one.

E.g., Joe, Mary and Helvetica are running in a race. If Joe has a one in three chance of winning the race and Mary has a one in two chance of winning the race, what is the chance that Helvetica will win?

Here's how to set it up:

Probability of each participant winning: $J = \frac{1}{3}$, $M = \frac{1}{2}$, $H = x$

All probabilities together = 100%, or 1 out of 1 [someone has to win the race], so

$$J + M + H = \frac{1}{1}, so$$

$$J + M + H = \frac{1}{3} + \frac{1}{2} + x = 1$$
$$\frac{2}{6} + \frac{3}{6} + x = 1$$
$$\frac{5}{6} + x = 1$$

$$x = \frac{1}{6}$$

Therefore, the chances that Helvetica will win the race are one in six $[\frac{1}{6}]$.

1ˢᵗ Ed. © ibidPREP llc

PROBABILITY

1. There are s shops on a street. If one shop is entered at random, the probability that a grocery store will be entered is $\frac{5}{8}$. In terms of s, how many shops are grocery stores?

   A. $\frac{s}{8}$

   B. $\frac{5s}{8}$

   C. $\frac{8s}{5}$

   D. $\frac{13s}{8}$

   E. $8s$

4, 6, 10, 12, 15, 18, 20, 24

2. A number is selected at random from the list above. What is the probability that the number selected will be a multiple of both 4 and 6?

   A. $\frac{1}{8}$

   B. $\frac{1}{4}$

   C. $\frac{1}{2}$

   D. $\frac{3}{4}$

   E. 1

Food Preferences of Students

	School A	School B
Like Hamburgers	50	60
Like Pizza	70	20

3. The table above shows students classified according to what school they go to and their food preference. If a student is picked at random from either school, what is the probability that he or she likes burgers AND attends School A?

   A. $\frac{1}{20}$

   B. $\frac{1}{5}$

   C. $\frac{1}{4}$

   D. $\frac{5}{12}$

   E. $\frac{5}{6}$

4. There are 12 pairs of socks in a drawer. Five pairs are gray, three are black and the rest are white. If one pair of socks is taken at random from the drawer, what is the probability that it is white?

    A. $\frac{1}{12}$

    B. $\frac{1}{8}$

    C. $\frac{1}{3}$

    D. $\frac{1}{2}$

    E. $\frac{2}{3}$

5. A bag of marbles contains only yellow, blue and green marbles. There are 4 yellow marbles and 2 blue marbles, and $\frac{1}{3}$ of the marbles are green. If a marble is picked out of the bag at random, what is the probability that it will be blue?

    A. $\frac{1}{9}$

    B. $\frac{1}{6}$

    C. $\frac{2}{9}$

    D. $\frac{1}{4}$

    E. $\frac{1}{3}$

6. David chooses numbers from two hats, one red and one blue. The red hat contains all even digits greater than zero, and the blue hat contains all odd digits greater than zero. The numbers picked are used to form fractions. The red number is the numerator, and the blue number is the denominator. What is probability that David's fraction will be greater than $\frac{1}{2}$ but less than 1?

1st Ed. © ibidPREP llc

Functions

Think of a function as a little machine. Each function is a different machine that does something to whatever you put into it. Let's say $f(x)$ is a juicer, a machine that turns whatever is inside the parentheses into juice, so f(carrot) = carrot juice and $f(2)$ = 2 juice and $f(x)$ = x juice. In most cases, we call whatever comes out of the function: y. As in, if f(carrot) = carrot juice, then y = carrot juice.

Of course the functions on the ACT are not as fruitful as juicer machines. Usually they are just simple double the x and add 2 kind of machines [$f(x) = 2x + 2$]. In those cases, just stuff **WHATEVER** is inside the parentheses into the place of the x in the 2x + 2 part.

E.g., if $f(x) = 2x + 2$ then when x = 3, then $f(3)$ = 2(3) + 2, so f(3) = 8, etc. Easy enough? Good. Now here comes the blow your mind part.

Blow your mind FUNCTION question:

1. If $f(x) = 2x + 2$, then when x = (2x + 2), what is the value of the function?
   A. 2x + 2
   B. 4x + 2
   C. 4x + 4
   D. 4x + 6
   E. 8x + 2

Remember, the x in the function **BECOMES** whatever that x is defined as, and you stuff ALL of the new x in place of plain old x, even if the new value of x has an x in it! [Whew!]

Sooooo...

If $f(x) = 2x+2$ then when x=(2x+2):
   $f(x) = 2(2x+2)+2$
   $f(x) = (4x+4)+2$
   $f(x) = 4x+6$

If you chose (D), you were right.
Remember: the answer you choose must look **exactly** like your answer. Exactly!

The other important thing to remember with functions is that sometimes you won't be given what goes **into** the function, but what **comes out** of the functions. You're given the y but not the x. Then you must work backwards to figure out the x!

2. If the function $f(t)=5t-3$ indicates how many pizzas Pepe can make per hour and t=hours, how many hours will it take him to make 7 pizzas?

Note here that t, hours, is what you're putting **into** your machine, and pizzas are what you're **getting out**, f(t)=pizzas. We know that we're getting out 7 pizzas, so now we need to find out how many hours it takes to get that. Just reverse engineer the equation and solve for (t)!

$$f(t) = 7 = 5t - 3$$
$$7 = 5t - 3$$
$$\underline{+3 = \quad +3}$$
$$10 = 5t$$
$$2 = t \quad \text{It takes Pepe 2 hours to make 7 pizzas!}$$

Practice

FUNCTIONS

1. The graph of y = s(a) is pictured at right. If s(7) = p, then what is the value of s(p)?

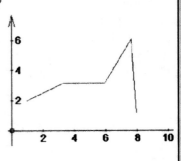

2. If $f(x) = \frac{(x^2 - 6)}{x}$ for all non-zero x, then what is the value of $f(3)$?

3. If the total profit p, in dollars, raised by selling c cookies is given by the function p(c) = 5c - 10 , then how many cookies must be sold in order to raise $325?

4. The speed of a car on a certain section of highway S, in miles per hour, is modeled by the function S(t)= 55 - 0.75t, where t is time in seconds. According to the model, for what value of t is the speed of the car 46 miles per hour?

5. Which of the following equations describes y in terms of x for all ordered pairs in the table below?
    A. y = 64 – x
    B. y = 64 – 4x
    C. y = 64 + x
    D. y = 64 – x²
    E. y = 64 + x²

(x,y)
(0,64)
(1,63)
(2,60)

1st Ed. © ibidPREP llc

6. If the function f is defined by $f(x) = 5x + 6$, then $3f(x) + 3 =$
   A. $15x + 9$
   B. $15x + 21$
   C. $18x + 9$
   D. $18x + 21$
   E. $18x - 21$

7. Let the function h be defined for all values of a by $h(a) = a(4 - a)$. If k is a positive number and $h(k - 4) = 4$, what is the value of k?

a	$f(a)$
-4	5
-3	7
-1	3
0	1
2	-4

8. The table above defines the function f. If the function h is defined as $h(a) = f(a) + 3$, what is the value of x when $h(2x) = 6$?
   A. -2

   B. $-\dfrac{3}{2}$

   C. $-\dfrac{1}{2}$

   D. 0

   E. 1

Practice

Funky Functions

Whenever you see a symbol [or anything] on this test that you don't recognize: REMAIN CLAM! Although we do like to assume the worst in moments like these ["We completely missed out on learning this," or "We learned and forgot," or "Our tutors sucked and forgot to tell us!!"], in truth if you see something on the test you haven't seen before, RELAX: No one else has either! What's more, I will bet you dollars to donuts [super old nonsensical expression] that the question is going to define the unknown symbol for you in the next phrase.

FUNKY FUNCTIONS

1. For all numbers s, let s∀ be defined as s∀=s^2 – s. What is the value of –3∀?
   A. –12
   B. –3
   C. 3
   D. 6
   E. 12

2. For all integers f, let f∩=f^2 – f(f + 3). If f ∩ = –12 what is f?
   A. –4
   B. –3
   C. 4
   D. 6
   E. 8

3. For all nonzero integers m, let m# be defined as $m\# = \dfrac{m^2(m-1)}{m}$. Which of the following is **NOT** a possible solution of m#?
   A. –1
   B. 0
   C. 2
   D. 6
   E. 20

4. For all numbers a and b, let a¤b be defined as a¤b =$2a^2$ – ab – b^2. What is the value of 5¤–3?
   A. 32
   B. 44
   C. 56
   D. 104
   E. 136

1st Ed. © *ibidPREP llc*

5. Let the operation ❂ be defined as $b ❂ c = bc - \dfrac{c}{b}$ for all nonzero values of b and c. What is the value of -3 ❂ 2?

   A. $-6\dfrac{2}{3}$

   B. $-5\dfrac{1}{3}$

   C. $-4\dfrac{2}{3}$

   D. $5\dfrac{1}{3}$

   E. $6\dfrac{1}{2}$

6. Let $p \sim q = \dfrac{p^2+p}{qp+p} \cdot \dfrac{q^2-q}{pq-p}$ for all nonzero integers p and q. What is the value of 3~5?

   A. $\dfrac{3}{5}$

   B. 1

   C. $\dfrac{10}{9}$

   D. 5

   E. 15

7. Let #x be defined as $\#x = x^2 + \sqrt{x^2} - 18$ for all integers x. Which of the following is equal to #3?
   A. # −6
   B. # −3
   C. # 0
   D. # 6
   E. # 18

8. Let a @ b be defined as $a @ b = \left(\dfrac{a}{b}\right)^2 + 1$ for all nonzero numbers a and b. Which of the following is NOT equal to 2 @ 3?
   A. -2 @ -3

   B. $\dfrac{1}{4} @ \dfrac{3}{8}$

   C. $\dfrac{3}{4} @ \dfrac{1}{8}$

   D. $\dfrac{2}{3} @ 1$

   E. 4 @ 6

Algebra

Functional Inequalities

Most basic functions are either linear or curved. That means when you plot them, they tend either to look like lines or curves. When you are given a functional inequality to evaluate over a set of values, 9 times out of 10 they'll give you a curve because 9 of out 10 students will assume that it's a line and get it wrong. Most students thinking it's a line and not a curve will automatically assume it's either going to get bigger or smaller across its domain. Therefore, most students will simply [and wrongly] plug the smallest and largest x values of the domain into the function, and wrongly think they have the range over that set of values. Of course, since 9 times out of 10 the function is a curve, it will probably *curve* over those values and the minimum or maximum values will NOT be on either side of the inequality, but somewhere in the middle. E.g.:

Q. What is the range of the function $f(x) = x^2 - 3$ for the domain $-2 \le x \le 3$?

If you plug in –2 and 3 [the first and last values of x], you get a range of $-1 \le x \le 6$. WRONG!

However, if you evaluate all values of x through the domain [you can try all integers or use your calculator[38]], you'll find a much different result:

For $f(x) = x^2 - 3$

x	y
–2	–1
–1	–2
0	–3
1	–2
2	1
3	3

So, the actual range for the function $f(x) = x^2 - 3$ for the domain $-2 \le x \le 3$ is:

$$-3 \le y \le 3$$

Charts, Diagrams & Graphs

If you are given a chart, diagram or graph, for heaven's sake, READ AND ANALYZE IT FIRST! There is a lot of info you can get from these things, and a lot of conclusions you can draw before you even read the question. If you are given a graph, read the labels on the x and y axes and see what's going on. If you are given a chart with a few columns, read down and across and see if there are any operations you can perform on the numbers [add, multiply, divide...?]. Once you get in the habit of filling in charts and processing diagrams, you'll be perfectly ready to deal with...

---

[38] Push $\boxed{y =}$
On line y_1 = enter $x^2 - 3$
Push $\boxed{\text{2nd}}$ then $\boxed{\text{Table (Graph)}}$
Find your x and y values there

1st Ed. © ibidPREP llc

CHARTS, TABLES, DIAGRAMS & GRAPHS

1. The table below gives the temperatures of five different substances at t seconds after the substance was exposed to water. The temperature of which substance decreases the most during the period from t = 10 to t = 15?

    A. 1
    B. 2
    C. 3
    D. 4
    E. 5

Temperature vs Time

Substance	Temperature at t Seconds (Celsius)
1	$-5t + 4$
2	$-\frac{1}{5}t - 4$
3	$-\frac{1}{5}t + 4$
4	$\frac{1}{5}t - 4$
5	$5t - 4$

2. The table below shows the inventory of sweaters and sweatshirts that are available at a clothing store. If the store has three times as many sweaters as sweatshirts, what is the value of x?

Inventory at Cliff's Edge Clothing Store

	Sweaters	Sweatshirts
Blue	17	4
Red	13	x
Yellow	20	5
Black	x	2
White	16	5

3. Nice Kicks, a shoe store, sold a total of 1750 shoes last year in the percentages shown in the circle graph below. Based on the graph, how many of the shoes sold were not green or blue?

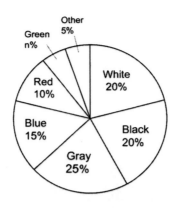

Shoes Sold by Nice Kicks Last Year

4. There are 25 students in Class K before Winter Break. After Winter Break, one more student joins Class K. Based on the information in the chart above, if the total number of video games the new student owns, T, is less than 4, T < 4, then what is the difference between the median number of videos owned by the original group and the median of the expanded group?

Number of Students in Class K [before Winter Break] with x Number of Video Games	Number of Video Games
3	0
5	1
2	2
4	3
5	4
6	6

1st Ed. © *ibidPREP llc*

GEOMETRY

1ˢᵗ Ed. © ibidPREP llc

HOW TO DO GEOMETRY

Words To Math: Still Applies, But More So

Just as with general word problems, it is vital in geometry problems that you translate words into math as you go and not try to take in the whole problem at once. Many times you will be setting up equations just as in algebraic word problems. However, with geometry problems, it's very important that instead of simply creating equations, you put down formulas as you go. There are very few formulas the ACT requires you know, but as with all basics, you must know them inside and out!

Fill In Figures—

When you are given a geo problem with a figure, always, always fill in everything you know about the figure and everything you are given about the figure BEFORE you start to tackle the question itself. Most of the time, in the process of filling in the info you will solve the problem!

Solve For Your Angle Last—

Just as students feel compelled to go after the hardest-looking part of the question first, we also usually feel compelled to go after the answer first. Who wants to spend any more time than necessary on a problem? Of course, that usually leads to a bigger problem and more time wasted—especially in geometry problems in which you are meant to solve for an angle inside a figure. Usually the figure will give you one or two actual angles or side values, a few additional unknowns and the unknown you need to solve for. The ONLY way to find your variable will be to figure out ALL the other unknowns first. In fact, one way I keep my students from going after their variable first is to cover the question and just make them figure out everything they can about the figure given. Once they do that, I uncover the question, and all they have to do is provide the right answer from their quiver[39] of knowledge.

Solve Like This:

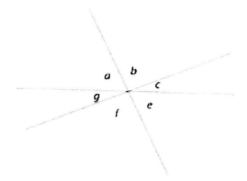

Q: In the figure above, three lines intersect at a point. If f = 85 and c = 25, what is the value of a?

---

[39] a case for holding arrows

In the drawing above, you will notice that they are vertical angles[40]: ∡a = ∡e, ∡b = ∡f, and ∡c = ∡g. Mark that info on the drawing clearly and not too hugely, like so:

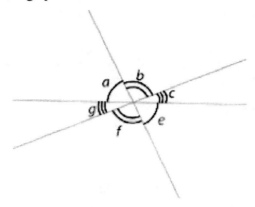

NOW read the problem and find out what they are giving you, i.e. what's given in the problem. Here we find out:

f = 85 and c = 25. Since we know what ∡f and ∡c are, we also know that ∡b = 85 and ∡g = 25. FILL THAT INFO IN on the figure, like so:

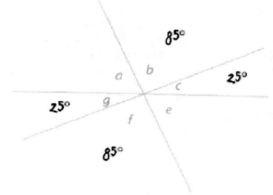

If you look at the figure again in light of the measures of several of the angles, you will now SEE that the last two remaining angles are equal to each other. Each angle is then half of whatever degree amount is left when you subtract these other known angles from some mysterious sum which isn't so mysterious at all if you re-member: All those angles that revolve around one central point add up to 360°, the central angle of a circle! Now we know that the two remaining angles [∡a & ∡e] together will equal:

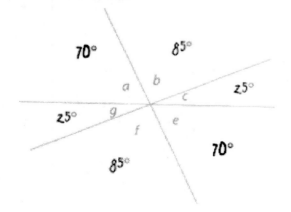

360 – 2(85) – 2(25) = 360 – 170 – 50 = 140,
therefore, ∡a + ∡e = 140, and, since ∡a = ∡e,
∡a must equal 70°!

---

[40] When two lines intersect to form an X, the angles across from each other at the intersection are equal; see p. 185.

1ˢᵗ Ed. © ibidPREP llc

Geo—Topics, Terms & Tips

Solve for Your Angle Last, for Reals

Q: In the figure below, solve for angle t.

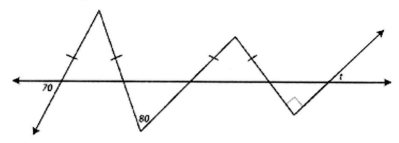

If you rush into trying to solve this by looking at ∡t first, then you'll never solve it. However, if you ignore ∡t and start filling in what you know as far away from it as possible, it's a pretty easy problem!

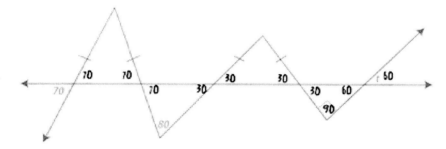

ESPECIALLY WHEN IT LOOKS HARD, FILL IN WHAT YOU KNOW

No matter how scary a figure looks, if you start filling in what you know even before you read the questions, you'll be able to solve ANY geometry problem.

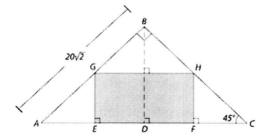

Q: In ∆ABC, point H is the midpoint of $\overline{BC}$. What is the perimeter of the shaded region?

Without even looking at the text of the question, there are many pieces of info we can fill in.

First: Since the three angles of any triangle are equal to 180° and ∡ABC=90° and ∡BCA=45°, then ∡BAC=45°.

Second: Since we also know that ∡GED=90° then ∡GEA=90° then ∡AGE=45°. The same can be said for the angles in ∆HFC, so then ∡FHC=45°

Third: Now we can find ∡EGH and ∡FHG because $\overline{GH}$ and $\overline{EF}$ have to be parallel. How do we know this? We know this because each segment is perpendicular to $\overline{BD}$. That means that ∡EGH and ∡FHG are both 90°.

Fourth: Therefore we also know that ∡BGH and ∡BHG are both 45° because they are part of line segments with two angles that add up to 135°.

All the above info tells us that we have four isosceles right triangles: ΔABC, ΔAEG, ΔGBH and ΔHFC, and we know all the angles without even having looked at the text of the question!

We can still find out EVEN more without even looking at the text. Because we know that ΔABC is an isosceles right triangle with one leg equal to 20√2, we know that $\overline{BC}$ must also be 20√2 , and $\overline{AC}$ must equal 40 (because we know our 45°, 45°, 90° triangles!).

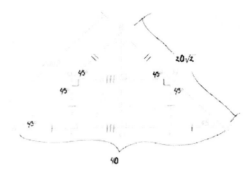

NOW we can move onto the text of the question. It says that "point H is the midpoint of $\overline{BC}$." This means that $\overline{BH} = \overline{HC}$, therefore we also know that $\overline{BH}$, $\overline{HC}$, $\overline{GB}$, and $\overline{AG}$ are all equal and equal to 10√2 which is half of 20√2.

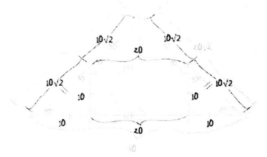

NOW see what the question is asking for: What is the perimeter of the shaded region?

EASY PEASY!

The sides $\overline{GE}$ and $\overline{HF}$ are the sides of isosceles right triangles with hypotenuses of 10√2. $\overline{GE}$ and $\overline{HF}$ are therefore equal to 10.

AND since ΔGBH is also an isosceles right triangle and $\overline{GB}$ and $\overline{BF}$ are each legs of 10√2, then hypotenuse $\overline{GH}$ is equal to 20, and, therefore, so is $\overline{EF}$.

Add up $\overline{GH}$, $\overline{EF}$, $\overline{GE}$, and $\overline{HF}$ and you get 60!

 1st Ed. © ibidPREP llc

COMBOS—Geometry & Algebra & Arithmetic

It might help to know that geometry, algebra and arithmetic are not really separate topics but one. Most arithmetic principles and rules of algebra came from geometry. Before we were able to think and solve problems arithmetically and algebraically, we had to SEE them geometrically. Then algebra was used to discover rules about geometry.

It's a lot easier to understand a picture and prove how something works by measuring it than by throwing around a bunch of x's. So when you have a problem with a line or a figure that will need solving for variables, start with the figure.

As we said above, draw it out and mark it with variables first, THEN construct your equation. To construct your equation, FIRST write out all formulas involved, if any. Write them out in their basic form without adding in any info from the question—yet.

Then, add your info as you go. Often as you add in given info in place of your variables you will be able to solve for other pieces of information. THEN use those other pieces of information to answer your question.

Once you're armed with a full arsenal of knowledge, answering the questions should be easier, if not downright easy!

Words to Math for Geometry

The words to math approach works super well for most of those classic algebra word problems everyone enjoys making fun of. It also works extraordinarily well for geometry questions if you not only set up equations as you go, but also write out formulas and fill in, draw or redraw figures as you go.

If the area of Circle A is three times its circumference, what is its radius?
...the area of Circle A
πr^2
is three times its circumference
$\pi r^2 = 3(2\pi r)$
STOP! Anytime you can solve an existing equation or simplify it, do so!!
$\pi r^2 = 3(2\pi r)$
$$\frac{\pi r^2}{\pi} = \frac{6\pi r}{\pi}$$
$$\frac{r^2}{} = \frac{6r}{}$$
$r = 6$
Now read the last part of the question: *...what is its radius?*
You've already solved it!!
Radius = 6

How to solve COMBOS:

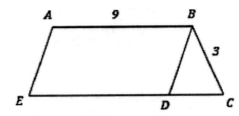

1. **In the diagram above ABDE is a parallelogram and BCD is an equilateral triangle. What is the perimeter of ABCE?**

In an equilateral triangle all sides are equal, so:

P = 2l + 2w = 2 [9] + 2 [3] + 3 = 27! EASY!!

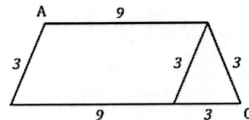

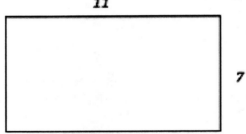

2. **What is the area of a Square S that has the same perimeter as the Rectangle R above?**

First:
Area of Sq = s²
Perimeter of Sq = 4s
P Rect = 2l + 2w
P Rect R = 22 + 14 = 36, SO:
P Sq S = 36

Therefore
4s = 36
s = 9
A Sq S = 81!

1st Ed. © ibidPREP llc

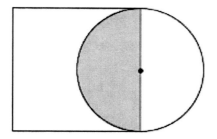

3. **A square and a circle are drawn above. The perimeter of the square is 8. What is the area of the shaded region?**

The first part of this question mentions a square and a circle, so write:

$$Area\ of\ Circle = \pi r^2$$
$$Circumference\ of\ Circle = 2\pi r$$
$$Area\ of\ Sq = s^2$$
$$Perimeter\ Sq = 4s$$
GIVEN: P = 8, so write P = 4s = 8, so s = 2

If s = 2, then you know from marking the figure that r will equal 1. That means

$$Area\ of\ Circle = \pi$$

But since we have HALF the circle shaded, then

$$\textbf{Area Semicircle} = \frac{\pi}{2}$$

4. **The perimeter of triangle ABC is 35. If AB is twice the length of BC and AC is one half the length of BC, then AC =**

$$P\ triangle = side\ 1 + side\ 2 + side\ 3 = AB + BC + AC$$

$$P\ triangle = s1 + s2 + s3 = AB + BC + AC = 35$$
$$AB = 2BC$$

$$AC = \frac{BC}{2}$$

Now we have everything in terms of BC, so we can **put** everything in terms of BC:
$$BC = BC\ [don't\ forget\ that!]$$
$$AB = 2BC$$
$$AC = \frac{BC}{2}$$

$$\text{so: } s1 + s2 + s3 = AB + BC + AC = 2BC + BC + \frac{BC}{2} = 35$$

$$2BC + BC + \frac{BC}{2} = 35$$
$$3.5BC = 35$$

$$BC = \frac{35}{3.5}$$
$$BC = 10, \text{ SO...}$$

$$\text{if } AC = \frac{BC}{2}$$
$$\text{then}$$

$$AC = \frac{10}{2} = 5!$$

5. **If the circumference of a circle is π, what is its area?**

Circumference= 2πr [C = 2πr is almost always better to use than C = πd]

SO

$$2\pi r = \pi$$

$$2r = 1$$

$$r = \frac{1}{2}$$

THEN

What is its area?

BECOMES

$$\text{Area of Circle} = \pi r^2 = \pi \left(\frac{1}{2}\right)^2 = \pi \frac{1}{4} = \frac{\pi}{4}$$

Now try the next problem set...or try them AFTER you've reviewed your GEO in MUST KNOW GEO [p. 183]:

1st Ed. © ibidPREP llc

GEO WORD PROBLEMS

1. A farmer wants to put up a fence costing $3 per foot around a rectangular pen whose area is 168 square feet and whose width is 12 feet. How much will it cost?
   A. $14
   B. $42
   C. $84
   D. $156

2. Sally wants to paint the four walls of her square room. The walls are ten feet high, and she uses $1\frac{3}{4}$ buckets of paint to cover them. Each bucket can cover 320 square feet. How wide is her room in feet?
   A. 7.5
   B. 10
   C. 12.5
   D. 14

3. How many cookies will be able to fit on a baking sheet if each cookie has a radius of 2 inches and the inner dimensions of the tray are 12" x 20"?
   A. 5
   B. 9
   C. 12
   D. 15

4. A farmer's plow is five feet wide and his ox moves the plow ten feet per minute. How much area, in square feet, can the farmer plow in an hour?
   A. 50
   B. 100
   C. 300
   D. 3000

1st Ed. © ibidPREP llc

Must Know Geometry

1st Ed. © ibidPREP llc

used to call this section GEO PALETTE because all the info below gives you ALL the geo you will ever need on ALL general standardized tests. When painters want to unify their image and make it work better visually, they limit the colors they choose to work with [their palette] and use those few colors really well. If you know this limited number of rules well and know how to apply them with a painter's touch, then the geometry questions might just be the easiest ones on the test. If you think you need to remember something about Side/Angle/Side or non-Euclidean geometry, you don't! But you must know your—

Vertical Angles & Lines Intersecting Parallel Lines

There is big money [points] to be made from being able to recognize and fill in info properly on vertical angles and alternate interior angles on parallel lines.

Vertical Angles Are:

- Equal

- Angles adjacent to vertical angles are supplementary to them (add up to 180°).

- Both pairs of vertical angles add up to 360°.

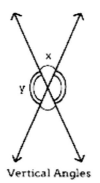

Vertical Angles

Alternate Interior Angles...

...on a line intersecting parallel lines [a transversal] are:

> EQUAL

So, if you combine the vertical-angle rule with the alternate-interior-angle rule, and you are given one angle that a transversal forms, then you will be able to determine all the angles a transversal forms.

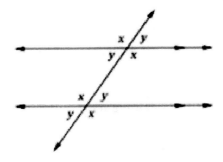

So if you know this:

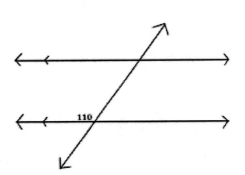

You know this:

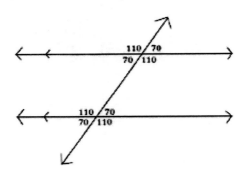

PARALLEL LINES
Try These!
Solve for all possible angles.

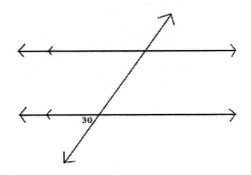

1.

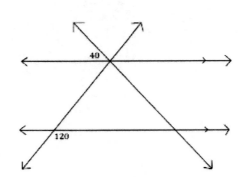

2.

1st Ed. © ibidPREP llc

LINES & ANGLES

1. In the figure to the right, three lines intersect at a point.
    If a = 65 and f = 40, what is the value of c?
    A. 45
    B. 55
    C. 65
    D. 75
    E. 85

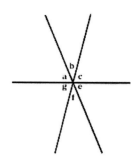

2. In the figure to the right, ABCD is a rectangle.
    What is the value of x?
    A. 5
    B. 6
    C. 9
    D. 15
    E. 30

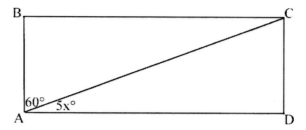

3. In the figure to the right, lines a and b intersect as shown.
    What is the value of x ?
    A. 115
    B. 125
    C. 135
    D. 145
    E. 155

4. In the figure to the right, which of the following angles is greatest?
    A. a
    B. b
    C. c
    D. d
    E. e

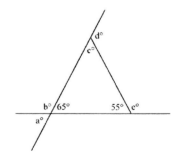

5. In the figure to the right, if a and b are parallel lines intersected by line c, what is the value of 7x?
    A. 12
    B. 15
    C. 45
    D. 84
    E. 96

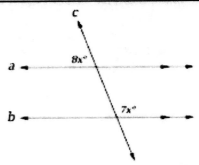

6. In the figure to the right, lines b and c are parallel. What is the value of x ?
    A. 15
    B. 30
    C. 36
    D. 75
    E. 105

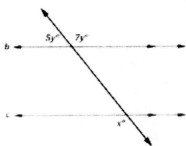

7. In the figure to the right, s ∥ t. What is the value of x?
    A. 35
    B. 75
    C. 105
    D. 110
    E. 145

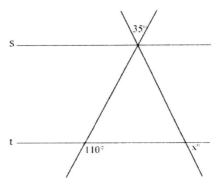

8. In the figure below, the four lines a,b,c, and d intersect to form 8 angles with equal measures. If the dotted segments bisect 2 of those angles, what is the measure, in degrees, of the angle indicated by the arrow?

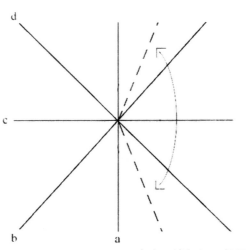

†angles (straight lines) are equal & dotted lines bisect the straight lines on either side of them.

1ˢᵗ Ed. © ibidPREP llc

TRIANGLES

- **The sum of the angles of a triangle = 180°**
- **Supplementary Angle Rule:**

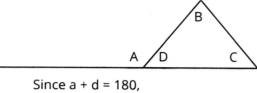

Since a + d = 180,
and b + c + d = 180,
then a = b + c

- **In a right triangle the side opposite the largest angle (and therefore the longest) is the:**
    Hypotenuse

- **In similar triangles**:
    All angles are congruent to their counterparts in the other triangle, and all sides are in equal ratios to one another.

- **The area of a triangle equals:**

$$\frac{1}{2}b \times h$$

    One half the triangle's base times the height drawn perpendicularly to that base

Remember:

Any leg of a triangle can be used as the base of the triangle, so long as you draw a line perpendicular to it that represents the apex (highest point) of the triangle from that specific base.

In a right triangle (a triangle with a 90 degree angle), the two legs that are perpendicular by definition represent a base and a height for the triangle.

Geometry

Some Triangles

An **isosceles** triangle has: two equal sides and two equal angles opposite them.

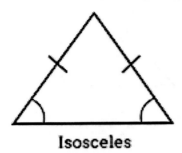

Isosceles

An **equilateral** triangle has: three equal sides and three 60° angles.

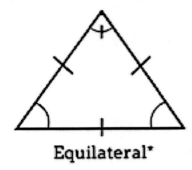

Equilateral*

In a **right*** triangle the side opposite the 90° angle [and therefore the longest] is the: hypotenuse—c.

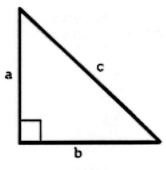

Right Triangle

*Careful though: as much as we wish it were the case, not every triangle is an equilateral or right triangle. Don't assume it is unless that info is given.

1ˢᵗ Ed. © ibidPREP llc

TRIANGLES: AREA & PERIMETER

1. An isosceles triangle is shown in the figure to the right (note: figure is not drawn to scale).
    If the perimeter of the triangle is 16, what is its area?
    A. $4\sqrt{2}$
    B. $8\sqrt{2}$
    C. 12
    D. $16\sqrt{2}$
    E. 24

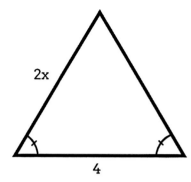

2. The two triangles below are both isosceles triangles. The length of line segment AB is 24. What is the combined perimeter of the two triangles?
    A. 24
    B. 48
    C. 56
    D. 72
    E. 96

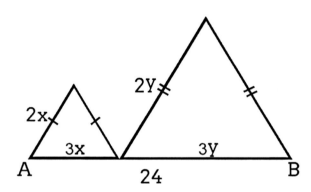

3. If the area of right triangle ABC is 12, and one of its legs has a length of 6, what is the perimeter of ABC?
    A. $2\sqrt{13}$
    B. $10 + 2\sqrt{13}$
    C. $16 + 2\sqrt{13}$
    D. $10 + 4\sqrt{13}$
    E. 52

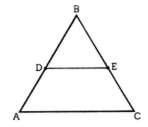

Note: Figure not drawn to scale.

4. In triangle ABC above, D is the midpoint of segment AB, and E is the midpoint of segment BC. If AB = 12, BC = 10, and AC = 9, what is the perimeter of triangle DBE?
   A. 12.5
   B. 13
   C. 15.5
   D. 21
   E. 30

5. An equilateral triangle has sides of length 6. What is the ratio of the perimeter of the triangle to its area?
   A. 1:√3
   B. √3:1
   C. 2: √3
   D. 2 √3
   E. 9√3

6. A ladder is leaning against a wall. The foot of the ladder is 6 feet away from the wall. The length of the ladder is 10 feet. What is the area under the ladder, in square feet?
   A. 8
   B. 24
   C. 36
   D. 48
   E. 60

1ˢᵗ Ed. © ibidPREP llc

THE PYTHAGOREAN THEOREM—
THE PYTHAGOREAN THEOREM IS THE TORTILLA/CREPE/PANCAKE
[OR DUMPLING/PIEROGI/GYOZA] OF MATH FORMULAS

There are certain items, especially foods, that pop up again and again across the world in essentially the same form but with different names. The pancake and the dumpling are such good ideas that they had to go viral. The same is true for the Pythagorean theorem. It is the most awesome of all theorems [it is the pizza of theorems], so naturally it pops up EVERYWHERE and in many different forms.

PYTHAGOREAN THEOREM & ITS DOPPELGÄNGERS[41]

Pythagorean Theorem: $a^2 + b^2 = c^2$

Distance Theorem: $\sqrt{(y_2 - y_1)^2 + (x_2 - x_1)^2} = \sqrt{d^2}$

Formula of a Circle: $x^2 + y^2 = r^2$ {when center is at (0,0)}

Trigonometric Identity: $\sin^2 + \cos^2 = 1$

Diagonal through a Box: $l^2 + w^2 + h^2 = d^2$

PYTHAGOREAN TRIPLETS

If the hypotenuse of a right triangle is 5 and the next longest side is 4, then the shortest side is: THREE.

The 3, 4, 5 triplet exists for all right triangles in similar proportions:

6, 8, 10 / 9, 12, 15/ 12, 16, 20/ etc... The other Triplet generally used on standardized tests is 5, 12, 13.

[41] twins, look-alikes

Practice

PYTHAGOREAN THEOREM

1. If the legs of right triangle XYZ have lengths 8 and 15, what is the area of a right triangle with each side twice the length of its corresponding side in triangle XYZ?
   - A. 17
   - B. 34
   - C. 60
   - D. 80
   - E. 240

2. What is the perimeter of the trapezoid to the right?
   - A. 71
   - B. 72
   - C. 102
   - D. 106
   - E. 118

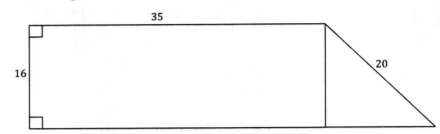

3. In the figure to the right, the triangle with legs of 4 and 5 is a right triangle. What is the area of square ABCD?
   - A. 39
   - B. 40
   - C. 41
   - D. 42
   - E. 43

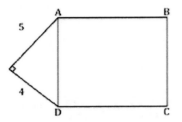

4. In the figure to the right, AB = 20, BC = 37, and AD = 22. What is the length of CD?
   - A. 15
   - B. 17
   - C. 22
   - D. 25
   - E. 30

5. The figure to the right shows a trapezoid divided into three triangles. What is the area of the middle triangle?
   - A. 100
   - B. 112.5
   - C. 144
   - D. 150
   - E. 200

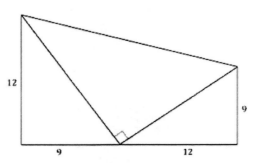

1st Ed. © ibidPREP llc

SPECIAL RIGHT TRIANGLES

It is vital that you learn these proportions—so you can recognize them in whatever guise they pop up. If you see a $\sqrt{2}$ or a $\sqrt{3}$ inside a figure then your SPECIAL RIGHT TRIANGLE sensors should go off.

Isosceles Right Triangles

In a 45°, 45°, 90° isosceles right triangle:

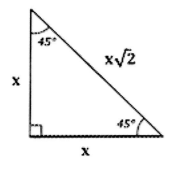 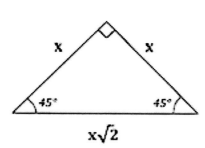

The two equal sides $= x$

The hypotenuse $= x\sqrt{2}$

So if $x = 3$, then: If $x\sqrt{2} = 4\sqrt{2}$,

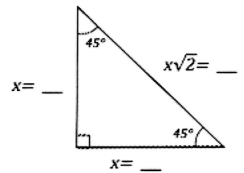 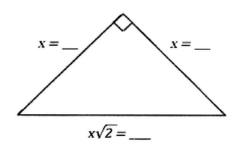

Try this:

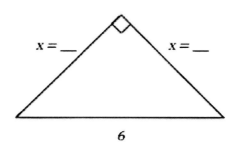

6

But if $x\sqrt{2} = 8$? Remember your Algebra!

If $x\sqrt{2} = 8$, then:

$$x = \frac{8}{\sqrt{2}}$$

$$x = \frac{8}{\sqrt{2}}\left(\frac{\sqrt{2}}{\sqrt{2}}\right) = \frac{8\sqrt{2}}{2} = 4\sqrt{2}$$

In a 30°, 60°, 90° triangle:

- The side opposite the 30° angle = x
- The side opposite the 60° angle = $x\sqrt{3}$
- The side opposite the 90° angle = 2x

So if :Then:

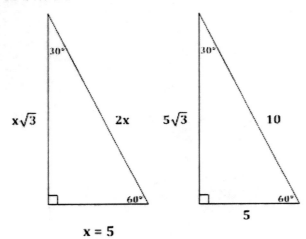

x = 5

And: Because {Remember your algebra!}:

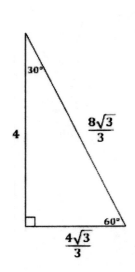

If 30° side = $\dfrac{4\sqrt{3}}{3}$ then 60° side = $\dfrac{4\sqrt{3}}{3}$ ($\sqrt{3}$)

$$= \frac{4 \cdot 3}{3}$$

$$= 4 \quad !!!$$

1st Ed. © ibidPREP llc

30°, 60°, 90° Triangle
Try These!

Solve for all sides.

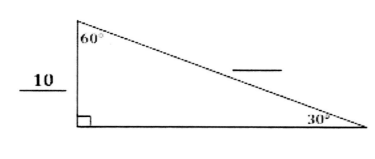

$\underline{\quad 10 \quad}$

1.

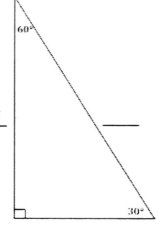

$\underline{\quad 7\sqrt{3} \quad}$

3.

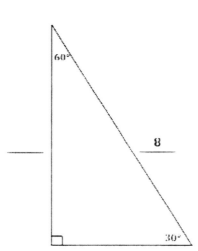

8

2.

$\underline{\quad 8 \quad}$

4.

Practice

SPECIAL RIGHT TRIANGLES

1. What is the second leg of the right triangle to the right?
   A. $20\sqrt{3}$
   B. $20\sqrt{5}$
   C. 40
   D. $40\sqrt{2}$
   E. 100

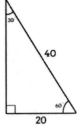

2. Using your knowledge of special triangles, determine x in the triangle to the right.
   A. 10
   B. $10\dfrac{\sqrt{3}}{2}$
   C. $10\sqrt{3}$
   D. $14\sqrt{3}$
   E. 21
   F. $20\sqrt{3}$

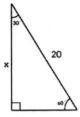

3. The area of rectangle ABCD above is 72. What is the length of segment CE?
   A. 6
   B. $6\sqrt{2}$
   C. $6\sqrt{3}$
   D. 12
   E. $12\sqrt{2}$

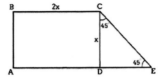

4. In a 30-60-90 triangle where the shorter leg is 20 ft, what is the length of the hypotenuse?
   A. 20
   B. $20\sqrt{2}$
   C. $20\sqrt{3}$
   D. 40
   E. $40\sqrt{3}$

5. What is the area of the rectangle in the diagram to the right? (Note: Figure not drawn to scale.)
   A. 0.5
   B. 1
   C. 2
   D. 3
   E. 6

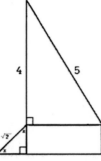

6. In the figure to the right, how long is the diagonal of the square?
   A. 5
   B. $5\sqrt{2}$
   C. $5\sqrt{3}$
   D. 55
   E. 5.5

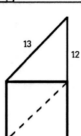

1ˢᵗ Ed. © ibidPREP llc

More Fun With Triangles—Triangle Basics

The later in the math section you see a triangle problem, the better the chances they will be testing you on a VERY basic fact of triangles, such as:

- The area of a triangle equals one half base times height of ANY side of the triangle and its corresponding height.
- If you are given two sides of a triangle, the third side of the triangle must be less than the sum of the other two and greater than their difference. *Wait what*? Very simple:
    - If you add any two sides of a triangle together their sum has to be bigger than the third side.
    - If you subtract two sides of a triangles, the third side has to be bigger than their difference.

TRIANGLE: ADVANCED BASICS [OXYMORON[42] INTENDED]

- The shortest distance between two points is a straight line
- One leg of a triangle must be:
    - GREATER than the difference of the other two and LESS than their sum

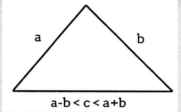

a-b < c < a+b

- The side opposite the largest angle in a triangle is: the largest side
- Area of a Triangle = $\dfrac{bh}{2}$ {regardless of which base and which height}

STUFF YOU'LL KNOW IF YOU KNOW SPECIAL RIGHT TRIANGLES

The height of an equilateral triangle with side of length s=

$$s\frac{\sqrt{3}}{2}$$

[Because it is really the side opposite the 60° angle in a 30°, 60°, 90° triangle].

The length of the diagonal of a square with side of length s =

$$s\sqrt{2}$$

[Because it is really the hypotenuse of an isosceles right triangle].

---

[42] contradiction in terms, e.g., jumbo shrmip

Circles

Every time you are given a fact about a circle, its area, circumference, etc., write it down as an equation!

Circles

- The **central angle** of a circle measures: 360°.
- **One revolution** of a circle is equal to the **circumference** of that circle.
- **Diameter** is the **longest chord** that can be drawn in the circle—it passes through the center. It is equal to two times the radius.
- The **radius** is a line drawn from the center to the circumference of a circle. It is **one half** the **diameter**.
- The **circumference** of a circle is the distance a **360°** arc around the circle covers [think of it as the perimeter of the circle].
- The **circumference** of a circle [its perimeter] = **πd = 2πr**
- The **area of a circle** = **πr²** [if you get area and circumference of circles confused, remember area always has the square in it: square feet, square meters, r²].

AND ANOTHER THING ABOUT CIRCLES:

LEAVE π ALONE![43]

Like a scab that we must pick, it is VERY hard to leave complicated math things alone on tests. We are afraid of them, so we think we MUST do something to them. However, on the ACT Test, **<u>never</u>** convert π.

---

[43] If you do need a solution without π in it, when you are completely finished solving your equation, THEN pop in your approximation—usually the problem will indicate which value to use. The same is true for other irrational numbers such as roots like $\sqrt{2}$ or $\sqrt{3}$. Instead of replacing them with approximate values and trying to schlep those ugly numbers around the equation, just move the roots around the same way you would x's.

1ˢᵗ Ed. © ibidPREP llc

Tangents

A tangent is not just your teacher veering off the topic; it is also a line diverging[44] from a point of intersection on a shape. A Line Tangent [Intersecting at One Point] to a Circle intersects the radius drawn to the point of intersection at an angle of 90°.

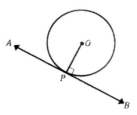

Sectors – Slices Of π

A sector is a part of a circle. It looks like a wedge, a piece of pie or a slice of pizza. For most, the sector problems seem like the hardest of all geometry problems, but if you keep one thing in mind, they're actually pretty straightforward.

If you take a slice out of a circle, all parts of the slice will be in the same ratio to the whole circle.

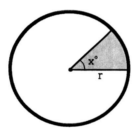

I.e., if the slice of pie is a 45° slice [1/8 of 360°- the central angle], then the area of that slice is 1/8 of the area of the circle, and the arc of that slice is 1/8 of the circumference of the circle [arc length seems to scare students the most, but it really just means a piece of the circumference].

---

[44] splitting off from, deviating, wandering, digressing

SECTORS

1. For a sector with an radius of 6 and a central angle of 30°, find:
   Arc length of sector—
   Area of sector—

2. For a 45° sector with an area of 8π, find:
   Radius of sector—
   Arc length of sector—

3. For a sector with a 120° central angle and an arc length of 6π, find:
   Radius of sector—
   Area of sector—

4. For a sector with a radius of 3 and an area of π, find:
   Central angle of sector—
   Arc length of sector—

5. For a sector with radius of 8 and arc length of 4π, find:
   Central angle of sector—
   Area sector—

1st Ed. © ibidPREP llc

CIRCLES

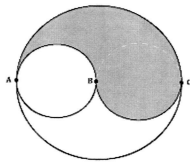

1. In the figure, the smaller circles each have a radius of 5. The small circles are tangent to the large circle at points A and C, and are tangent to each other at point B. Point B is the center of the large circle. What is the perimeter of the shaded region?
    A. 9π
    B. 10π
    C. 12π
    D. 15π
    E. 20π

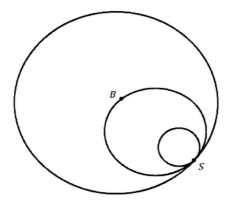

2. The center of the three circles lies on segment $\overline{BS}$ (not shown). The three circles are mutually tangent at point S. The center of the largest circle is point B, and the center of the middle circle lies on the smallest circle. The radius of the smallest circle is 8. What is the circumference of the largest circle?
    A. 16π
    B. 32π
    C. 64π
    D. 80π
    E. 128π

3. In the figure to the right, the circle has a center, A.
    If the measure of the arc BAD is 48°, what is the value of x?

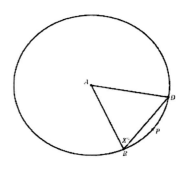

Note: Figure not drawn to scale

4. Point C is the center of both circles in the figure to the right. The circumference of the smaller circle is 18, and the radius of the small circle is one third of the radius of the large circle. What is the length of the darkened arc?

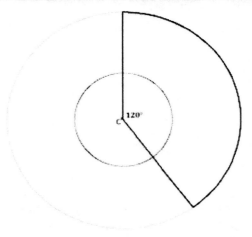

5. In the figure below, the two semicircles have radii of lengths a and b, respectively. Which of the following expressions gives the length of the curved path shown from Z to X?
    A. abπ
    B. (a + b)π
    C. a² b² π
    D. 2aπ + 2bπ
    E. $\dfrac{2ab}{\pi}$

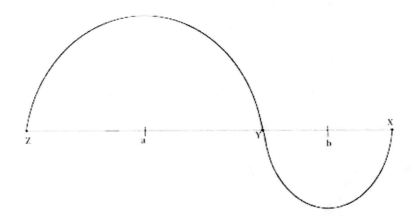

1ˢᵗ Ed. © ibidPREP llc

COMBOS—CIRCLES & TRIANGLES

These tests love, love, love to put triangles into circles. The reason they love to put triangles into circles is that if they put one vertex of the triangle on the center of the circle and the other two on the circumference of the circle, then two legs of the triangle are radii and the students who know that realize they have an isosceles triangle and life gets easier.

Triangles In Circles

If a triangle is inscribed in a circle and one of its vertices is the center of the circle, then that triangle is an isosceles triangle with two legs equal to the radius.

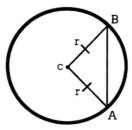

$\triangle$ ABC = Isosceles$\triangle$

Practice

CIRCLES WITH TRIANGLES

1. In the figure to the right, line segments BP and SP are tangent to the circle at points B and T, respectively. If the center of the circle is M, what angle must have the same degree measure as ∠BPS?

    A. ∠BMT
    B. ∠BSP
    C. ∠SMT
    D. ∠STM
    E. ∠MST

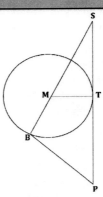

2. In the figure to the right, triangle PNO is inscribed in the circle with center M and diameter NO. If NP = NM, what is the degree measure of ∠NOP?

    A. 90°
    B. 60°
    C. 45°
    D. 30°
    E. 15°

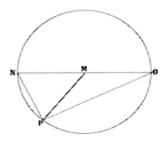

3. In the circle to the right, point A is the center, and BD is a diameter of the circle. If the length of arc $\overline{BED}$ is 6π, what is the length of arc $\overline{CFE}$?

    A. $\dfrac{2\pi}{3}$

    B. π

    C. 2π

    D. 3π

    E. 4π

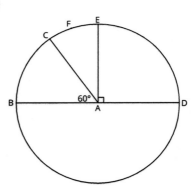

1ˢᵗ Ed. © ibidPREP llc

4. A circle and a triangle lie in the same plane. What is the maximum number of points at which the circle and triangle can intersect?
    A. 0
    B. 2
    C. 3
    D. 5
    E. 6

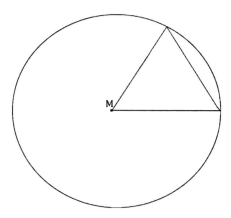

5. In the figure above, the circle has a center M, and the equilateral triangle inscribed in the circle has a perimeter of 24 cm. What is the area of the circle to the nearest square centimeter?

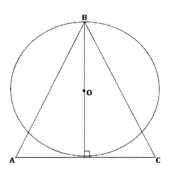

6. In the figure above, the circle with a center O has an area of 36π. What is the area of the equilateral triangle ABC?
    A. 64
    B. 72
    C. 108
    D. $36\sqrt{3}$
    E. $48\sqrt{3}$

Geometry

Other Combos

Inscribed Shapes

- If a circle is inscribed in a square, the length of a side of the square equals the diameter of the circle.

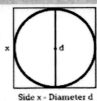

Side x - Diameter d

- If a square is inscribed in a circle, the diameter of the circle equals the diagonal of the square.
- If a cube is inscribed in a sphere, the diagonal of the cube = the diameter of the sphere.

- If a sphere is inscribed in a cube, the diameter of the sphere = the side of the cube.

Quadrilaterals

- A **Quadrilateral** is: any four-sided polygon [a closed figure with straight sides] with four interior angles that add up to 360°.
- A **Parallelogram** has: two pairs of opposite but equal sides [the two pairs may be equal to each other] and two opposite pairs of equal angles [these two pairs may be equal to each other]. Each pair of sides is parallel and the diagonals are congruent.
- All **Rectangles** are parallelograms with four 90° angles and equal diagonals that bisect one another. Not all parallelograms are rectangles, but all rectangles are parallelograms.
- All **Squares** are parallelograms with four equal sides, four 90° angles and diagonals that bisect one another at 90° angles. Squares are parallelograms and also rectangles, but not all rectangles and parallelograms are squares.
- **Area of a Parallelogram** = *Base × Height = bh*.
   Base × height [Height of parallelogram is the same as its side only if it is a rectangle.]

   [Since a rectangle is a type of parallelogram, **Area of a Rectangle** *also equals Base × Height = bh*]
- The **Area of a Square** equals: side times side, $s × s$, i.e. side *squared*, s^2 — get it?
- The **Perimeter of a Rectangle** equals: 2 Length + 2 Height =$2l + 2w$.
- The **Perimeter of a Square** equals: four times Side, $4s$.
- The **Diagonals of a Square** are equal to: the side of the square [s] times $\sqrt{2} = s\sqrt{2}$.

   [Because they are also the hypotenuses of isosceles right triangles]
- **Area of a Trapezoid**:

$$\frac{1}{2}h(b_1 + b_2)$$

Average of the parallel bases × height

1st Ed. © ibidPREP llc

INSCRIBED SHAPES

1. In the figure above, a circle with center C is inscribed in a square of area 64 square centimeters. What is the area of the circle, in centimeters?
    A. 4π
    B. 8π
    C. 16π
    D. 32π
    E. 64π

2. A square and triangle are inscribed inside of a circle as shown in the figure above. Which of the following statements must be true?

    I. If Z is a point inside of the triangle, then Z is inside of the square.
    II. If Y is a point inside the square, then Y is inside of the circle.
    III. If X is a point inside of the circle, then X is inside of the triangle.

    A. I only
    B. II only
    C. III only
    D. I and II only
    E. I, II, and III

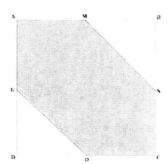

3. In the Square ABCD above, points L, M, N, and O are midpoints of the sides. If the area of the square is x, what is the area of the non-shaded regions in terms of x?
    A. $\frac{1}{4}x$

    B. $\frac{1}{2}x$

    C. $\frac{3}{4}x$

    D. $\frac{2}{3}x$

    E. $\frac{7}{8}x$

4. A square with an area of 4 is inscribed in a circle. What is the area of the circle?
    A. π
    B. 2π
    C. 4π
    D. 8π
    E. 16π

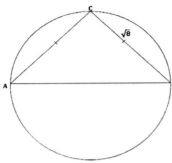

5. An isosceles triangle, △ABC, is inscribed in a circle as shown in the figure above. AC = BC and AB is equal to the diameter of the circle. Find the circumference of the circle.
    A. π
    B. √8 π
    C. 2π
    D. 2√8
    E. 4π

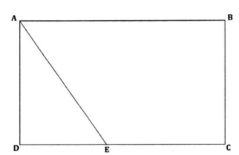

6. In the figure above, ABCD is a rectangle. The area of triangle ADE is 24 and DE = $\frac{1}{3}$ AD. If the area of rectangle ABCD is 168, what is the length of EC?
    A. 8
    B. 9
    C. 10
    D. 11
    E. 12

1st Ed. © ibidPREP llc

IRREGULAR SHAPES

If you see a circle with a shaded *yin* area within it, do not freak thinking that you were taught the area of a *yin* sign and forgot, or weren't paying attention, or should have been taught it by your tutor. Instead, please try to **see the shape as the sum or difference of shapes you do know** the area of -- circles, triangles, rectangles and that's it. The entire visual world can be broken down into those shapes when drawing *or* doing geometry. It is nice to work with an alphabet that has only three letters!

[The area of the shaded region in a yin-yang shape is simply half the area of the surrounding circle!]

The Hardest Thing About Perimeter

The hardest thing about perimeter is remembering to answer for it. In other words, many ACT perimeter questions like to combine area and perimeter in one question in order to make you think you are solving for area when in fact they want the perimeter of a shape.

Ex. The area of a rectangle is equal to two times its length plus five. If the length of the rectangle is 5 what is its perimeter?

SPANISH STEPS PROBLEM

HERE'S ONE OF THOSE PROBLEMS THAT LOOKS A LOT HARDER THAN IT IS.

IF THE SPANISH STEPS [A VERY FAMOUS OUTDOOR STAIRCASE IN A ROMAN PLAZA, SEE RIGHT] ARE 120 FEET TALL AND 240 FEET LONG, HOW MANY FEET OF CARPETING WOULD IT TAKE TO COVER THE STEPS FROM THE BOTTOM OF THE PLAZA TO THE TOP?

IT IS EASY TO GET SUPER REVVED UP BY THIS PROBLEM AND TRY DUSTING OFF YOUR TRIG, CURSING ME, WHIPPING OUT YOUR SLIDE RULE [NEVER MIND WHAT THAT IS] OR JUST FLEEING. HOWEVER, IF YOU LOOK CLOSELY AT THE DRAWING, YOU MIGHT NOTICE THAT ALL YOU HAVE TO DO IS CARPET THE HORIZONTAL TOPS OF THE STEPS AND THE VERTICAL FRONTS OF THE STEPS. IF YOU CONNECT ALL THE HORIZONTALS [FLATTENING THEM], YOU REALIZE YOU HAVE THE LENGTH OF THE STEPS. IF YOU CONNECT ALL THE VERTICALS, YOU HAVE THE HEIGHTS. SO:

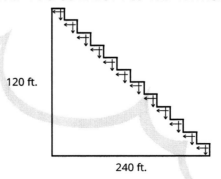

120 ft.

240 ft.

YOU WOULD SIMPLY NEED 120 FEET + 240 FEET = 360 FEET OF CARPETING TO CARPET THE SPANISH STEPS!

Practice

AREA & PERIMETER OF REGULAR & IRREGULAR SHAPES

1. The figure to the right represents a skyscraper with an off-center spire.
    If $\overline{BC} \parallel \overline{DE}$, what is the combined area of ΔABC and ΔDEF?
    A. 32
    B. 32+8√3
    C. 48
    D. 32√3
    E. 48+16√3

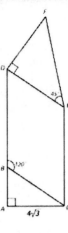

2. What is the perimeter of the figure to the right?
    A. 32
    B. 50
    C. 99
    D. 100
    E. 101

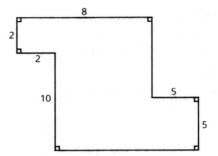

3. Find the area of the figure to the right.
    A. 36
    B. 24
    C. 48
    D. 60
    E. 72

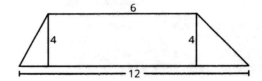

1ˢᵗ Ed. © ibidPREP llc

More Stuff—Polygons

Generally, there are not many questions involving polygons on the ACTs. However, you might as well get the few ones there are correct!

There are fairly simple formulas for determining the interior angles of regular polygons[45] [the only kind you'll be tested on]. However, if you forget the formula [not included in front of MATH Sections], there is a very simple way to look at polygons that should help you remember. Polygons are constructed of lots of triangles. If you draw lines from the center of a polygon to each of its vertices, then you will see that a square is made up of four isosceles triangles, a pentagon is made up of five and so on...

Since each triangle is 180° the total of the angles inside the polygon is equal to the number of triangles times 180°.

$$5 \times 180° = 900°$$

Then to find the total of just the interior angles of the polygon, merely subtract 360° from that total because that is what all the tips of the triangles add up to as they form the central angle!

$$900° - 360° = 540°$$

Now, to figure out what each interior angle equals, merely divide the total number of interior angles by the number of sides in the polygon.

$$\frac{540}{5} = 108$$

Diagonals Of Polygons:

Here's a fun one...Occasionally you will encounter questions that give you a polygon, and ask you to figure out the number of distinct [different] diagonals that can be drawn inside it. It seems simple to thoroughly and carefully draw in all the diagonals and count them as you go, but you would be amazed how difficult that can be under pressure. Hopefully your nerves have improved through reading this book, but should they fail you, here are the formulas for the numbers of diagonals in a polygon. Of course, if your memory of the formula fails you, Remain Clam! and systematically draw the diagonals.

Polygons

Total of Interior Angles of a Polygon with "N" number of sides = $180(N-2)$

Interior Angle of a Polygon with "N" number of sides = $\dfrac{180(N-2)}{N}$

Diagonals of a polygon = $\dfrac{N(N-3)}{2}$

---

[45] A polygon in which all sides and all interior angles are equal.

3D GEO

Cubes & Boxes [Rectangular Prisms]

- A cube is a box whose dimensions [length, width & height] are all equal.

- Every box, rectangular prism, has SIX faces and EIGHT vertices [corners].

- The volume of a cube = s^3 which is side times side times side, i.e.: side cubed.

- The volume of a box [rectangular prism] = Length times width times height = lwh.

[Remember: Cubes are Also Boxes]

- The surface area of a box [rectangular prism] =The sum of the area of the faces of a box [a.k.a. surface area] = 2lw + 2hw + 2hl.

- The surface area of a cube = The sum of the area of the all six square faces of the cube = $6s^2$.

- The diagonal of a box goes from one vertex of the box through the shape to the vertex directly across from it.

- Diagonal of a rectangular box [including cubes] goes from one corner to its opposite through the box

$$\sqrt{l^2 + w^2 + h^2}.$$

- Diagonal of a cube with side s then would be: $\sqrt{s^2 + s^2 + s^2} = \sqrt{3s^2}$

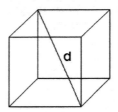

3D Is Really 2D

Most students are terrified of three dimensional shapes. Don't be. A lot of times they aren't even really questions about 3D shapes. If you look closely you realize they are really just questions about 2 dimensional shapes. Think fast, if you see a cylinder head-on as a silhouette, what shape does it make? From the top down it's a circle, but from the side it's a rectangle – weird! If you squash a cone, it becomes a triangle. A sphere becomes a circle and so on.

1st Ed. © ibidPREP llc

3D Is Really 2D

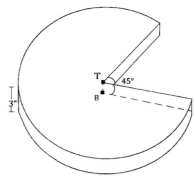

1. A right circular cylindrical wheel of cheese of uniform density weighs 4 pounds. The wheel of cheese has had a 45° wedge cut out as shown. All cuts made are perpendicular to the base and radiate from points T and B, the respective centers of the top and bottom. What is the weight (in pounds) of the cheese wedge that was cut out?
    A. 1/4
    B. 1/2
    C. 1
    D. 2
    E. 3

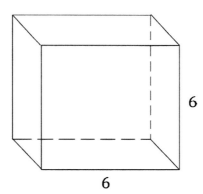

2. In the figure above a cube is shown with dimensions of 6 x 6 x 6. If a line is drawn from the midpoint of one edge to the midpoint of an adjacent edge, what would be the length of this line?
    A. 3
    B. $3\sqrt{2}$
    C. $2\sqrt{6}$
    D. 6
    E. 12

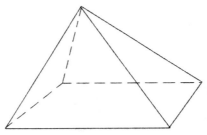

3. An equilateral pyramid has a base with an area of 36. If the 4 triangular sides of the pyramid were to be unfolded onto the same plane as the base, what would be the perimeter of this object?
    A. 48
    B. 42
    C. 36
    D. 30
    E. 24

4. A right cylinder has a volume of 36π and a radius of 2. What is the combined surface area of top and bottom of the cylinder?
    A. 9
    B. 4π
    C. 8π
    D. 18π
    E. 72π

5. The cube to the right has the dimensions 4 x 4 x 4. What is the length of $\overline{AH}$?
    A. 4√2
    B. 4√3
    C. 8
    D. 16
    E. 64

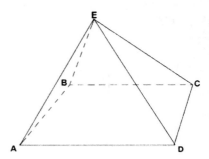

6. The figure to the right is a pyramid. ABCD is a square and each triangle is isosceles. If $\overline{AB}$ is 8 and the height of the pyramid is 4√2, what is the combined area of all the faces including the base?
    A. 128
    B. 64 +128√3
    C. 64 + 64√3
    D. 64 + 32√2
    E. 32 + 96√3

1ˢᵗ Ed. © ibidPREP llc

Cylinders

A cylinder is a circle raised up along a height. Therefore:

Volume of a cylinder = Area of the base circle times the height of the cylinder, or V= $\pi r^2 h$.

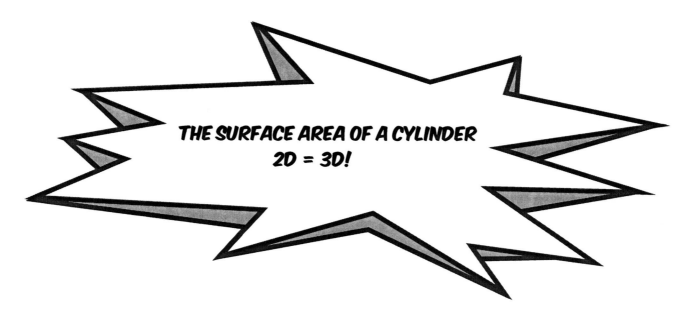

THE SURFACE AREA OF A CYLINDER
2D = 3D!

Here's an odd one:

The surface area of a cylinder is equal to the area of the **two circles** on the top and bottom of the cylinder **AND** THE AREA OF THE RECTANGLE DEFINED BY THE CIRCUMFERENCE OF THE CYLINDER AND ITS HEIGHT.

Wait. What? Where did the **rectangle** come from?

Take a piece of paper. Make a tube out of it [now it's a cylinder!]. Open it up again [it's a rectangle again!]. The lateral part of a cylinder [the part that goes up] is really just a rectangle.

Practice

3D GEOMETRY

1. A rectangular prism has a volume of 360 cubic centimeters. The height of this prism is 6 cm, while the width is 5 cm. Find the surface area.
   - A. 300
   - B. 324
   - C. 360
   - D. 432
   - E. 720

2. The volume of the rectangular solid above is 480. If AG = 3x, GH = 5x, and CH = 5x, what is the value of x?
   - A. 1
   - B. 1.5
   - C. 2
   - D. 3
   - E. 4

3. Determine the surface area of a cube with a volume of 343.
   - A. 49
   - B. 252
   - C. 294
   - D. 307
   - E. 343

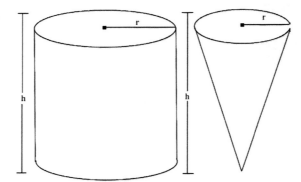

4. Both the cylinder and cone shown in the figure above have the same radius, r, of 8 cm and a height, h, of 12 cm. If the cylinder is completely filled with water, and then water is poured out of the cylinder to fill the cone, what will be the depth in cm of the water remaining in the cylinder? (Volume of cone = $\frac{1}{3}\pi r^2 h$)
   - A. 4
   - B. 6
   - C. 8
   - D. 9
   - E. 10

1st Ed. © ibidPREP llc

COORDINATE GEOMETRY

At least 95% of the time when students get these types of questions wrong, it's because they confuse the x and y coordinates in their calculations or plotting. Really. It's as simple as that. Problems involving coordinate geometry [points with x and y coordinates plotted on x and y axes] can be made much, much easier if you are extra careful and double check your coordinates before and after you use them.

Equation Of A Line

For all points x and y on a line, the formula for the equation of the line is:

- $y = mx + b$
- y: value of y coordinate
- m: value of slope
- x: value of x coordinate
- b: value of y intercept

REMEMBER: y **intercept** is the value of y when x=0. This makes sense if you think about it [and even if you don't] because if you put 0 in for m in the equation of the line, you get:

$$y = mx + b$$

$$y = m(0) + b$$

$$\therefore y = b \quad !$$

What makes the equation of the line helpful [and not just something to memorize] is that if you know the slope and y intercept of the line [m and b respectively], you can use that info to figure out the y coordinate for any x you choose and vice versa. Furthermore, if you are given three of these variables, you can figure out the fourth. I.e., if you are given the slope, y intercept and any old value of x, you can figure out y and vice versa.

Domain & Range

Domain: all possible x values of a function or a part of the function—

More often defined by what it excludes than what it includes:

$$f(x) = \frac{27}{x-3} + \sqrt{x} \text{ , Domain: } 0 \leq x \text{ and } x \neq 3$$

{negative numbers and 3 would make the function undefined as you can't divide by zero or take the square root of a negative number}.

Range: all possible y values of a function or part of a function—e.g.:

For f = x + 1, Range: y = all real numbers

For f = x², Range: y ≥ 0 {since any number squared ≥ 0}

For $f(x) = \frac{2}{x}$, Range: y ≠ 0

{since x cannot equal 0, there is no way for y to equal 0}

You can also use the equation to construct the line without being given any coordinate points. Because you only ever need two points to construct a line, and since in the equation of a line you are given the slope and the y intercept, you automatically know Point, P_1, the y intercept. To find your second point, P_2, find the x in-tercept [the value of x when y = zero]. To do that, set y equal to zero [just as you made x zero to find your y intercept] and solve for x. Now you have two points with which to draw your line.

Slopes—How To Read Them, & Everything Else You Ever Wanted To Know

$$\text{Slope} = m = \frac{y_2 - y_1}{x_2 - x_1} = \frac{\text{rise}}{\text{run}} = \frac{\Delta y}{\Delta x} = \frac{\text{change in y}}{\text{change in x}}$$

- When calculating slope: Make sure you put the y's OVER the x's !!!!!!
- The slope of a line is read from left to right [just like we read English]:
    - if it goes down the slope is negative.
    - if it is horizontal the slope is zero—Slope of a Horizontal line: m = 0.
    - if the line is vertical the slope is undefined—Slope of a Vertical line:
      m = undefined [you can't divide by zero which is the run {change in x} on a vertical line].
- If for a line, m = 1 or –1:
    - The line forms a 45° angle to the x axis.
    - If a line forms an angle of greater than 45° with the x axis, then its slope will be greater than 1.
    - If a line forms an angle less than 45° with the x axis, then its slope will be less than 1.

1ˢᵗ Ed. © ibidPREP llc

- If a line passes through the origin and a point (x,y), the slope of that line will simply equal $\frac{y}{x}$.
- The slopes of parallel lines are EQUAL to each other.
- The slopes of perpendicular lines are NEGATIVE RECIPROCALS of each other.
    - E.g. slope of l_1 = 2; slope of $l_2 \perp l_1$ = $-\frac{1}{2}$.
- The slope of the reflection of a line across another line or axis is the NEGATIVE of the original line.
    - E.g. slope of l_1 = 2; slope of l_2 reflection of l_1 = –2.

Functions To Know On Sight!

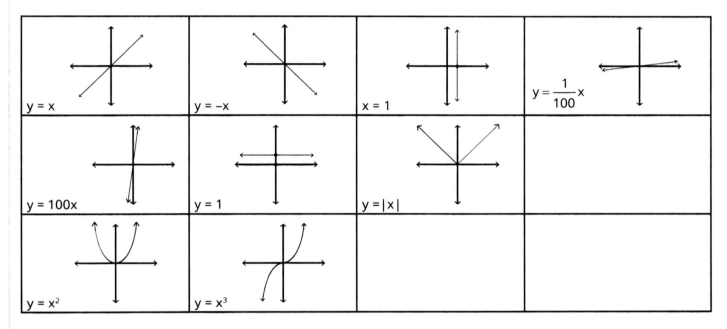

$y = x$	$y = -x$	$x = 1$	$y = \frac{1}{100}x$
$y = 100x$	$y = 1$	$y = |x|$	
$y = x^2$	$y = x^3$		

Intersections

If two functions intersect at one point, then the x and y coordinates of that point will fit into both equations as their x and y variables, AND **the two functions can be set as equal to each other**.

Practice

COORDINATE GEOMETRY

1. In the coordinate plane to the right, the points A (-2, 2), B (1, 5), and C (4, 2) lie on a circle with center P. What are the coordinates of point P?
   A. (0, 0)
   B. (1, 1)
   C. (0, −1)
   D. (1, 2)
   E. (2, 1)

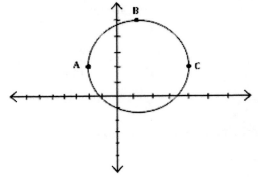

2. In the xy-coordinate plane, the distance from point P to point (3,2) is 8. If the y-coordinate of point P is 2, which of the following could be the x-coordinate of P?
   A. −3
   B. 4
   C. 7
   D. 8
   E. 11

3. In the xy plane, three of the vertices of a square are (0,0), (0,4), and (4,0). If the square is reflected about the line y = −x, which of the following is one vertex of the resulting square?
   A. (−4, −4)
   B. (−4, 4)
   C. (0, 4)
   D. (4, −4)
   E. (4, 0)

4. In the figure to the right, point A is the center of the circle. What is the slope of segment AR?

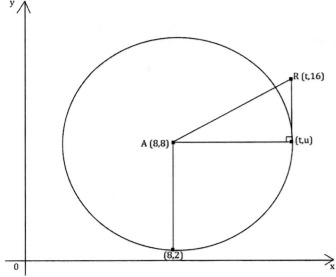

1st Ed. © ibidPREP llc

5. Based on the portions of the graphs of the functions of
    f and g shown to the right, what are all the values of x
    between –8 and 8 for which g > f?
    A.   –8 < x < –5 only
    B.   –5 < x < 0 only
    C.   0 < x < 5 only
    D.   5 < x < 8 only
    E.   –8 < x < –5 and 0 < x < 5

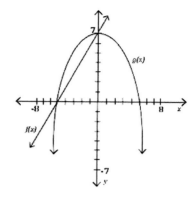

6. In the figure below, the points (a,0) and (-a,b) lie on the graph of y= 4 – x³.
    What is the value of b?
    A.   4
    B.   8
    C. $\sqrt[3]{4}$
    D. $2\sqrt[3]{4}$
    E. $\sqrt[3]{2}$

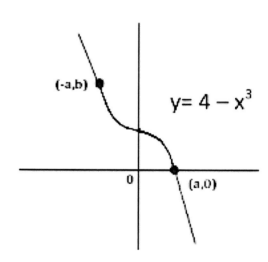

1ˢᵗ Ed. © ibidPREP llc

SPECIAL ACT MATH

1st Ed. © ibidPREP llc

Welcome to the MATRIX!

Matrices [the plural of "matrix"] are used to crush statistics and all sorts of real world info—later in your mathematical for life. For now, they are mostly a minor annoyance on the ACT. But since a point is a point, here you go...

Let's take a simple real world example of how you might construct and use a matris.

Example One: Two families A and B (though you may easily deal with more than two) have monthly expenses for food, utilities, and health.

How can you represent the data collected in those categories? Many ways are available, but a matrix allows us to combine the data, so that it is easy to manipulate.

Let's write it like this:

$$\text{Month} = \begin{pmatrix} \text{Family} & \text{Food} & \text{Utilities} & \text{Health} \\ \text{A} & a & b & c \\ \text{B} & d & e & f \end{pmatrix}$$

If you have no problem confusing the names and what the expenses are, you may write:

$$\text{Month} = \begin{pmatrix} a & b & c \\ d & e & f \end{pmatrix}$$

This is a **Matrix**.

The SIZE of the matrix is defined as:

- the number of Rows and the number of Columns. In this case, the above matrix has 2 rows and 3 columns. You may easily come up with a matrix which has m rows and n columns. In this case, we say that the matrix is a (m x n) matrix (read as "m-by-n matrix").
  - Remember
    - m = number or rows, and
    - n = number of columns.

Our matrix above is a (2 x 3) matrix.

When the numbers of rows and columns are equal, we call the matrix a **square matrix**. A square matrix of **order n** is a (n x n) matrix.

Matrix Addition and Matrix Subtraction

Just like ordinary algebra, matrix algebra has operations like addition and subtraction.

How to Add and Subtract Matrices

Two matrices may be added or subtracted only if they have the same <u>dimension</u>—that is, they must have the same number of rows and columns.

Addition or subtraction is accomplished by adding or subtracting corresponding elements. For example, consider matrix A and matrix B.

$$A = \begin{pmatrix} 1 & 2 & 3 \\ 7 & 8 & 9 \end{pmatrix} \quad B = \begin{pmatrix} 5 & 6 & 7 \\ 3 & 4 & 5 \end{pmatrix}$$

Both matrices have the same number of rows and columns (2 rows and 3 columns), so they can be added and subtracted. Thus,

$$A + B = \begin{pmatrix} 1+5 & 2+6 & 3+7 \\ 7+3 & 8+4 & 9+5 \end{pmatrix} = \begin{pmatrix} 6 & 8 & 10 \\ 10 & 12 & 14 \end{pmatrix}$$

And,

$$A - B = \begin{pmatrix} 1-5 & 2-6 & 3-7 \\ 7-3 & 8-4 & 9-5 \end{pmatrix} = \begin{pmatrix} -4 & -4 & -4 \\ 4 & 4 & 4 \end{pmatrix}$$

And finally, note that the order in which matrices are added is not important; thus, A + B = B + A.

EXAMPLE PROBLEM
Consider the matrices shown below - A, B, C, and D

$$A = \begin{pmatrix} 1 \\ 2 \end{pmatrix} \quad B = \begin{pmatrix} 3 & 5 \\ 4 & 6 \end{pmatrix} \quad C = \begin{pmatrix} 4 & 5 \\ 6 & 6 \end{pmatrix} \quad D = \begin{pmatrix} -1 & 0 \\ -2 & 0 \end{pmatrix}$$

1. Which of the following statements are true?
    I.   **A + B = C**

    II. **B + C = D**

    III. **B - C = D**

    A.   I only
    B.   II only
    C.   III only
    D.   I and II
    E.   I and III

1st Ed. © ibidPREP llc

SOLUTION
The correct answer is C, as shown below.

$$\mathbf{B\text{-}C} = \begin{pmatrix} 3-4 & 5-5 \\ 4-6 & 6-5 \end{pmatrix} = \begin{pmatrix} -1 & 0 \\ -2 & 0 \end{pmatrix} = \mathbf{D}$$

Note that Matrices **A** and **B** cannot be added, because **B** has more columns than **A**. Again, matrices may be added or subtracted only if they have the same number of rows and the same number of columns.

Matrix Multiplication

In matrix algebra, there are two kinds of matrix multiplication: multiplication of a matrix by a number and multiplication of a matrix by another matrix.

How to Multiply a Matrix by a Number

When you multiply a matrix by a number, you multiply every element in the matrix by the same number. This operation produces a new matrix, which is called a **scalar multiple**.

For example, if x is 5, and the matrix A is:

$$\mathbf{A} = \begin{pmatrix} 100 & 200 \\ 300 & 400 \end{pmatrix}$$

Then, $x\mathbf{A} = 5\mathbf{A}$ and

$$5\mathbf{A} = 5\begin{pmatrix} 100 & 200 \\ 300 & 400 \end{pmatrix}$$

$$5\mathbf{A} = \begin{pmatrix} 5\cdot100 & 5\cdot200 \\ 5\cdot300 & 5\cdot400 \end{pmatrix}$$

$$5\mathbf{A} = \begin{pmatrix} 500 & 1000 \\ 1500 & 2000 \end{pmatrix} = \mathbf{B}$$

In the example above, every element of **A** is multiplied by 5 to produce the scalar multiple, **B**.

Note: Some texts refer to this operation as multiplying a matrix by a scalar [a scale multiplier].

Identity Matrix

The identity matrix is an n x n diagonal matrix with 1's in the diagonal and zeros everywhere else. The identity matrix is denoted by I or In. Two identity matrices appear below.

$$\mathbf{I}_2 = \begin{pmatrix} 1 & 0 \\ 0 & 1 \end{pmatrix} \quad \mathbf{I}_3 = \begin{pmatrix} 1 & 0 & 0 \\ 0 & 1 & 0 \\ 0 & 0 & 1 \end{pmatrix}$$

The identity matrix has a unique talent. Any matrix that can be premultiplied or postmultiplied by I remains the same; that is:

$$\mathbf{AI} = \mathbf{IA} = \mathbf{A}$$

Special Math

1. Consider the matrices shown below—A, B, and C

$$A = \begin{pmatrix} a & b \\ c & d \end{pmatrix} \quad B = \begin{pmatrix} e & f \\ g & h \end{pmatrix} \quad C = \begin{pmatrix} w & x \\ y & z \end{pmatrix}$$

Assume that **AB** = **C**. Which of the following statements are true?
   A. $w = a*e + b*h$
   B. $x = a*f + b*h$
   C. $y = c*g + d*h$
   D. All of the above
   E. None of the above

SOLUTION

The correct answer is B. To compute the value of any element in matrix C, we use the formula $C_{ik} = \Sigma_j A_{ij}B_{jk}$.

In matrix C, x is the element in row 1 and column 2, which is represented in the formula by C_{12}. Therefore, to find x, we use the formula to calculate C_{12}, as shown below.

$$x = C_{12} = \Sigma_j A_{1j}B_{j2} = A_{11}B_{12} + A_{12}B_{22} = a*f + b*h$$

All of the other answers are incorrect.

How to Multiply a Matrix by a Matrix

As with addition of matrices, you can definitely multiply matrices of the same dimensions and here's how:

$$\begin{pmatrix} a & b \\ c & d \end{pmatrix}\begin{pmatrix} e & f \\ g & h \end{pmatrix} = \begin{pmatrix} ae+bg & af+bh \\ ce+dg & cf+dh \end{pmatrix}$$

However, you do not need to have two matrices of the same size in order to multiply them. Below, we will multiply a (2 x 2) matrix with a (2 x 1) matrix (which gave a (2 x 1) matrix).

BUT BE CAREFUL: You can only multiply matrices of different dimensions when only when the number of **columns** in the first matrix is **equal** to the number of **rows** in the second matrix. And the order of the matrices does matter!

YES:

$$\begin{pmatrix} a & b & c \\ d & e & f \end{pmatrix}\begin{pmatrix} \alpha \\ \beta \\ \upsilon \end{pmatrix} = \begin{pmatrix} a\alpha+b\beta+c\upsilon \\ d\alpha+e\beta+f\upsilon \end{pmatrix}$$

NO:

$$\begin{pmatrix} \alpha \\ \beta \\ \upsilon \end{pmatrix}\begin{pmatrix} a & b & c \\ d & e & f \end{pmatrix}$$

If this is still confusing, set up your matrix multilplication in a grid, with the first matrix on the left of the grid, and the second on the top. Just like so:

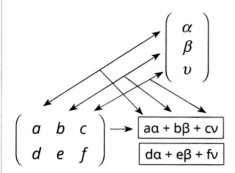

So you have to be very careful about multiplying matrices. Sentences like "multiply the two matrices A and B" do not make sense. You must know which of the two matrices will be to the right (of your multiplication) and which one will be to the left. In other words, you have to know whether you are asked to perform **A × B** or **B × A**. Even if both multiplications do make sense (as in the case of square matrices with the same size), you still have to be very careful. Consider the two matrices:

$$\begin{pmatrix} 0 & 1 \\ 0 & 0 \end{pmatrix} \text{ and } \begin{pmatrix} 0 & 0 \\ 1 & 0 \end{pmatrix}$$

You have

$$\begin{pmatrix} 0 & 1 \\ 0 & 0 \end{pmatrix}\begin{pmatrix} 0 & 0 \\ 1 & 0 \end{pmatrix} = \begin{pmatrix} 1 & 0 \\ 0 & 0 \end{pmatrix}$$

and

$$\begin{pmatrix} 0 & 0 \\ 1 & 0 \end{pmatrix}\begin{pmatrix} 0 & 1 \\ 0 & 0 \end{pmatrix} = \begin{pmatrix} 0 & 0 \\ 0 & 1 \end{pmatrix}$$

So what is the conclusion behind this example? The matrix multiplication is not commutative, the order in which matrices are multiplied **is important**. In fact, this little setback is a major problem in playing around with matrices. This is something that you must always be careful with. Let us show you another setback. You could have

$$\begin{pmatrix} 0 & 1 \\ 0 & 0 \end{pmatrix}\begin{pmatrix} 0 & 1 \\ 0 & 0 \end{pmatrix} = \begin{pmatrix} 0 & 0 \\ 0 & 0 \end{pmatrix}; \text{ i.e.,}$$

the product of two non-zero matrices may be equal to the zero-matrix.

So, you have to be very careful about multiplying matrices.

Practice

MATRICES

1. Multiply the following matrices: $\begin{pmatrix} 3 & 4 \\ 5 & 6 \end{pmatrix}\begin{pmatrix} 6 & 5 \\ 4 & 3 \end{pmatrix}$.

   A. $\begin{pmatrix} 34 & 27 \\ 54 & 43 \end{pmatrix}$

   B. $\begin{pmatrix} 36 & 27 \\ 54 & 45 \end{pmatrix}$

   C. $\begin{pmatrix} 70 & 56 \\ 110 & 88 \end{pmatrix}$

   D. $\begin{pmatrix} 288 & 180 \\ 720 & 450 \end{pmatrix}$

   E. These matrices cannot be multiplied.

2. What is $\begin{pmatrix} 1 & 10 & 3 \\ 17 & 3 & 4 \end{pmatrix}+\begin{pmatrix} 2 & 1 & 6 \\ 5 & 1 & 8 \end{pmatrix}$?

   A. $\begin{pmatrix} 2 & 10 & 18 \\ 22 & 3 & 32 \end{pmatrix}$

   B. $\begin{pmatrix} 3 & 11 & 9 \\ 22 & 4 & 12 \end{pmatrix}$

   C. $\begin{pmatrix} 8 & 12 & 17 \\ 24 & 5 & 18 \end{pmatrix}$

   D. $\begin{pmatrix} 7 & 11 & 5 \\ 25 & 4 & 9 \end{pmatrix}$

   E. These matrices cannot be added.

3. $\begin{pmatrix} 1 & 2 \\ 3 & 4 \\ 5 & 6 \end{pmatrix}\begin{pmatrix} 5 \\ 17 \\ 6 \end{pmatrix}$

   A. $\begin{pmatrix} 10 \\ 204 \\ 180 \end{pmatrix}$

   B. $\begin{pmatrix} 28 & 56 \\ 84 & 112 \\ 140 & 168 \end{pmatrix}$

   C. $\begin{pmatrix} 1 & 2 & 5 \\ 3 & 4 & 17 \\ 5 & 6 & 6 \end{pmatrix}$

   D. $\begin{pmatrix} 5 & 10 \\ 51 & 68 \\ 30 & 36 \end{pmatrix}$

   E. These matrices cannot be multiplied.

1ˢᵗ Ed. © ibidPREP llc

MUST KNOW Trigonometry

SOH CAH TOA

S = Sine

C = Cosine

T = Tangent

O = Side opposite angle being evaluated

H = Hypotenuse

A = Side adjacent to angle being evaluated

SOH means Sine = Opposite over [divided by] Hypotenuse

CAH means Cosine = Adjacent over Hypotenuse

TOA means Tangent = Opposite over Adjacent

So...

If you're given the sides of a right triangle and want to find its angles, use **SIN** key on calculator [or **COS** or **TAN**— before the start of your test make sure you check that your calculator is in DEGREE not RADIANS]:

$$\sin(x) = \frac{\text{Opposite}}{\text{Hypotenuse}}$$

$$\sin(30) = \frac{\text{Opposite}}{\text{Hypotenuse}} = \frac{1}{2}$$

[remember your 30°,60°,90° triangle here,and you' ll recall that the side opposite the 30° angle is equal to 1 when the side opposite the 90° angle is equal to 2]

If you're given the sides of a right triangle and want to find out what an angle in the triangle is, use your calculator buttons : $\sin^{-1}(\theta)$, $\cos^{-1}(\theta)$, or $\tan^{-1}(\theta)$

e.g. $\sin^{-1}(.5) = 30°$

What's up Trigonometry?

Many students are a little scared of trig, but the ACT seems to overcompensate for that fact by testing trig in an pretty straightforward way. ACT trig is basically all about right triangles. If you felt comfortable in the triangle section above, trig will be a breeze. If you didn't feel too comfortable, learning a bit of trig can help you. When it comes down to it, you only have to be comfortable with the most basic aspects of trig to do well on the ACT trig questions.

Finally, there will only be four trig questions on the Math Test, so even if you aren't comfortable with trig, it won't destroy your Math score. The topics of trigonometry covered by the ACT are:

1. SOHCAHTOA
2. Solving Triangles
3. Trigonometric Identities
4. Trigonometric Graphs

SOHCAHTOA: Sine, Cosine, and Tangent

Most of the trig questions come down to knowing SOHCAHTOA. It's as easy as that. This acronym captures almost everything you'll need to know to answer ACT trig questions. It means:

SOH— Sine = Opposite over Hypotenuse
CAH—Cosine = Adjacent over Hypotenuse
TOA—Tangent =Opposite over Adjacent

All of this opposite-adjacent-hypotenuse business in the parentheses tells you how to determine the sine, cosine, and tangent of a **right** triangle. *Opposite* means the side facing the angle; *adjacent* means the side that's next to the angle, [NOT the hypotenuse—the side opposite the 90° angle].

Say you have the following right triangle:

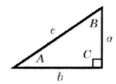

To find the *sine of A* just think of SOH, divide a, the opposite side, by c, the hypotenuse of the triangle. Get the idea?

So, for the triangle above:

$$\sin A = \frac{a}{c} \qquad \sin B = \frac{b}{c}$$

$$\cos A = \frac{b}{c} \qquad \cos B = \frac{a}{c}$$

$$\tan A = \frac{a}{b} \qquad \tan B = \frac{b}{a}$$

1ˢᵗ Ed. © ibidPREP llc

There are some values for the sine, cosine, and tangent of particular angles that you should learn for the ACT. ACT trig questions often test these angles, and if you know these trig values, you can save a great deal of time.

Angle	Sine	Cosine	Tangent
0°	0	1	0
30°	1/2	√3/2	√3/3
45°	√2/2	√2/2	1
60°	√3/2	1/2	√3
90°	1	0	undefined

Even if you don't remember these values for these special angles, they're easy enough to determine using the Unit Circle. The unit circle is also a great way to determine whether the sin/cos/tan of a certain angle is positive or negative.

Unit Circle

A unit circle is a circle of radius = 1, drawn over the x and y axes with its center at (0,0)

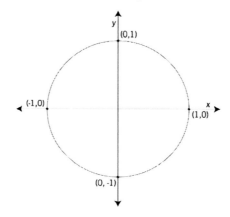

If you want to measure a central angle drawn with the origin as its vertex, there's a neat way to measure and determine the measure of the interior angle.

If you pick a point on the circle, any point, you may call that point (x,y). If you drop a line down [or up] from that point to the x axis, and if that line is perpendicular to the x axis, then you can draw a line from where it hits the x axis to the origin, and what do you have?

Triangle A: a right triangle with a hypotenuse of 1 [because the hypotenuse of the triangle overlaps the radius of the circle!], and legs of length x and y respectively.

PICK A POINT ON CIRCLE WITH A RIGHT TRIANGLE CONSTRUCTED FROM POINT (X,Y) WITH SIDES LABELLED X, Y AND ONE.

Now, if you pick an angle created with the center of the circle as its vertex and you call it θ ["theta"], then the fun begins. We measure that angle using the positive side of the x axis as 0° and rotating counterclockwise from there around the circle until we've rotated 360° and end up back at 0°.

Special Math

Find the sinθ

$$\sin\theta = \frac{\text{Opposite}}{\text{Hypotenuse}} = \frac{y}{1} = y$$

SO, for the unit circle s

Find the cosθ

$$\cos\theta = \frac{\text{Adjacent}}{\text{Hypotenuse}} = \frac{x}{1} = x$$

Find the tanθ

$$\tan\theta = \frac{\text{Opposite}}{\text{Adjacent}} = \frac{y}{x}$$

Since the sinθ = y, cosθ = x and tan$\theta = \frac{y}{x}$, then you know:

- if the y coordinate of your point is negative then the sin will be negative,
- if the x is negative the cos will be negative, and
- if the either the x or y is negative then the tan is negative. However, if both the x and y are negative than the tan is positive because tan is y/x and a negative divided by a negative is, of course, positive!

Radians

Radians are based on the unit circle.

We mentioned above that in the unit circle angles are formed by travelling around the circle. The positive side of the x axis is used as the first ray of the angle, and the second ray is formed from another radius drawn to a point anywhere on the circle.

Although radians seems bizarre, there's really a simple explanation for them. They are a way of measuring angles by distance rather than degrees. Radians give a measure of an angle relative to the arc length of that angle rather than its degree measure. Since the unit circle has a radius of 1, then its circumference is 2π, that means that $360° = 2\pi$ radians or 2π rad.

Going with that info, it's easy to convert most common angles to radians.

$$360 = 2\pi \text{ rad}$$

$$270 = \frac{3}{2}\pi \text{ rad}$$

$$180 = \pi \text{ rad}$$

1st Ed. © ibidPREP llc

$$120 = \frac{2\pi}{3} \text{ rad}$$

$$90 = \frac{\pi}{2} \text{ rad}$$

$$60 = \frac{\pi}{3} \text{ rad}$$

$$45 = \frac{\pi}{4} \text{ rad}$$

$$30 = \frac{\pi}{6} \text{ rad}$$

Solving Triangles

Once you understand the trigonometric functions of sine, cosine, and tangent, you should be able to use these functions to "solve" a triangle. In other words, if you are given some information about a triangle, you should be able to use the trigonometric functions to figure out the values of other angles or sides of the triangle. For example,

What is the length of $\overline{BC}$ in the triangle below?

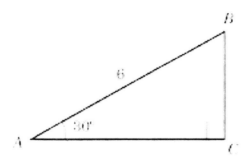

In this problem, you are given the measure of ∠A, as well as the length of $\overline{AB}$. The image also shows that this triangle is a right triangle. You can use this information to solve for $\overline{BC}$ if you can figure out which trigonometric function to use. You have to find the value of side $\overline{BC}$, which stands opposite the angle you know. You also know the value of the hypotenuse. To figure out $\overline{BC}$, then, you need to use the trig function that uses both opposite and hypotenuse, which is sine. From the chart of the values of critical points, you know that sin 30° = ½.

To solve:

$$\sin 30 = \frac{x}{6}$$

$$\frac{1}{2} = \frac{x}{6}$$

$$x = 3$$

Another favorite ACT problem is to combine the Pythagorean theorem with trig functions, like so:

What is the sine of ∠A in right triangle ABC below?

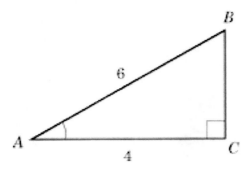

To find the sine of ∠A , you need to know the value of the side opposite ∠A and the value of the hypotenuse. The figure gives the value of the hypotenuse, but not of the opposite side. However, since the figure does provide the value of $\overline{AC}$, you can calculate the value of the opposite side, $\overline{BC}$, by using the Pythagorean theorem.

$$AB^2 = AC^2 + BC^2$$

$$6^2 = 4^2 + x^2$$

$$36 = 16 + x^2$$

$$x^2 = 20$$

$$x = \sqrt{20} = 2\sqrt{5}$$

Now that you know the value of $\overline{BC}$, you can solve for sin A:

$$\sin A = \frac{2\sqrt{5}}{6}$$

$$\sin A = \frac{\sqrt{5}}{3}$$

Trigonometric Identities

A trigonometric identity is an equation involving trigonometric functions that holds true for all angles. For the ACT test, trigonometric identities, on those few occasions when they come up, will be helpful in situations when you need to simplify a trigonometric expression. The two identities you should know are:

$$\tan\theta = \frac{\sin\theta}{\cos\theta}$$

$$\sin^2\theta + \cos^2\theta = 1$$

1st Ed. © ibidPREP llc

If you see an expression that contains either $\dfrac{\sin\theta}{\cos\theta}$ or $\sin^2\theta + \cos^2\theta$, you should immediately substitute in its identity.

Trigonometric Graphs

The ACT will include one or two questions covering the graphs of the trigonometric functions. You should be able to match each graph with each function, and you should know when the different functions reach their highest point and lowest point.

Graph of y = sin x

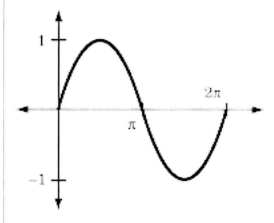

Graph of y = cos x

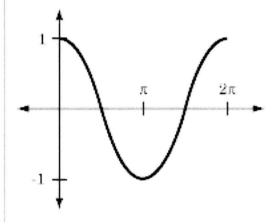

Graph of y = tan x

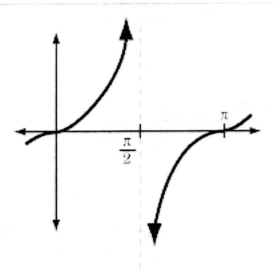

Stretching the Trigonometric Graphs

In addition to knowing the graphs of the trigonometric functions, you should also know how the graphs can be stretched vertically or horizontally. Vertical stretches affect the graph's amplitude, while horizontal stretches change the period.

Stretching The Amplitude

If a coefficient is placed in front of the function, the graph will stretch vertically: its highest points will be higher and its lowest points will be lower. Whereas the function y = sin x never goes higher than 1 or lower than –1, the function y = 3 sin x has a high point of 3 and a low point of –3. Changing the amplitude of a function does not change the value of x at which the high and low points occur. In the figure below, for example, y = sin x and y = 3 sin x both have their high points when x equals –3π/2 andπ/2.

1ˢᵗ Ed. © ibidPREP llc

TRIGONOMETRY

1. According to the following diagram, which of the following statements is true?

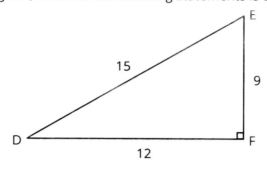

A. $\cos E = \dfrac{5}{3}$

B. $\sin E = \dfrac{3}{5}$

C. $\cos D = \dfrac{4}{5}$

D. $\sin D = \dfrac{4}{5}$

E. $\tan E = \dfrac{3}{4}$

2. According to the following diagram, which of the following statements is true?

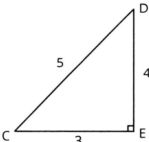

A. $\sin C = \dfrac{7}{5}$

B. $\sin C = \dfrac{3}{5}$

C. $\sin C = \dfrac{5}{3}$

D. $\sin C = \dfrac{4}{5}$

E. $\sin C = \dfrac{5}{4}$

3. According to the following diagram, which of the following statements is true?

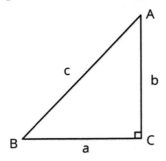

A. $\cos B = \dfrac{c}{a}$

B. $\tan B = \dfrac{c}{a}$

C. $\cos B = \dfrac{b}{a}$

D. $\tan B = \dfrac{b}{a}$

E. $\sin A = \dfrac{c}{a}$

4. According to the following diagram, which of the following statements is true?

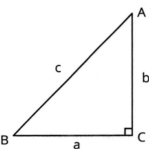

A. $\cos A = \dfrac{b}{c}$

B. $\sin A = \dfrac{b}{c}$

C. $\tan A = \dfrac{b}{c}$

D. $\sec A = \dfrac{b}{c}$

E. $\csc A = \dfrac{b}{c}$

1ˢᵗ Ed. © ibidPREP llc

5. Law of Cosine: for triangle ABC with sides opposite the angles A, B, C, as a,b,c, respectively, $c^2 = a^2 + b^2 - 2ab \cos C$. What is the length of side c?

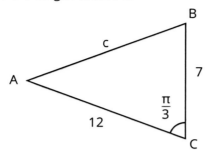

A. $\sqrt{(12)^2 + (7)^2 - 2(12)(7)\cos\frac{\pi}{3}}$

B. $\sqrt{(12)^2 + (7)^2 + 2(12)(7)\cos\frac{\pi}{3}}$

C. $\sqrt{(12)^2 + (7)^2 - 2(12)(7)\cos\frac{\pi}{6}}$

D. $\sqrt{(12)^2 + (7)^2 + 2(12)(7)\cos\frac{\pi}{6}}$

E. $\sqrt{(12)^2 + (7)^2}$

6. What is the length of side a?

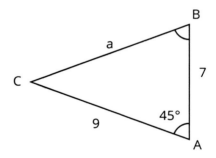

A. $\sqrt{(9)^2 + (7)^2 - 2(9)(7)\cos 25°}$

B. $\sqrt{(9)^2 + (7)^2 - 2(9)(7)\cos 45°}$

C. $\sqrt{(9)^2 + a^2 - 2(9)(a)\cos 25°}$

D. $\sqrt{(7)^2 + a^2 - 2(7)(a)\cos 45°}$

E. $\sqrt{(7)^2 + 9^2}$

7. For which value of $\cos\theta$ is the following answer true given $2\pi > \theta > \dfrac{3\pi}{2}$?
   A. -1
   B. -.806
   C. -.237
   D. 0
   E. .468

8. For which value of $\sin\theta$ is the following statement true given $\dfrac{\pi}{2} > \theta > \pi$?
   A. 1
   B. .735
   C. 0
   D. -.283
   E. -1

9. For which value of $\tan\theta$ is the following statement true given $-\dfrac{\pi}{4} > \theta > \dfrac{\pi}{4}$?
   A. -1
   B. -.685
   C. 0
   D. .999
   E. 1

10. If $\sin\theta = \dfrac{6}{10}$ and $0 < \theta < \dfrac{\pi}{2}$ then $\cos\theta = ?$
   A. $\dfrac{6}{10}$
   B. $\dfrac{10}{6}$
   C. $\dfrac{8}{10}$
   D. $\dfrac{10}{8}$
   E. $\dfrac{6}{8}$

1st Ed. © ibidPREP llc

11. If $\tan\theta = \dfrac{1}{2}$ and $\pi < \theta < \dfrac{3\pi}{2}$, then $\sin\theta = ?$

A. $\dfrac{1}{2}$

B. 2

C. $\dfrac{1}{5}$

D. $\dfrac{2}{5}$

E. $\dfrac{1}{\sqrt{5}}$

12. When the angle θ lies in $\dfrac{\pi}{2} < \theta < \dfrac{3\pi}{2}$ and $\sin\theta < 0$, which of the following statements is true?
A. $\theta = 145°$
B. $\theta = 45°$
C. $\theta = 245°$
D. $\theta = -45°$
E. $\theta = -75°$

13. When the angle θ lies in $0 < \theta < \pi$ and $\cos\theta < 0$, which of the following statements is true?
A. $\theta = 30°$
B. $\theta = 90°$
C. $\theta = 135°$
D. $\theta = 190°$
E. $\theta = 275°$

Logs

C'mon. You're afraid of these? Really? These cute little systems of dealing with exponents can and should be quite simple if you remember what the heck they mean. Rest assured too, that LOG questions on the ACTs will follow the "hard topic/easy question" rule because **EVERYONE** freaks out on LOGS, so they can't make them **too** hard because **someone** has to get them right!

LOGS are simply exponential numbers turned inside out.

Basically, logs turn one little algorithm into another! Instead of writing $4^3 = 64$ we write $\log_4 64 = 3$, so the result of a LOG is not the product of number taken to a power, but the exponent you needed to get that product. Here's one way to remember it.

Let B = Base; e = exponent; and R = Result

$B^e = R$

[BER]

$\log_b R = E$

[BRE]

Here is a how it works basically:

$$5^3 = 125$$

SO

Base = 5

Exponent = 3

Result = 125

Changes to:

B = 5

R = 125

E = 3

Which translates to:

$$\log_5 125 = 3$$

Using logs allows us to manipulate exponents in all kinds of interesting ways—if we remember our rules of

1st Ed. © ibidPREP llc

exponents [p. 113].

For example if we remember that $x^y \cdot x^z = x^{y+z}$, then it may be easier to understand that:

$$\log_x(x^y \cdot x^z) = \log_x x^y + \log_x x^z = y + z$$

This works for any **product**, so...

$$\log_x(ab) = \log_x a + \log_x b$$

For example:

$$\log_3(243) = \log_3(9 \times 27) = \log_3 9 + \log_3 27$$

At this point, it may be good to remember that $9 = 3^2$ and the $27 = 3^3$, so...

$$\log_3(243) = \log_3(9 \times 27) = \log_3 9 + \log_3 27 = 2 + 3 = 5$$

$$\log_3(243) = 5$$

$$3^5 = 243$$

Let's do the same thing with division. If we remember that $\dfrac{x^y}{x^z} = x^{y-z}$, then it may be easier to understand that:

$$\log_x\left(\frac{x^y}{x^z}\right) = \log_x x^y - \log_x x^z = y - z$$

This works for any quotient, so...

$$\log_x\left(\frac{a}{b}\right) = \log_x a - \log_x b$$

For example:

$$\log_3\left(\frac{243}{27}\right) = \log_3 243 - \log_3 27$$

At this point, it may be good to remember that $243 = 3^5$ and that $27 = 3^3$, so...

$$\log_3\left(\frac{243}{27}\right) = \log_3 243 - \log_3 27 = 5 - 3 = 2$$

$$\log_3\left(\frac{243}{27}\right) = 2$$

SO

$$\frac{243}{27} = 3^2 = 9$$

Lastly, if we remember that $(x^y)^z = x^{yz}$, then it may be easier to understand that:

$$\log_x((x^y)^z) = z\,(\log_x(x^y)) = zy$$

This works for any number raised to a power, so...

$$\log_x(a^b) = b\,(\log_x(a))$$

At this point, it may be good to remember that $25^3 = 625$, so...

$$\log_5(25^2) = 2\,\log_5 25$$

$$\log_5(25^2) = 3\,(\log_5(25)) = 3\,(2) = 4$$

SO

$$5^4 = 625$$

Log Rules

$$B^e = R \rightarrow \log_b R = E$$

$$\log_x(ab) = \log_x a + \log_x b$$

$$\log_x\left(\frac{a}{b}\right) = \log_x a - \log_x b$$

$$\log_x(a^b) = b\,(\log_x(a))$$

1st Ed. © ibidPREP llc

LOGARITHMS

1. If b is a positive number such that $\log_b\left(\dfrac{1}{125}\right) = -3$, then b =
   A. 5
   B. 25
   C. 375
   D. $\dfrac{1}{5}$
   E. $\dfrac{1}{25}$

2. If R is a positive number such that $\log_6 R = 3$, then R =
   A. $\dfrac{1}{2}$
   B. 9
   C. 18
   D. 36
   E. 216

3. The value of $\log_7 7^{\frac{19}{7}}$ is between which of the following pairs of integers?
   A. 0 and 1
   B. 1 and 2
   C. 2 and 3
   D. 3 and 4
   E. 196 and 197

4. The value of $\log_2(39.5)$ is between which of the following integers?
   A. 2 and 3
   B. 4 and 5
   C. 5 and 6
   D. 9 and 10
   E. 18 and 19

5. For all the values of t greater than 1, $\log_t \dfrac{t^9}{t^{-1}} =$
   A. -9
   B. $\dfrac{1}{9}$
   C. 8
   D. 9
   E. 10

6. If $t > 1$, then $\log_t\left[\dfrac{\left(t^7\right)^3}{t^2}\right] =$
   A. 2
   B. 5
   C. 11
   D. 19
   E. 23

Extra ACT Rules

Standard Form of the Equation of a Circle:

$$(x-h)^2 + (y-k)^2 = r^2$$

Center of circle is at (h,k)

General Equation of an Ellipse:

$$\frac{(x-h)^2}{a^2} + \frac{(y-k)^2}{b^2} = 1$$

Center of ellipse is at (h,k)
and (b) are the values of one half the major and/or minor axes

General Equation of a Hyperbola:

$$\frac{(x-h)^2}{a^2} - \frac{(y-k)^2}{b^2} = 1$$

Repeated Percent Increase:

$$\text{Final} = \text{Original} \cdot (1 + \text{rate})^{\text{\# of changes}}$$

Log Identities:

$$\log_b(xy) = \log_b x + \log_b y$$

$$\log_b(x/y) = \log_b x - \log_b y$$

$$\log_b(x^r) = r \log_b x$$

Quadratic Formula:

$$x = \frac{-b \pm \sqrt{b^2 - 4ac}}{2a}$$

Area of a Trapezoid:

$$A = \frac{(b_1 + b_2)}{2}h$$

Sum of the Internal Angles of a Polygon with n Sides:

$$\text{Sum of Angles in n-sided Polygon} = (n - 2) \cdot 180°$$

$$\text{Interior Angles of Regular n-sided Polygons} = \frac{(n-2) \cdot 180°}{n}$$

   1st Ed. © *ibidPREP llc*

Trigonometric Identity:

$$\sin^2\theta + \cos^2\theta = 1$$

Law of Cosines:

$$c^2 = a^2 + b^2 - 2ab\,\cos C$$

Inverse Functions:

Switch x for y in f(x) = y and solve for y
e.g., When f(x) = 2x + 1, y = 2x + 1, so
for $f^{-1}(x)$:

$$x = 2y + 1$$
$$x - 1 = 2y$$
$$\frac{x-1}{2} = y$$

$$f^{-1}(x) = \frac{x-1}{2}$$

Powers of i:

$$i = i$$
$$i^2 = -1$$
$$i^3 = -i$$
$$i^4 = 1$$

Arithmetic Series:

First Term	Second Term	Third Term	Nth Term
x	x + y	x + 2y	x + (n-1)y

Geometric Series:

First Term	Second Term	Third Term	nth Term
$x \cdot y$	$x \cdot y$	$x \cdot y^2$	$x \cdot y^{n-1}$

Sum of an Infinite Geometric Series:

If $|y| < 1$, the infinite Geometric Series:

$x + x \cdot y + x \cdot y^2 + x \cdot y^{n-1}$

converges to the sum s = x / (1 - y).

If $|y| > 1$, and x does not = 0, then the series diverges.

A series that diverges means either the partial sums have no limit or approach infinity.

Diagonal of a rectangular box [that includes cubes]:

$$\sqrt{x^2+y^2+z^2} = d^2$$

1ˢᵗ Ed. © ibidPREP llc

Chapter Four

Reading
Comprehension

1st Ed. © ibidPREP llc

Section 3 – Reading   40 Questions   35 minutes

Four Reading Passages
40 Multiple Choice Questions—Ten questions per section
Four Choices per Question

1. **Reading Section; Timing [35 minutes]**—The Reading section is comprised of four reading passages. These passages always occur in the same order.
   a. Fiction
   b. Social Sciences
   c. Humanities
   d. Natural Sciences

2. Each passage has ten questions which means that you should allot about nine minutes per passage! That does not seem like a lot of time, but if you read well and briskly, you will have enough time. Although moving quickly is important, it is still important to read each passage well enough to grasp the Three T's: Theme, Thesis and Tone.

3. **Time saving approach**—
   a. **Read the whole thing**—The non-fiction readings on the ACT are generally fairly straightforward. That means that determining the three T's should not be too difficult or lead you too far into the passage.

   If you read and process as you go, it is almost always better to read through the entire passage. It is better to read and process through the entire passage because:

   You get a grasp on the entirety of the author's argument. Grasping the entirety of the argument is good especially as on occasion, things change in the author's argument especially by the conclusion.

   You know where to find things. Most of the questions about specific details or parts of a non-fiction passages are in order. That is, the questions will address issues and details in they order they arise in the passage. If you've gone through the passage and processed those details and issues, you'll be able to hone in on them instantly.

   b. **Don't read the whole thing[46]**— If you have practiced with a few Reading Comprehension sections in the manner suggested above and continue to have problems with time, try this:

   Determine the three T's, if you've had trouble with time, then simply read through the rest of the passage gleaning the topic of each remaining paragraph. To figure out the topic of each paragraph, you may usually read the first sentence of the paragraph, but that is not always the case. As with the THESIS of the entire passage, the topic of a paragraph may not be revealed until the second or third or...of the paragraph. As with everything: if you're not sure, just read more!

   IF YOU'RE EVER NOT SURE, JUST READ MORE!

   Then feel free to go to the questions and follow our procedure for answering them [See How to Read, etc.].

Finding facts in order—One of the reasons you don't absolutely need to read the entire passage on the non-fiction portion of the ACT is that, for the most part, when you are asked questions that pertain to specific details or portions of the passage, those sections are dealt with in order. The questions will not give you line readings, but they will point to the paragraphs that you need to look in. When they don't point to the paragraphs you need to look in, simply look to the point in the passage that the last question left you at. The answer to the question your on now will be shortly after that.

---

[46] Unlike the non-fiction passages, **you must read the entirety of the fiction passage**. The reason you must read all of it is because you rarely know the the point of the story until you get to the end. In some fiction pieces it's can be hard to tell even what the heck is going on unless you take in the whole passage from beginning to end. But don't despair: every story like every essay you read does get somewhere eventually and absolutely will make sense!

4. Reading section: Timing—With four passages each with ten questions, you wind up with eight to nine minutes per passage. As you work through the practice sections, you will find out which types of passages, if any, give you the most trouble. For some it's the fiction and for others it's the natural science passage, etc. Feel free to save those for last, but when you get to them don't rush. Work through them as you are mean to.

    If the FIVE MINUTE time mark gets called, don't panic. Remember, you're only meant to have 8-9 minutes per passage, so five minutes leaves you with enough time to get through almost an entire passage. Read the passage until you get the THESIS, run through for the topic of each paragraph after that, and then read the conclusion. Armed with this, go to the questions. If you know the answer to a question answer it. If you know where to find the answer to a question, go for it. But if you can't process either the questions or envision the answer SKIP IT.

Vocabulary & The ACT

There is no specific vocabulary requirement for the ACTs beyond having a grasp of second and third level definitions for the occasional ENGLISH question. **However**, the better your vocabulary the easier the reading comprehension passages will be. There is no way around that fact. If you continually need to try to figure out words by context or find ways to work around words you don't know, it will slow you down and impair your comprehension of the passage. So work on the words in the appendix and build up your vocab day by day, week by week. Also, please be sure to STOP and look up words you don't know. IT'S NOT HARD! Your phone, computer, mom, teacher, and good old fashioned dictionary are all capable of providing you with definitions without your having to expend even the smallest puff of energy. So don't let words you don't know slide by—grab them and learn them!

To succeed on most reading comprehension sections you need to master two skills:

1. **Refuse to be bored!** Learn to read and process everything you read no matter how excruciatingly boring you might find the material.
2. **Make up your <u>own</u> mind!!** Change your habits; process questions and establish your own answers to them **<u>BEFORE</u>** picking through the multiple-choice offerings.

Revolutionary Reading Strategy

Students come to me all the time with amazing [not] reading comprehension strategies. Some have been told just to read the first lines of each paragraph, the first and last paragraphs, read the questions first, etc.

HERE'S MY STRATEGY:
READ THE DARN
PASSAGE!

1ˢᵗ Ed. © ibidPREP llc

'BLAH, BLAH, BLAH, GOLF!'

MY YOUNGER SON NOTICED I HAD A SUNBURN. I TOLD HIM, "YEAH. I USUALLY ONLY WEAR A HAT OUTSIDE WHEN I PLAY GOLF. YESTERDAY I WAS OUTSIDE IN THE SUN, BUT I DIDN'T PLAY GOLF, SO I DIDN'T WEAR A HAT AND GOT A SUNBURN BECAUSE OF IT."

HE REPLIED, "BUT YOU DIDN'T PLAY GOLF YESTERDAY."

I LAUGHED AND SAID, "YOU KNOW, WHEN I TALKED JUST NOW ALL YOU HEARD WAS 'BLAH, BLAH, BLAH, GOLF!'"

HE LAUGHED AND GRUDGINGLY AGREED.

How To Read

You know in your dark, beating heart that the title "How to Read" is not a joke. You know that deep down you don't always really read. You are not alone. Most people, young and old, read poorly. We scan and skim rather than pore over the details of our reading. The reality of poor reading makes it possible for unscrupulous businessmen, lawyers, advertisers [and test makers] to write things in which are embedded hidden costs, loopholes, and meanings. Of course, in reality, these costs and loopholes are usually hidden in plain sight. No one is stopping people from reading these details; most small print is not even really smaller than the rest of the print, but the sad fact is that most people simply don't read more than a few words deep.

Think of when your parents talk to you. You probably listen to the first six words or so of what they say, listening for any big words like "money," "college," "vacation," and then tune out the rest assuming you get the gist of what they've said and whether you need to bother catching the rest [we know the answer to that one]. Test makers are **counting** on your doing this. They pray to whatever higher power they pray to that you do this. They get excited and rub their antennae together in a really creepy way when you do this. **Don't do this.**

That is not to say that it won't be easy **not** to do this. Test makers select readings whose main point is not revealed until later in the passage. Also (AND THIS IS REALLY IMPORTANT), they like to pick passages that start out seeming as if they are saying one thing, only to change midstream, i.e., after most readers have tuned out. And just in case you manage to avoid those pitfalls, they throw one extra curve at you: they like to choose passages that are mind-numbingly boring.

There is no way around it. No way to sugarcoat it: your parents are right! The students who are longtime habitual readers have little trouble with their verbal sections. There, I said it [I'm just full of painful truths]. Obviously, those students who got into the habit of reading probably like reading, and if you were never a reader it could be because you have processing difficulties or never found a book you liked or because your mom [dad, other dad, other mom, grandma, grandpa, warden, etc...] read to you until you were ten years old, and you got to be too lazy to read. Whatever the reason, it's not too late to start.

Learning to read carefully and well is a great skill. Now is the perfect time to develop that skill!

The Two T's

The best readers are constantly asking questions of themselves and, more importantly, the material in front of them. "Why is that author going on for so long about this tiny thing?" "Why is he asking us this question?" "Why am I having problems getting through this part?" "Why is this mind-numbingly boring?" Good readers do not accept confusion as a natural state while reading. If something doesn't make sense, they stop and try to figure it out.

The Two T's:

1. What is the **THEME** of this piece:
   a. what is its **TOPIC**?
2. What is the **THESIS** of the piece:
   b. what is the author trying to say about the THEME
   c. what is the **POINT OF THE PIECE**?

Two T's EXAMPLE:

Emanuel Bronner

Emanuel H. Bronner (born Emanuel Heilbronner, 1908–1997) was the maker of Dr. Bronner's castile soap. Bronner, whose parents were killed in the Holocaust, promoted a belief in the goodness and unity of humanity.

Bronner started his business in his home and made all his products by hand. He used the labels of his products to promote his personal philosophy, which he called his "Moral ABC." The labels of his products were famously covered with writings in tiny print from all sorts of sources from Jewish and Christian texts, such as the Shema and the Beatitudes, to poets such as Rudyard Kipling. These labels became famous for their idiosyncratic[47] style, including hyphens that joined long strings of words and the liberal use of exclamation points.

After moving his family several times, Bronner settled in California, where eventually his soap-making operation grew into a small factory. At his death in 1997, it produced more than a million bottles of soap and other products a year—all still by hand!

[47] unique, individual

1st Ed. © ibidPREP llc

The company continues producing Bronner's original, natural product with minute messages on each label. The firm also continues his beliefs by supporting many, many charitable causes.

THEME:

__The theme, subject, of this piece is Dr. Bronner and his company.__

THESIS:

__Bronner did more than make soap. He made a natural product that carried messages of goodness and unity, and he tried to have his company follow those messages.__

THE POINT NEVER IS...

ALTHOUGH SOMETIMES YOU READ A SENTENCE AND YOU FEEL LIKE THEY MUST BE SAYING SOMETHING LIKE: ME LIKE CRAZY TALK, YOU CAN'T UNDERSTAND FISH PANTS BECAUSE BLADDERS ARE FULL OF SKEPTICISM...

OR

THE FLOWERS ON PLANET ZUDON ARE POISONOUS SO THAT MEAT PIES HAVE HAIR...

REMEMBER:

NO MATTER HOW OBTUSE AND OBSCURE THE LANGUAGE OF A SENTENCE MIGHT BE, THE POINT IT IS MAKING, THOUGH OCCASIONALLY COMPLEX OR SLIGHTLY LAYERED, IS NOT!

Finding The Main Idea—Thesis

Your Assumptions Will Be Used Against You

If you get to a passage about global warming and you've already heard or read a lot about this topic, chances are that your initial reaction will be, "Yeah, yeah, global warming is bad, yadda, yadda, yadda..." And that's when they've got you, because these tests love, love, love picking passages that go against expectations. And they don't just go against expectations, they do it by first laying out what your expectation might be. I call this:

Banana, Banana, Banana, Banana, Banana but *Really* <u>Strawberry</u>

Because the test makers know that most people skim, they pick readings that really penalize the skimmer. What kinds of passages penalize the skimmer? Passages that do not make their main point right off the bat, for one. I call these passages "Banana, banana, banana, banana, banana but ***really*** strawberry," because they start by offering one point of view [banana]. This point of view is what is known as a red herring. It does not offer the writer's point of view but involves him or her setting out others' points of view for the main purpose of contradicting those points of view with his or her own point later in the passage. The test makers know that after our parents make the same point two or three times, we generally tune out, after which time they could be saying anything! **Do not do this here.**

HOW TO FIND THE STRAWBERRY—ALWAYS LOOK FOR THE "BUT"

One way to know when the author is finally putting forward her main point is to look for the "but" [aka the "however," the "although," the "yet," the "actually"—you get the idea]. The "but" marks the shift in the piece from the author recounting what everyone else thinks to her laying out what the truth really is [according to her point of view of course].

> *Most people believe that science is a rational process based on cool, dispassionate evaluation of facts and data. The majority of books and movies portray scientists as cold, clinical beings more at home with test tubes than other warm blooded living creatures.* **HOWEVER***, the truth is that most scientists are passionate, highly social beings who rely as much on feeling and intuition as they do on cold-blooded, rational evaluations of their subjects.*

Reading Comprehension: Finding The Two T's Passage #1
Please read the following passage and identify the Two T's: Theme and Thesis. Write about these on the questions that follow.

1st Ed. © ibidPREP llc

The Printing Press and the Internet

The printing press is a device used for printing ink onto paper or other materials through a transferring process. Printing presses are typically used to produce texts, often in mass quantities. The printing press made its appearance in the West around 1450. Before the invention of the printing press, there was no method of quickly producing a large print run of a text; in other words, people had to hand-write books. This process was very time-consuming. Therefore, books were luxury possessions and very expensive, and the majority of people were illiterate. The invention of the printing press changed all of this. It also prompted the mass circulation of information and revolutionary ideas, thus altering the very structure of society. The invention of the printing press is seen as one of the most influential events in history, marking the beginning of modernity.

The invention of the Internet is akin to the invention of the printing press in many ways. Today, the Internet is even more accessible than books—most people have access to the Internet in their homes, at school or in public places such as libraries and coffee shops. Many people even have portable access to the Internet via smart phones, tablets or laptop computers. Never has such a high volume of information been so readily accessible to so many people at such a low cost. People used to have to look up information in books, which were not always available, or ask other people for help. Now we can answer most of our own questions with a simple click of a mouse. The Internet has already changed society in substantial ways and continues to do so every day. However, the Internet only really came into use the early 1990s. So as of now, there is insufficient evidence to say that the Internet has been as influential an invention as the printing press. We will need to wait many more years to see how history unfolds before we make such a claim.

What is this passage about (**THEME**)?

_____

_____

_____

What is the main point of the passage (**THESIS**)?

_____

_____

Reading Comprehension: Finding The Two T's Passage #2
Please read the following passage and identify the Two T's: Theme and Thesis. Write about the Two T's on the questions that follow.

Penguins

Everyone is familiar with penguins, but few people know just how unique they are. Scientifically, penguins are classified as birds, but they are aquatic and flightless. They are also the only birds that can swim. They are highly adapted to the water, and their wings have evolved into flippers. Penguins spend about half their lives on land and half their lives in the water. Although penguins are native to the southern hemisphere and many of them live in Antarctica, not all species of penguins live in cold climates—in fact, some live in temperate or even tropical climates! Some prehistoric penguins became as large as adult humans. Penguins are also camouflaged—to a predator lurking in deeper waters, penguins' white bellies resemble reflective water surfaces. Their dark backs camouflage them from above. Unlike most animals, penguins are monogamous!

Most people think that one of the strangest things about penguins is that they are classified as birds even though they cannot fly. This is not actually that strange, though, because the scientific classification of an animal as a bird does not require that the animal fly. Penguins are considered birds because they have wings, beaks, and feathers, and because they lay eggs.

What is this passage about (**THEME**)?

_____

_____

_____

What is the main point of the passage (**THESIS**)?

_____

_____

Reading Comprehension: Finding The Two T's Passage #3

Please read the following passage and identify the Two T's (Theme and Thesis). Write about the Two T's on the page that follows.

Are Superstores Good for American Communities?

The time for fighting back against the supposed "super" stores is long since past! Wal*Mart, the big blue box store full of plastic junk made in sweatshops, is now the world's largest corporation. How does that happen? At the expense of all the businesses they have crushed in their growth, their expansion, their tyranny over little mom and little pop and their little shop! We have let these "super" stores squash what makes us unique just to pay a few pennies less for a box of soap. Is that what Americans are made of? Are we that cheap? And don't tell me you're that poor! You wouldn't need to worry about a few pennies if you could get a proper job, but how are you going to get one when Wal*Mart is the only chain gang in town willing to hire you? They're going to pay you as little as they can, and when you tell them it's not enough to support your family they'll tell you to go on welfare! That means everyone pays for Wal*Mart except Wal*Mart itself! The time has come to band together and fight back. If they won't let their workers form a union, it is up to us to fight for them! Unite and fight to get your communities back!

What is this passage about (**THEME**)?

_____

_____

_____

_1st_ Ed. © _ibidPREP llc_

What is the main point of the passage (**THESIS**)?

_____

_____

She Who Does Not Get Bored Wins!!!

If the critical reading passages were interesting, most students would get most questions right. Therefore, the test would not be an effective measure of differences among readers. One way to separate students out is to present passages that are progressively more boring.

How do the test makers succeed in boring you? Either they choose topics that are duller than watching your fingernails grow, or they choose passages that are so obtusely[48] and banally[49] written that no one save[50] the author's mother could slog through the pieces. Sometimes they even select passages that are both deadly dull topics AND incredibly densely written! Ouch. Your goal as a student is to refuse to be bored. When you feel yourself pulling away from the reading, that is the time to redouble your attention because, rest assured, you will be asked a question or a bunch of questions about the very place at which you start to get bored.

If You Skim, You're Sunk!

If you skim through the passage, you'll miss the point of the passage and misunderstand what you're being asked.

If you skim through the answers, you'll invariably be fooled into picking the wrong answer, usually an answer that is word for word about 80% correct but contains a word or words that make it 100% incorrect.

To avoid skimming, you first have to realize you're doing it. We all do it. But you have to realize when you're not committing yourself to the passage and just trying to get by glossing over the surface of the piece. Chances are if you've been going through our educational system, whether it is public or private, you've been forced to schlep through a lot of material and just cover it with your eyes. I'm telling you now that every time you skim and don't absorb the material, you're wasting your time, energy and points.

The sections we all tend to zone out on are those that are particularly dense, poorly written or simply difficult to comprehend. If these parts are poorly written, chances are that the author has made the unfortunate choice of using a complex or flashy way of saying something simple. Be aware that while the thoughts expressed by the writers of the reading passages are not simplistic or unsophisticated, they are rarely beyond the comprehension of most students. They might not be as simple or straightforward as you would like them to be, but be confident that if you apply yourself to the reading you will be able to discern their meanings.

If You're Ever Not Sure—Read Some More!

The nice thing about reading comprehension is that ALL the answers are in the text! In math or grammar, if you have forgotten a concept or approach, you may have no way of finding it out during the exam. In reading, however, if you're not sure of a detail, instead of staring off into space, look back to the text! It's all there!! It's the same for questions regarding specific lines. If you can't determine an answer from the specific lines given, read more before or after the lines to make better sense of them!

[48] dim, dense, dull-witted
[49] boring, dull, ordinary
[50] except

HEAR THE WORDS

I HAD A NOT-SO-GOOD READER WHO BECAME A VERY GOOD READER SEEMINGLY OVERNIGHT. HER SECRET? SHE STARTED READING ALOUD TO HERSELF IN HER HEAD [OXYMORON[51] INTENDED]. SOME READERS DO THIS NATURALLY. THE WORDS FLOW THROUGH THEIR HEADS ON A SEMI-AUDIBLE LEVEL, AND THAT MAKES IT EASIER FOR THEM TO "HEAR" AND UNDERSTAND WHAT THE AUTHOR IS SAYING. IF YOU DON'T DO THIS, TRY. EVEN IF YOU HAVE TO ACTUALLY READ OUT LOUD* FOR A LITTLE WHILE—JUST MAKE SURE YOU'RE NOT DOING THIS DURING THE ACTUAL TEST!

*THIS IS NOT TO BE CONFUSED WITH BEING READ TO. AS MUCH AS OUR PARENTS, TEACHERS OR CAREGIVERS MAY LOVE US, IT IS VERY IMPORTANT THAT THEY STOP READING TO US AT A CERTAIN AGE [PROBABLY AROUND 2ND GRADE]. BEING READ TO TENDS TO PROMOTE PASSIVE READING, MAKING IT AKIN[17] TO WATCHING TV OR BEING SPOON-FED. STUDENTS MUST LEARN TO CHEW THEIR OWN FOOD!

SPECIAL KINDS OF READING COMPREHENSION QUESTIONS

There are basically three kinds of reading comp questions: general, vocabulary and specific questions. Reading for the main idea takes care of the general questions (and we've already covered that in depth), and, as we'll see, basic sentence-completion techniques will take care of the vocab questions. Here's how we do them.

Reading For Detail

It is easy to spot Reading for Detail questions because they usually direct you to certain lines and ask factual questions pertaining to the material in the passage. In order to solve them, you must read them sequentially[52]. and not leap to conclusions. You must also make sure to read before and/or after the cited material until you find an answer! If the quoted material starts with THIS shows...you MUST go to the preceding sentence and find out what THIS is. If the quoted materials do not clear things up for you, keep going. In either case, don't just skim the cited text and despair if you can't find an answer. It's always in there somewhere!

Please read the following short passages and keep in mind what you have learned about "How to Read" and "How to Answer," then answer the multiple choice questions.

[51] a contradiction in terms
[52] in order, consecutively, in sequence [duh]

HARPER LEE

We often believe that, in order to be successful, we must have a long list of impressive accomplishments to brag about. For example, we might be impressed by someone who invented five computer programs, can speak eight languages, or directed 17 films. Success should not always be measured in numbers alone. Take for example Harper Lee, author of the best-selling, Pulitzer Prize-winning novel To Kill a Mockingbird. This was Lee's only published book, and yet her contribution to literature was so important that she won the Presidential Medal of Freedom. She also received honorary degrees from various colleges, although she never agreed to make a speech on any of these occasions. There are many authors who write dozens of books, none of which is as influential as To Kill a Mockingbird.

1. Which point is the author trying to make about success?
   A. Authors are more impressive than film directors.
   B. Harper Lee is more successful than any other author.
   C. Success is not only about numbers.
   D. Someone who speaks eight languages is more impressive than someone who speaks five languages.
   E. Someone who has earned honorary degrees is successful.

2. Based on the information in the passage, which of the following is not an honor that Harper Lee received?
   A. She received honorary degrees from many colleges.
   B. She received the Pulitzer Prize.
   C. She won the Presidential Medal of Freedom.
   D. She spoke many languages.
   E. Her novel was a best seller.

CICADAS

We all know about cicadas: those large, flying insects that make strange noises in the summer. Cicadas are often called locusts, like the insects in the Biblical plague, but cicadas are not actually related to locusts. According to the Ancient Greeks, at least, their origins were quite special. As one of their myths has it, cicadas used to be regular people. Then the muses—goddesses of inspiration—came along. The muses were always singing, and the cicada people were so enchanted that they wanted to sing too. They started singing all the time, 100% of the time, so much that they forgot to eat or sleep. Soon all the cicada people died—literally killed by their passion. They were then re-born as cicadas, and that is why they are constantly making that sound in the summer—all they want to do is sing.

1. According to the Greek myth, what killed the cicada people?
   A. The muses killed the cicadas.
   B. The cicadas accidentally killed themselves because they forgot to eat.
   C. The cicadas killed themselves because they didn't want to live if they couldn't be muses.
   D. Zeus killed the cicadas.
   E. The locusts killed the cicadas.

2. How would the Greeks likely explain the sound cicadas make?
   A. They are trying to annoy the muses with this sound.
   B. They are crying—mourning the loss of their human status.
   C. They make the sound in an attempt to attract the muses.
   D. They make this sound because they want to sing constantly.
   E. They are trying to imitate the locusts.

Reading Formally

Reading formally is one of the hardest things for most teenagers to do. I don't know if it's because you rarely have been asked to, OR if you can only read for what's being said instead of how it's being said because you can't see beyond your own four walls just yet. In any case, in order to read formally:

1. Become aware of how or why a thing is said as opposed to what it's saying.
    a. Remember what the functions of various parts of a passage are:
    b. Introductions introduce and offer the theme and thesis
    c. Body paragraphs provide examples
    d. Conclusions conclude
    e. Examples are used to illustrate the author's point or its contrary
    f. Each sentence is linked to the next via subject/predicate links. I.e. the subject of Sentence 1 takes a predicate. The predicate of Sentence 1 becomes the subject of Sentence 2, etc. [A great way to structure any writing!]
    g. Quotation marks around words of groups of words indicate the author's opinion toward the word or words. I.e. he may take their meaning or sense in an ironic or mocking fashion.
        People think scientists are "cold," but really they are often passionate, creative thinkers.

READING FOR INFERENCE AND SUGGESTION

What is an inference?

Unlike in the Logical Reasoning section, in Reading Comprehension you may be called on to make inferences. For the purposes of standardized tests, a reading comp inference is a two-step logical conclusion that can be drawn from the text. However, just as in the Logical Reasoning section, inference in Reading Comprehension is NOT based on assumption or your own opinions. Here too you must be careful not to draw conclusions that are overly broad or not truly supported.

For example:

If you read, "the boys had not eaten all day," you might be able to infer that:
    a. They were hungry.
    b. They had been unable to eat food.

You cannot infer that:
    a. They were poor.
    b. They were punished.
    c. They were anorexic, etc.

How to determine what answer **is** a logical inference:

• Check answer offered.
    o Go to passage where answer under consideration is discussed.
        • Is the gist of the answer stated in the lines cited?
            • If "yes," then don't pick the answer—if it's explicitly stated, then it's not an inference!
                o If "no," then evaluate the answer choice to see if it can be inferred from the text in a simple two-step process as mentioned above.
                    • If "yes," pick it!

1st Ed. © *ibidPREP llc*

Reading Comprehension: Reading for Inference

Please read the following passages keeping in mind what you have learned about reading for inference. Answer the questions that follow each passage.

IMPRESSIONISM

Since the Impressionists are so well-loved today, it may come as a surprise that Impressionism was initially met with harsh opposition. Critics at the time valued images that looked realistic when examined closely. Impressionists were interested in portraying momentary effects of sunlight—they liked how the appearance of a scene changed with the time of day. They focused on overall visual effects rather than details, and they used short, broken brushstrokes. One of the primary Impressionists is Claude Monet, known for his Water Lily paintings. Monet created about 250 such paintings in his life, in an attempt to explore how the season, the type of light, and the kind of day affected the appearance of his subject, the water lilies. The Impressionists paved the way for many avant-garde art movements in the years to come.

1. Which of the following can be inferred from the passage?
   A. Critics did not think Impressionist paintings looked realistic when examined closely.
   B. The critics were wrong about Impressionism.
   C. Critics never appreciate art until later.
   D. Impressionist paintings were too repetitive for critics.
   E. Although critics did not like most Impressionist paintings, they did like the Water Lily paintings.

2. Which of the following can be inferred from the last sentence in the paragraph?
   A. No art movement would be met with as much critical opposition as Impressionism.
   B. Impressionism was the first avant-garde art movement.
   C. Every movement in art has its roots in Impressionism.
   D. Impressionism had a big influence on the art movements that came after it.
   E. Had it not been for Impressionism, we never would have had Cubism.

COGNATES

Learning another language may seem daunting; however, cognates make the process a bit easier. Cognates are words in different languages that have a common origin and therefore sound similar and often have the same meaning. For example, English shares many cognates with French. One example is *bleu* in French, which means "blue." Another example is the French *orange*, which refers to both the color and the fruit, just like in English. Learning cognates can make language apprehension easier, but it is important to watch out for false cognates, or words that look or sound the same but do not have the same meaning. One example is *chance* in French, which means "luck," not "chance."

1. Which of the following can be inferred from the passage?
   A. French and English have more cognates than French and Spanish.
   B. All colors are cognates in French and English.
   C. If you memorize cognates, you will have no problem learning French.
   D. If a French word looks the same as an English word, you can assume it has the same meaning.
   E. If a French word looks the same as an English word, you cannot assume it has the same meaning.

2. Which of the following can be inferred from the following sentence: "Cognates are words in different languages that have a common origin and therefore sound similar and often have the same meaning."
   A. Any two given languages have some cognates.
   B. Only Romance languages have cognates.
   C. Sometimes words that sound the same don't actually have the same meaning.
   D. Words that sound the same always have the same meaning.
   E. There are more cognates than we realize.

<u>**SIGN LANGUAGE**</u>

Humans have been attempting to teach sign language to animals, particularly chimpanzees, for many years. We chose sign language rather than spoken language because chimpanzees' mouths are not structured in a way that would allow them to make the sounds of our language. We have taught many chimps to use signs, but it is a matter of debate to what extent the animals are really "learning" the language. Many scientists hypothesize that the chimps are simply imitating the signs humans show them, without exercising the generative function of language. This is akin to an infant hearing her mother say "dog," and then saying "dog" without really knowing what a dog is. Human infants, of course, eventually get to a point where they can describe the world around them using words—they can say that a dog is yellow or that their mom is tall. New findings in chimp research present a new problem, though: one chimp saw a swan and, not knowing the sign for "swan," combined the sign for "water" and the sign for "bird," naming the swan a "water bird."

1. Which of the following best describes what is implied by the last sentence in the paragraph?
    A. Chimps have the same ability as humans to use language.
    B. Chimps can use language only as well as human infants.
    C. The reason chimps don't seem to be able to use the generative function of language is because we have not taught them enough signs.
    D. Chimps may in fact be able to use the generative function of language.
    E. Chimps have their own language and do not need to learn human language.

2. Which of the following does the passage imply about what it means to learn language?
    A. Language involves a creative function—not just using words, but putting words together in meaningful ways.
    B. Any appearance of the generative function in language is an illusion.
    C. All language is really just pointing at things and naming them.
    D. Our language is really much less sophisticated than it appears.
    E. Sign language is more sophisticated than spoken language.

How to Read Fiction

Just as we have the Two T's for most expository [essay] writing, we like to use something like it for fiction and memoir writing. We call it:

STEW

Just as there are three main things to look for in most other kinds of prose[53] passages, there are four main things to look for in fiction and memoir reading.

S—Subject
T—Tone
E—Eyesight
W—What Happened?

How does it work? Let's take a story most everyone knows: Cinderella![54]

53 Prose is the opposite of poetry. This sentence is prose.
54 In case you don't know it or don't remember—Cinderella is a mistreated step-child who only gets to go to the royal ball because her fairy godmother helps her with an enchanted spell. At the ball the prince falls in love with her, but she has to run off before he can find out more about her. She leaves only a glass slipper behind, and he tries it on all the feet of all the women in the land until he finds her. They live happily ever after.

1st Ed. © ibidPREP llc

SUBJECT—What is the story about?

The story is about Cinderella, a girl who wants to go to a dance but is not allowed to by her mean stepmother.

TONE—How is the author telling the story?

The author of "Cinderella" uses a light, descriptive tone to tell the story.

To determine tone, it can be helpful to think about what the author's attitude is and to describe that attitude as a feeling. So an author may write in a reflective, wistful, regretful, affectionate or _____ tone. The list goes on.

If you are having a hard time figuring out tone, think of tone in terms of shading in pictures from dark to light. Something funny like The Diary of Wimpy Kid might have a light tone, something scary or sad like a horror story might have a dark tone, while most articles and textbooks are written with a neutral [middle], gray tone.

In "Cinderella," the author uses a light, descriptive storyteller tone to tell the story.

The author is using a gray to light voice to describe the action and tell the story. He is not really showing too much opinion even when talking about the stepsisters.

But...

Be careful! Tone is different from Eyes.

EYES—Through whose EYES are we seeing the narrative unfold? Who's seeing the story?

In Cinderella we see the story through Cinderella's eyes.

To find the EYES, ask yourself:

 Who is seeing the story?

- A character? (first person)
- An outside narrator? (third person limited)
- An all-knowing observer? (third person omniscient)
- What is THAT person's attitude toward the story?

Remember: Each character has his or her unique attitude [point of view], and each of these might be different from the narrator's attitude, and both of those might be different from what the author thinks. Got that? It's tough at first, but just try to notice who's telling the story, whose EYES we're seeing the story through, and what the author might be trying to tell us about what's going on.

Finally:

What Happened & Why?!

The What Happened is like the THESIS of a work of non-fiction—it's the point of the piece, which in this case is to tell us what happened and why. It's also the most IMPORTANT part of your reading.

Cinderella gets to the ball and meets the Prince who falls in love with her. All this happens because she is good, kind and hard-working.

When you read fiction, your job is to follow the narrative like a detective or a reporter. You must follow all the knots and loops of the thread of the story to make sure you notice EVERYTHING and how the EVERYTHING adds up to WHAT HAPPENED!

Come to think of it, that's not a bad way to read all kinds of writing!!

In fiction, this job can be a little tricky because the author is not always making it super clear what happened. Sometimes, because the author is telling the story through the EYES of a certain character, we can't always trust what that character is telling us. Then we have to interpret what that narrator is telling us to figure out what's really happening.

What does this mean?

Does your mom ever ask you a question like:

Are you going to eat your greens?

She isn't really asking you what your plans are and whether or not you really want to eat your greens. She's really TELLING you to EAT YOUR GREENS.

Or did you ever tell your dad:

I don't need the light on...

What you were really probably saying was, "I don't want you to think I need the light on, but I really, really hope you leave it on anyway!"

This is the same thing that happens in fiction. Depending on whose eyes you're seeing the story through, figuring out what's really happening can be tricky.

Like in this passage told through the eyes of a 6th grader:

I didn't care what the bully said. Big Alice didn't scare me. I wasn't leaving the playground because she told me to. Or because I was scared of her. It was just because I knew my grandma wanted me to take out the garbage, and it was probably getting stinky, so I thought it would be a good idea to hurry home. So, I ran out of the playground as fast as my feet could carry me. I was glad to be getting away; I mean getting home to help my grandma!

Can you figure out what's really happening here? How do you know?

Short story and/or novel excerpts are ironic mine fields. Be very careful in all passages, but especially in fiction passages, not to take what you read too literally. Tone in these is often ironic and, so, things that are

1st Ed. © *ibidPREP llc*

said are often the opposite of what they mean. This is a situation known as the unreliable narrator. In these situations, you must deduce what is going on in the passage through clues dropped by the narrator—not necessarily by what she is saying directly. Furthermore, in all reading passages the ACT likes to pick pieces in which the author paraphrases another point of view as if it were his. Be very careful not to attribute the beliefs being paraphrased to the author. There are two types of fiction authors/narrators to beware of:

SPECIAL FICTION—BRITISH AUTHOR [DEADLIEST AND MOST FEARED OF ALL]

Sometimes the fiction passage in the Reading Comp includes passages by British authors or those who would write like British authors. By British authors, here I primarily mean those writers from the turn of the 20th century, Victorian Era mainly, who wrote about minute details of life among the British upper classes. They are usually passages about people and their tiny little lives that manage to say a lot about a very little. You will not be told that the passage you are reading is a Britshy o' Brit passage, but you will be able to tell it's fiction and then if the story is about Mindy and life in the cottage, or leaving the manor to become a woman of means, etc. you will know. You will also know mainly if the passage starts talking about people and you have NO IDEA what's going on. The biggest thing to remember about Britishy O' Brit passages is that these types of authors NEVER, EVER say what they mean. It's like against the law for them or something. EVERYTHING is ironic or has a double entendre. Tone is HUGE in these pieces. If it seems like the author or a character likes someone, he probably doesn't. If it seems like they are against someone, they probably aren't. Ugh.

Unreliable Narrator or Seeing Through the Eyes of an Unreliable Character

If a passage is a first person narration, be careful. If a passage is third person narration but the narrator says: Jackson believed [and then they go on to tell you Jackson's opinion as if it were fact], BE CAREFUL. Usually, Jackson is somehow deluded and reality is quite different from how it is being portrayed through his eyes...

(A)   Jackson knew that the geese were looking at him in an odd way. It wasn't so much that they resented him as that they were suspicious of him. They knew. Somehow they knew. It's not like he wanted to throw that rock. And it's certainly not like he had wanted to hit anything with it. It was just that there had been so much noise, and no way to stop it, and all of sudden there was the rock, in his hand and then not. It flew through the air in a perfect trajectory and then, the dull thud. He hadn't meant it, but still the geese were looking at him funny.

(B)   Grandmother would show you what for. Her hands were big as shovels and if she was mad enough she could chase you around the house faster than an angry dog even though she normally walked with a cane. Grandma liked her tea and she liked to have her lady friends over to drink tea with her. Usually they made special tea that smelled strong and wasn't for children to go sipping no how. They made it by pouring already made tea from a dark bottle into their hot tea. Some days they kept topping off their mugs with the made tea and started laughing like school girls. That's what grandma said, "Laughing like school girls." I didn't mind those days because those days when grandma got mad and tried to chase me around the house, she'd be so full of tea she'd usually tip over before she'd catch me...

Putting it all together: How To Answer

In multiple choice questions most of us read through the question and then pick through the answers for something reasonable.

This is not a good way to proceed.

On most standardized tests the answers are there to confuse you and not to help you. If you rely on the answer choices to do your thinking for you, you will waste time AND make mistakes. Here's a better way to proceed:

How to Answer READING COMPREHENSION questions.

1.   Read the question.
2.   Paraphrase[55] the question, so you're sure what it's asking.
3.   Answer the question.
4.   If you can't answer the question, look back in the passage.
5.   THEN look at the answer choices.
6.   Choose the answer closest to yours.

Stop the Multiple Choice Madness [and Other Bad Habits We Pick Up in School]

Conventional wisdom has it that multiple choice questions are great if you're not entirely sure about what you are doing. They give you something to get you moving in the right direction. Right? Wrong. Not on these tests. If you have no idea or only a partial idea of what you're doing on a question, the answer choices are going to be there to distract, annoy, confuse you further OR sucker you into the wrong answer right away. The multiple choice answers help give you a confidence boost only when you already know what you are doing in a question.

When your teacher gives a multiple choice test, she is probably using those multiple choices to help you. The answers act as prompts that are meant to steer students toward the correct answers and reward those who, even though they may not remember the exact answer to a question, have a general sense of the topic and what are reasonably correct answers. This is NOT AT ALL what goes on in most standardized tests!

Almost every kid, when left to his or her own devices, will tackle most multiple choice problems pretty much the same way: look at the problem, get a rough idea of what's being asked, and then pick through the answers for something that looks good. I would like to break you of that habit, not because it doesn't work on the problems on which it works, but because it really doesn't work on the problems on which it doesn't work. If you don't know the answer to a question and start picking through the answers, you are very likely to pick an answer that is partially correct and therefore completely incorrect. Most standardized tests are loaded with incorrect answer choices placed there to tempt and weed out the lazy.

How to combat these false answers? Come up with your own answer first! Don't just jump to the answer choices. For reading especially: figure out your own answer to the question FIRST, before you start shopping around from among the multiple choice selections. Then pick the answer choice that is closest to your own answer. You'll save time, energy and points!

Look for the <u>Least</u> Wrong Answer, Not the Right Answer

It is very important NOT to get hung up looking for the perfect answer; it might not be there. It is far more important to get good at choosing the least wrong answer!! One of the best ways of finding the least wrong answer is by finding the wrong wrong answers and eliminating them. Wrong wrong answers are generally easier to spot. These includes answers that:

- include absolutes that can't be proven. [An absolute is anything that does not allow for an exception. These include always, all, never, only, etc.]
- include direct repetition of quoted text.
- are just plain dopey.
- are 80–90% correct but contain one or two words that make them 100% WRONG.

[55] put into your own words

If you're prone to just reading the beginnings of answers to grab and go, these answers will get you every time. Eliminating bad answers can usually help you shake out two or three bad answers. The three or two that are left are generally not as tough to choose from as you might think. After you've done enough practice, you can begin to smell the right answers. That's right; there is a certain whiff to these kind of answers. It smells not too vague but not too specific. It qualifies[56] what it's saying to cover its butt and is generally about 90% right. The missing 10% usually frustrates good readers, sometimes to the point of forcing them to pick an answer that is more like 60% wrong. Don't do that.

The other thing about wrong answers is that they often seem correct at first glance. That is, 90% of the answer seems correct, but perhaps one or two wrong or misplaced words make the entire answer wrong. Readers who skim the answers, just like readers who skim the passages, are sunk. Make sure you read through the entire answer to be certain that **everything** it is saying is correct.

For example:

(D) The cotton gin was the most influential invention of the 19th century.

While it is true that the cotton gin was a very influential invention, it was invented in the **18th century**, and the passage most assuredly would have mentioned that fact!

Lastly, If You're Going to Get It Wrong, Get It Wrong Quickly

Studies [mine] show that the longer a reading comprehension question takes to answer, the greater the odds are that the student answering that question is going to get it wrong. Therefore, if you're going to get a reading comprehension question wrong, if you have no feel for the question, if you were able to get rid of only a few bad answers, if the answers remaining are all blurring together, don't agonize, don't sit there thinking "A no E no A...screw it, C." In these situations, if you get it down to two or three, cover the possibilities, GUESS **ONE** and MOVE ON (aka GTHOOT—get the heck out of there!). Some questions are just lost causes, and it's not worth agonizing over them when there are others to tackle (unless you have extra time at the end of the test after you've checked all your other answers). You will probably get it wrong, but you will save time, energy and confidence.

---

[56] tempers, modifies, puts conditions on

PLEASE SIT DOWN BEFORE YOU READ THIS: NO ONE CARES ABOUT YOUR OPINION!

IF YOU'VE BEEN IN SCHOOL SOMETIME DURING THE PAST THREE DECADES, AND I'M ASSUMING YOU HAVE, THERE IS A GOOD CHANCE YOU'VE GONE TO A SCHOOL THAT, THEORETICALLY ANYWAY, IS CONCERNED WITH YOU AS A THINKER AND PERSON [OR MAKES IT SEEM THAT WAY]. IN THESE SCHOOLS, TEACHERS WANT TO KNOW YOUR THOUGHTS AND OPINIONS ON EVERYTHING. SO MUCH SO THAT STUDENTS RARELY, IF EVER, LEARN TO FIGURE OUT THE THOUGHTS AND OPINIONS OF, YOU KNOW, OTHER PEOPLE, LIKE, FOR EXAMPLE, THE AUTHORS THEY'RE READING.

WELL, HERE'S A SHOCK: IF YOU ARE UNABLE TO TAKE IN AND PROCESS THE THOUGHTS AND OPINIONS OF AUTHORS WHO HAVE SPENT COPIOUS[57] AMOUNTS OF TIME RESEARCHING, WRITING AND EDITING THEIR PIECES, THEN YOUR OPINION WILL BE WORTHLESS. IT'S LIKE ASKING A FOUR-YEAR-OLD TO PLAN A DINNER PARTY. CHANCES ARE HE KNOWS ONLY ABOUT THREE THINGS TO EAT, AND NONE OF THEM IS THAT INTERESTING UNLESS YOU'RE ALSO FOUR. NOT A GREAT PARTY.

[57] vast, many

1st Ed. © ibidPREP llc

NUTS & BOLTS OF READING COMPREHENSION

1. Read the passage.

2. Keep reading until you've got your two T's. Usually you'll know your Theme and Thesis by the first few sentences of the second paragraph, but sometimes the author doesn't spit it out until much later. Hang in!

   a. Make sure you are clear on what the topic truly is [THEME]: Just because they're talking about bananas, it doesn't mean that the topic is really bananas.

   b. Make sure you are clear on what the author's viewpoint is [THESIS]. I.e., look for the "but." Just because the author writes "most people think bananas," it doesn't mean the author thinks "bananas." In fact he probably thinks "not bananas."

3. Once you've established what the "but" and/or author's point is, you will see that every body paragraph is designed to support that point.

4. Occasionally, authors will devote a body paragraph to a contrary example—something that seems to contradict their point of view. Authors do this in order to:

   a. Seem fair—they want to create the appearance of examining all sides of an argument and demonstrating their awareness of all sides of an argument, or

   b. Strengthen their point—by raising and then dismissing or diminishing contrary points of view, authors ultimately hope to reinforce the strength of their points of view.

5. Every passage makes one and only one point, and most of the questions hinge on your being aware of what that point is.

6. The questions:

   a. Read the question.

   b. Paraphrase the question so as to be sure you know what it's asking.

   c. Determine your answer to the question. If you don't have one, look back to the passage. Don't flip back to the question until you've figured something out.

   d. Then, once you have an answer in mind:

      i. Read the answers given.

      ii. Eliminate any answers which seem wrong outright.

      iii. If you find the answer during your first read through of the answers—pick it.

      iv. If you don't find the answer you want, but have one or two choices left, look closely at the remaining answers and try to find one or two words in an answer that would make it wrong.

      v. If you are still left with more than one answer choice, pick the answer that seems the most qualified [some, often, occasionally, etc.] and the most like previous answers to other questions in the section, and then,

      vi. Move on! Remember, the longer you spend on a reading comprehension question the more likely you are to get the question wrong anyway, SO save time, energy and points and GTHOOT!

Now let's practice reading [and answering] the right way. In the texts below, you will practice finding the Two T's and then you will read and answer questions about a longer passage. We'll help you with that first full passage by explaining the answers and how we got them. Then, you're on your own!

Now let's practice reading [and answering] the right way. In the texts below, you will practice finding the Two T's and then you will read and answer questions about a longer passage. We'll help you with that first full passage by explaining the answers and how we got them. Then, you're on your own!

READING COMPREHENSION—1

President Theodore Roosevelt's 7th Annual Message To Congress

Optimism is a good characteristic, but if carried to an excess it becomes foolishness. We are prone to speak of the resources of this country as inexhaustible; this is not so. The mineral wealth of the country, the coal, iron, oil, gas, and the like, does not reproduce itself, and therefore is certain to be exhausted ultimately; and wastefulness in dealing with it today means that our descendants will feel the exhaustion a generation or two before they otherwise would. But there are certain other forms of waste which could be entirely stopped— the waste of soil from irrigation, for instance, which is among the most dangerous of all wastes now in progress in the United States, is easily preventable, so that this present enormous loss of fertility is entirely unnecessary.

The preservation or replacement of the forests is one of the most important means of preventing this loss. We have made a beginning in forest preservation, but it is only a beginning. At present lumbering is the fourth greatest industry in the United States; and yet, so rapid has been the rate of exhaustion of timber in the United States in the past, and so rapidly is the remainder being exhausted, that the country is unquestionably on the verge of a timber famine which will be felt in every household in the land. There has already been a rise in the price of lumber, but there is certain to be a more rapid and heavier rise in the future.

The present annual consumption of lumber is certainly three times as great as the annual growth; and if the consumption and growth continue unchanged, practically all our lumber will be exhausted in another generation, while long before the limit to complete exhaustion is reached the growing scarcity will make itself felt in many blighting ways upon our National welfare. About 20 percent of our forested territory is now reserved in National forests; but these do not include the most valuable timber lands, and in any event the proportion is too small to expect that the reserves can accomplish more than a mitigation of the trouble which is ahead for the nation. Far more drastic action is needed.

What is this passage about (**THEME**)?

_____

_____

What is the main point of the passage (**THESIS**)?

_____

_____

1st Ed. © ibidPREP llc

THE BASQUE PEOPLE

The region straddling northeastern Spain and southwestern France is the homeland of the Basques, a unique people of unknown origins. They were long suspected to differ from their neighbors because of their unique language, which, unlike almost every other language in Europe, is not a descendant of a language called Indo-European. The Basques' distinct heritage has in recent years been confirmed by genetic testing.

Today, the elements that distinguished Basque culture from others in Europe have faded. In the past, however, differences were stark. For example, women in traditional Basque society were far more powerful than in other European societies. They owned property, acted as judges and clerics, and, perhaps most remarkably, the mother was the parent through which lineage was traced.

Being different came at the cost of conflict with the neighboring French and Spanish, each of which once controlled the most powerful empires of their age. Amazingly, though the Basques were unable to maintain autonomy over their land, for centuries they managed to maintain their culture in the face of foreign occupation. A similar situation exists today: the French and Spanish control the land on which the Basques live, but have not succeeded in assimilating the Basque people, despite having banned the use of the Basque language for several years earlier in the 20th century.

Over the generations, many Basques have responded to their lack of autonomy in different ways. Some, hoping for a better life elsewhere, left their homeland. In new countries, they have maintained their culture within distinct communities around the globe, some of which are more than a million strong. Others, however, were not willing to give up the fight for autonomy: some formed the secessionist group ETA, which bombed sites in Europe for more than fifty years in the hopes of being granted their own state. ETA has disbanded, however, and, at least for now, the Basque people are simply one people among many in pluralistic societies.

1. Which of the following best states the author's purpose?
   A. To explain the origins of the Basque language.
   B. To describe the circumstances of a unique European people.
   C. To argue for the creation of a Basque nation.
   D. To discuss the pros and cons of immigration and assimilation.
   E. To lament the loss of traditional Basque society.

2. Based on the passage, which of the following is not true about the Basque people?
   A. They are fighting for their own nation.
   B. The origins of their language are different from the origins of French and Spanish.
   C. Their traditional land is presently held by more than one nation.
   D. They have managed to maintain their culture in new countries.
   E. They have a long history of conflict with their neighbors.

3. What reason can be inferred for the French and Spanish ban on use of the Basque language?
   A. Indo-European languages are superior to other languages.
   B. The French and Spanish wished to assimilate the Basque people.
   C. There were communication problems between the Basque people and the occupying powers.
   D. Basque was the language of the terrorist group ETA.
   E. To encourage Basque people to emigrate to the New World.

4. In the context of the passage, "pluralistic societies" most closely means:
   A. Societies in which some people are oppressed.
   B. Societies in which all people agree to speak the same language.
   C. Societies in which one group's land is controlled by another group.
   D. Societies in which different groups coexist and maintain their identities.
   E. Societies in which many groups are fighting for independence.

5. What can be inferred from the passage about French and Spanish societies?
   A. Most Spanish and French people dislike Basque people.
   B. Most Spanish and French people were more interested in creating empires than Basque people were.
   C. Women in French and Spanish societies had less power than women in Basque society.
   D. People in French and Spanish societies never had to deal with occupation.
   E. People in French and Spanish societies had more money than people in Basque society

6. Which reason does the passage suggest for the Basque emigration to countries in the New World?
   A. Many Basque people wanted to create their own nation in the New World.
   B. Many Basque people were frustrated with their situation in Spain and France.
   C. Many Basque people were indifferent to their homeland.
   D. Many Basque people could not practice their religion as they wanted in Spain and France.
   E. Many Basque people wanted their women to be more powerful once again.

A Little Help—Questions and Answers with Explanations.

1. Which of the following best states the author's purpose?

If you've been reading for your Two T's, then you are ready for these questions. The topic of this passage is obviously the Basque people. To find the thesis, see what each paragraph is doing. Remember, every reading passage you will face has one big idea or purpose that every paragraph supports. Before we even look at the answer choices, we need to come up with the answer in our own words. So what is each paragraph doing? Each paragraph in this passage tells us something about who the Basque people are, what their experience has been at different times and how being different has affected them. So now let's look at the answer choices to find something along those lines.

A. To explain the origins of the Basque language. This answer is wrong because the author never explains the origins of the Basque language. Although the author tells us that the language is unusual, that is only in the first paragraph and is therefore certainly not the main point of the essay.

B. To describe the circumstances of a unique European people. This is pretty similar to what we came up with, but let's check the other answer choices just to be sure.

C. To argue for the creation of a Basque nation. While it's true that the author does talk about how ETA has been trying to create a Basque state, this is only a brief part of the article. Furthermore, we have no idea if the author is for or against the creation of such a state. This answer is totally wrong.

D. To discuss the pros and cons of immigration and assimilation. Maybe you don't know what "assimilation" means, but you can still rule out this choice. Why? Because you do know what "immigration" means, and the article certainly is not taking a stance about immigration. This answer must be wrong.

E. To lament the loss of traditional Basque society. Let's pretend you don't know what "lament" means, [though of course you know it means to feel sad about something]. However, you don't need to know what "lament" means because you know that the passage is not about the loss of traditional Basque society. Most of it is not about how Basque society has changed over the years, and certainly there is no sense of loss. Therefore we were right to choose B. **B** is the right answer!

2. *Based on the passage, which of the following is not true about the Basque people?*

What kind of question is this? This is a Reading for Detail question. We know that one of the answer choices will make a claim that is not supported by the article. This is one situation in which we can't come up with an answer before looking at the choices because we don't know which false claim will be made. What we need to do instead is evaluate each answer choice by comparing it to the text. If a choice makes a claim the text does not support, that will be the right answer. It is important to treat these questions like true or false questions, so you don't forget what you're looking for. If you see four trues and one false, pick the false. And vice-versa.

A. They are fighting for their own nation. This seems likely to be the right answer. Why? Because even though ETA was fighting for an independent state, the text also says they are no longer fighting. There isn't any evidence that the Basque are still fighting for their own state. False.

B. The origins of their language are different from the origins of French and Spanish. True. We know this is true because this is something we learn about the Basques in the first paragraph. Next!

C. Their traditional land is presently held by more than one nation. Refer to that first paragraph again. First line: the Basque land is in Spain and France. True.

D. They have managed to maintain their culture in new countries. Second sentence, final paragraph: "They have maintained their culture." The text explicitly says the Basques have done this, so this is true.

E. They have a long history of conflict with their neighbors. The third paragraph tells us that the Basque land was routinely occupied by other people. If that's not conflict, I don't know what is. True!

Which is the only answer of its type? A. It's the only false one, so pick A.

3. *What reason can be inferred for the French and Spanish ban on the use of the Basque language?*

What kind of question is this? The key word here is "inferred." That is the past tense of "infer," which is the same word we get "inference" from. This is an Inference problem! Remember: for these problems we are looking for a piece of information that we can conclude is true from the text, but which the text does not explicitly state. We also cannot come up with an answer before we look at the choices because we don't know what kind of inference the test makers are looking for. But we know that the answer choice will have to fit with the end of the third paragraph, where we learn that the French and Spanish banned the use of the Basque language.

A. Indo-European languages are superior to other languages. Can we infer this? No. There is no part of the text that tells us how to compare languages based on how "good" or "bad" they are. This is wrong.

B. The French and Spanish wished to assimilate the Basque people. This is a little tough because you have to know what "assimilate" means. The quick definition is to "absorb" or "integrate." So we can rephrase the answer like this: The French and Spanish wished to absorb the Basque people. Can we infer this? Look at the second sentence in the third paragraph: they were able to maintain their culture in the face of foreign occupation. We know then that the Spanish and French wanted to assimilate the Basques, but failed. This is correct, but let's look at the other choices, too.

C. There were communication problems between the Basque people and the occupying powers. We have no evidence whatsoever to support this. Could be true, could be false, but it can't be inferred. It's wrong.

D. Basque was the language of the terrorist group ETA. Not only do we not know that the members of ETA spoke Basque, we don't know if this is why the language was banned. Can't be inferred, even though it's possible.

E. To encourage Basque people to emigrate to the New World. Again, this could be true—maybe the French banned the language to make people feel less welcome—but we have no way of inferring it. It's wrong.

4. In the context of the passage, "pluralistic societies" most closely means:

What kind of question is this? Obviously, this is a vocab question! We've got a phrase here that you likely don't know, but you have to figure out a guess about what it means. For these problems, remember, we create a Sentence Completion, taking the words out of their original context. Like so: Others, however, were not willing to give up the fight for autonomy: some formed the secessionist group ETA, which bombed sites in Europe for more than fifty years in the hopes of being granted their own state. ETA has disbanded, however, and, at least for now, the Basque people are simply one people among many in _____. Ouch, this is tough! But let's try to fill in the blank in our own words.

We do this by picking out some key words. "One people among many" is a key phrase. Also, in the previous sentence, "autonomy," because we know the Basques are no longer fighting to be autonomous. So we can rewrite the last sentence like this: ETA has disbanded, however, and, at least for now, the Basque people are simply one people among many in a society where there are many groups and the groups are not autonomous. Ugly for sure, but let's see if we can find a choice that matches it.

A. Societies in which some people are oppressed. That doesn't really fit. If the Basque are "one society among many" in a larger society, there isn't really any evidence of oppression. Next!

B. Societies in which all people agree to speak the same language. Given that much of the text is about how the Basques have maintained their language, this doesn't seem very likely. It also doesn't match our predicted definition. Next!

C. Societies in which one group's land is controlled by another group. This is a tricky one. It's true that the Basque land is controlled by other people, but that doesn't really fit what we were looking for. We also don't know that they're oppressed anymore. Definitely the best choice so far, but let's see if we can do better.

D. Societies in which different groups coexist and maintain their identity. This not only matches what we were looking for, but it seems like a good summary of the whole passage. The Basques have their own identity, but they live alongside different groups. That means they live in pluralistic societies. Correct choice!

1ˢᵗ Ed. © ibidPREP llc

E. Societies in which many groups are fighting for independence. This can't be right because the sentence before it just said that ETA is no longer fighting for independence. This is wrong.

5. *What can be inferred from the passage about French and Spanish societies?*

This one should be easy now because it's another inference problem! We'll just tackle it the same way we did problem three.

A. Most Spanish and French people dislike Basque people. We have no idea how the French and Spanish feel about Basque people. We know that they want Basque land, but it's possible they really love Basque people. We can't choose this.

B. Most Spanish and French people were more interested in creating empires than Basque people were. Since we know that Basque people were oppressed, it's tempting to conclude this is true. But we can't. Just because they were oppressed doesn't mean they didn't also want to make their own empire. They could have wanted it more than anybody else!

C. Women in French and Spanish societies had less power than women in Basque society. Here we go. Look at the second sentence in the second paragraph. It says that Basque women were more powerful than women in other European societies. We know that the French and Spanish are Europeans, so we can infer that women there did not have as much power. This is the right answer!

D. People in French and Spanish societies never had to deal with occupation. This article tells us very little about French and Spanish history. We have no idea whether or not this is true. Also beware of absolutes here; "never" can almost "always" be disproven.

E. People in French and Spanish societies had more money than people in Basque society. Again, this is likely true given how strong France and Spain were, but we can't infer it from the text. The text tells us nothing about levels of wealth.

6. *Which reason does the passage suggest for the Basque emigration to countries in the New World?*

This is another of those reading for detail questions. Let's look back at the text and try to determine why the Basque people left for new countries. Looking at the final paragraph, we can deduce that they left because they were looking for a better life somewhere else. Let's see if we can find an answer that says something along those lines.

A. Many Basque people wanted to create their own nation in the New World. This is a possibility, but the text does NOT say that they were looking to make a new nation. All it says is that they went to live in new nations. Not right.

B. Many Basque people were frustrated with their situation in Spain and France. This sure sounds a lot like what we were looking for! It's probably right, but let's keep looking to be sure.

C. Many Basque people were indifferent to their homeland. This is clearly false. We know that ETA was fighting for a long time to get their independence. This one is just wrong.

D. Many Basque people could not practice their religion as they wanted in Spain and France. Again, this could be true, but there's nothing in the text to suggest it. This is just totally random and therefore wrong.

E. Many Basque people wanted their women to be more powerful once again. Same as D, this could be true but is totally unsupported by the text. We know that women used to be very powerful in Basque society, but we don't have any idea how any Basque people feel about it.

In addition to being alert to any of the narrator's deviations from reality, you must with all prose fiction be sure to **read until the end** of the passage to make sure you know what really happened!

TYPES OF ACT READING

Prose Fiction—

These passages are pretty much as described: prose fiction. They are generally excerpts from short stories or novels and often are told in first person in order to mix it up a little from the third person prose you'll be reading in the next three passage.

As with all first person narration, you must stay alert to the fact the your narrator might not always be the most reliable storyteller. I.e., what she's **saying** is happening might not jibe exactly with what is **actually** happening in the story.

Humanities—

Art and artists. Different kinds of art, art movement and the lives of those involved in them: writers, artist, musicians and odd variations thereof.

Natural Sciences—

Just before you start the SCIENCE section, you're given the Natural Science section reading comprehension passage. Yay! This passage is packed with all those things that test some kids boredom meter to the max. Fight on! Learn to love passages about weather, astrophysicists, medicine, and, for some reason, sea life. These people love sea life!

Social Sciences—

Social science in real life is a VERY broad category that includes anthropology, economics, geography, history, political science, psychology, social studies, and sociology. Generally, speaking it covers most things that have to do with stuff that happens between and among groups of people and individuals. On the ACT, it generally means passages about important occurrences in human development and history like great inventions, huge weather events, key migrations, changes in food patterns, etc.

AGAIN—INSTRUCTIONS AND INTRODUCTIONS ARE NOT YOUR PARENTS; LISTEN TO THEM.

At the start of each reading passage there is a brief intro with info on the piece you are about to read. READ IT. IT often provides useful info that can help locate you in the text VERY quickly.

 1st Ed. © ibidPREP llc

MORE PRACTICE

Now let's practice more reading [and answering] the right way. In the texts below, you will practice finding the Two T's and then you will read and answer questions to a longer passage. We'll help you with that first full passage by explaining the answers and how we got them. Then, you're on your own!

READING COMPREHENSION—NOW YOU'RE ON YOUR OWN!

FICTION

THE TURN OF THE SCREW
by Henry James

The story had held us, round the fire, sufficiently breathless, but except the obvious remark that it was gruesome, as, on Christmas Eve in an old house, a strange tale should essentially be, I remember no comment uttered till somebody happened to say that it was the only case he had met in which such a visitation had fallen on a child. The case, I may mention, was that of an apparition in just such an old house as had gathered us for the occasion—an appearance, of a dreadful kind, to a little boy sleeping in the room with his mother and waking her up in the terror of it; waking her not to dissipate his dread and soothe him to sleep again, but to encounter also, herself, before she had succeeded in doing so, the same sight that had shaken him. It was this observation that drew from Douglas—not immediately, but later in the evening—a reply that had the interesting consequence to which I call attention. Someone else told a story not particularly effective, which I saw he was not following. This I took for a sign that he had himself something to produce and that we should only have to wait. We waited in fact till two nights later; but that same evening, before we scattered, he brought out what was in his mind.

"I quite agree—in regard to Griffin's ghost, or whatever it was—that its appearing first to the little boy, at so tender an age, adds a particular touch. But it's not the first occurrence of its charming kind that I know to have involved a child. If the child gives the effect another turn of the screw, what do you say to TWO children—?"

"We say, of course," somebody exclaimed, "that they give two turns! Also that we want to hear about them."

I can see Douglas there before the fire, to which he had got up to present his back, looking down at his interlocutor with his hands in his pockets. "Nobody but me, till now, has ever heard. It's quite too horrible." This, naturally, was declared by several voices to give the thing the utmost price, and our friend, with quiet art, prepared his triumph by turning his eyes over the rest of us and going on: "It's beyond everything. Nothing at all that I know touches it."

"For sheer terror?" I remember asking.

He seemed to say it was not so simple as that; to be really at a loss how to qualify it. He passed his hand over his eyes, made a little wincing grimace. "For dreadful—dreadfulness!"

"Oh, how delicious!" cried one of the women.

He took no notice of her; he looked at me, but as if, instead of me, he saw what he spoke of. "For general uncanny ugliness and horror and pain."

"Well then," I said, "just sit right down and begin."

He turned round to the fire, gave a kick to a log, watched it an instant. Then as he faced us again: "I can't begin. I shall have to send to town." There was a unanimous groan at this, and much reproach; after which, in his preoccupied way, he explained. "The story's written. It's in a locked drawer—it has not been out for years. I could write to my man and enclose the key; he could send down the packet as he finds it." It was to me in particular that he appeared to propound this—appeared almost to appeal for aid not to hesitate. He had broken a thickness of ice, the formation of many a winter; had had his reasons for a long silence. The others resented postponement, but it was just his scruples that charmed me. I adjured him to write by the first post and to agree with us for an early hearing; then I asked him if the experience in question had been his own. To this his answer was prompt. "Oh, thank God, no!"

"And is the record yours? You took the thing down?"

"Nothing but the impression. I took that HERE"—he tapped his heart. "I've never lost it."

"Then your manuscript—?"

"Is in old, faded ink, and in the most beautiful hand." He hung fire again. "A woman's. She has been dead these twenty years. She sent me the pages in question before she died." They were all listening now, and of course there was somebody to be arch, or at any rate to draw the inference. But if he put the inference by without a smile it was also without irritation. "She was a most charming person, but she was ten years older than I. She was my sister's governess," he quietly said. "She was the most agreeable woman I've ever known in her position; she would have been worthy of any whatever. It was long ago, and this episode was long before. I was at Trinity, and I found her at home on my coming down the second summer. I was much there that year—it was a beautiful one; and we had, in her off-hours, some strolls and talks in the garden—talks in which she struck me as awfully clever and nice. Oh yes; don't grin: I liked her extremely and am glad to this day to think she liked me, too. If she hadn't she wouldn't have told me. She had never told anyone. It wasn't simply that she said so, but that I knew she hadn't. I was sure; I could see. You'll easily judge why when you hear."

1. For what reason does the narrator think Douglas does not immediately share his story?
   A. He doesn't remember it immediately.
   B. He is reluctant to speak in front of others.
   C. Another person was already telling a story.
   D. It is late and he wants to go to bed.

2. The narrator would most likely characterize Douglas' story telling ability in which of the following ways?
   A. understated skillfulness
   B. awkard shyness
   C. overbearing verboseness
   D. clumsy wordiness

1st Ed. © ibidPREP llc

3. The passage implies that the manuscript Douglas is referring to has not been out of its drawer for years for which reason?
   A. He had forgotten about it.
   B. He had lost the key.
   C. The account is too horrifying to read.
   D. No one had asked him about it.

4. As it is used in the 10th paragraph, what does "adjured" most nearly mean?
   A. Pestered
   B. Demanded
   C. Urged
   D. Argued

5. Based on the passage, stories told on Christmas Eve should be:
   A. humorous
   B. fantastical
   C. long
   D. horrifying

6. What is most likely the "inference" that is referenced in the last paragraph?
   A. Douglas is a part of the story he will tell.
   B. That he was romantically involved with the woman who wrote the story.
   C. He is lying about the story.
   D. The story is terrifying.

SOCIAL SCIENCES

FROM DWIGHT EISENHOWER'S FAREWELL ADDRESS IN 1961

Our military organization today bears little relation to that known by any of my predecessors in peacetime, or indeed by the fighting men of World War II or Korea.

Until the latest of our world conflicts, the United States had no industry just for making arms. American makers of plowshares [or anything else] could, with time and as required, make swords [or any other weapons] as well. But now we can no longer risk emergency improvisation of national defense; we have been compelled to create a permanent armaments industry of vast proportions. Added to this, three and a half million men and women are directly engaged in the defense establishment. We annually spend on military security more than the net income of all United States corporations.

This merging of an immense military establishment and a large arms industry is new in the American experience. The total influence—economic, political, even spiritual—is felt in every city, every State house, every office of the Federal government. We recognize the imperative need for this development. Yet we must not fail to comprehend its grave implications. Our toil, resources and livelihood are all involved; so is the very structure of our society.

In the councils of government, we must guard against the military industrial complex gaining too much influence. The potential for the disastrous rise of misplaced power exists and will persist.

We must never let the weight of this combination endanger our liberties or democratic processes. We should take nothing for granted. Only an alert and knowledgeable citizenry can compel the proper meshing of the huge industrial and military machinery of defense with our peaceful methods and goals, so that security and liberty may prosper together.

Akin to, and largely responsible for, the sweeping changes in our industrial-military posture has been the technological revolution during recent decades.

In this revolution, research has become central; it also becomes more formalized, complex, and costly. A steadily increasing share is conducted at the direction of the Federal government.

Today, the solitary inventor, tinkering in his shop, has been overshadowed by task forces of scientists in laboratories and testing fields. In the same fashion, the free university, historically the fountainhead of free ideas and scientific discovery, has experienced a revolution in the conduct of research. Partly because of the huge costs involved, a government contract virtually becomes a substitute for intellectual curiosity.

The prospect of domination of the nation's scholars by Federal employment, project allocations, and the power of money is ever present and is to be regarded very seriously.

It is the task of statesmanship to mold, to balance, and to integrate these and other forces, new and old, within the principles of our democratic system—ever aiming toward the supreme goals of our free society.

Another factor in maintaining balance involves the element of time. As we peer into society's future, we—you and I, and our government—must avoid the impulse to live only for today, robbing, for our own ease and convenience, the precious resources of tomorrow. We cannot mortgage the material assets of our grandchildren without risking the loss also of their political and spiritual heritage. We want democracy to survive for all generations to come, not to become the bankrupt ghost of tomorrow.

1. What does President Eisenhower say about solitary American inventors?
   A. They have been replaced by researchers at universities.
   B. The country would develop better technology if there were more of them at work.
   C. They helped give rise to the military-industrial complex.
   D. The country should help them adjust to the new economic conditions.

2. What risk from the military-industrial complex does President Eisenhower advise the country to resist?
   A. The risk that the military-industrial complex will be unable to meet the nation's technological demands.
   B. The risk that the military-industrial complex will come under communist influence.
   C. The risk that the military-industrial complex will exert too much control over the government's decisions.
   D. The risk that the military-industrial complex will waste the nation's resources.

1st Ed. © *ibidPREP llc*

3. What reason does President Eisenhower give for spending so much on defense?
   A. There will soon be another war and it is necessary that the country be ready.
   B. Having a strong military will persuade other countries not to attack America.
   C. The government spending is all that keeps millions of Americans employed.
   D. It helps expand human understanding of science.

4. Why is President Eisenhower wary about the presence of so much government money going to American universities?
   A. He does not value higher education.
   B. The universities are wasting the money.
   C. The universities already have too much influence over the national government.
   D. He is worried that the money will suppress free thinking.

5. President Eisenhower warns against using up the nation's resources too quickly. Doing so, he says, would have which adverse effect:
   A. Life would become less comfortable.
   B. It would threaten the existence of democracy.
   C. It would threaten the fragile environment.
   D. It would contribute to rising inequality.

6. What does "imperative" most closely mean as it is used in the third paragraph?
   A. optional
   B. judicial
   C. unnecessary
   D. crucial

HUMANITIES

FROM "THE LAST GREAT EXPLORER"

The quest to find the Garden of Eden sounds like a pursuit that should have fallen by the wayside well before the 19th century. No longer did the fantastic medieval geographies of John Prester or Columbus allow for the existence of an exotic, unspoiled earthly paradise. This was a newer, wiser age. We had conquered the wild regions of the world. And Darwin's Origin of Species, published in 1859, was slowly proving that man and, say, the birds of the air, were not created all at once in a single spot on the globe.

Darwin himself dismissed the search for a geographical point of origins in his 1871 Descent of Man. He allowed that: "It is somewhat more probable that our early ancestors lived on the African continent than elsewhere." But, he declared, there was also a large ape that roamed Europe not so long ago, and anyway the earth is old enough for primate species to have migrated all the way around it by now. So, "It is useless to speculate on this subject."

Victoria Woodhull, feminist radical and free-love advocate, was less diplomatic in her epic speech "The Garden of Eden," which she delivered frequently in the 1870s. Eden on Earth was nonsense: "Any school boy of twelve years of age who should read the description of this garden and not discover that it has no geographical significance whatever, ought to be reprimanded for his stupidity." Although she never said, this comment might have been meant for the missionary-explorer David Livingstone, who had declared, while crazed with malaria in 1871, that Paradise existed at the source of the Nile, which he judged to be in the Lake Bangweulu region of Zambia.

Livingstone was not the only one still looking for Eden. This brave new world was turning time-honored beliefs upside down. Evolution was suggesting that man had ascended over time from our less-intelligent, animalistic primate origins. But Christianity had been insisting for centuries that man had descended, through original sin, from near-divine heights in the Garden of Eden to the miserable, depraved society of the late 19th century. What was a modern person of faith to believe? Enter William Fairfield Warren, distinguished Methodist minister and educator. As the president of Boston University, he knew science was going to define the future, but he was unwilling to give up his theology to the new discipline. How to knit the two perspectives together?

Surprisingly, Warren looked to Eden itself. He set about translating the Bible into science. Since Genesis says Eden contains "every tree that is pleasant to the eye or good for food"; Warren supposed "flora and fauna [plants and animals] of almost unimagined vigor and luxuriousness." He took note of a newly discovered fact: millions of years ago, the earth had been much warmer. He followed the uncovering of fantastic creatures at once familiar and mythical, like the woolly mammoth, the dinosaur and the giant sequoia. He knew there was still one blank spot on the world map, a place where nobody had been that might have held them all. He arrived at his "inevitable" conclusion: The Garden of Eden is at the North Pole! It made sense, in a way. Both Eden and the Pole had frustratingly resisted explorers' attempts to discover and claim them, despite centuries of dangerous, expensive expeditions.

1. Why did William Fairfield Warren feel compelled to express his religion in scientific terms?
    A. He liked science more than he liked religion.
    B. People had always tried to express Christian beliefs in scientific terms.
    C. He saw that science was going to dominate future understandings of the world and wanted to reconcile his faith with it.
    D. He was losing his faith in God.

2. Why did Charles Darwin think it was not worthwhile to speculate about where human beings originally evolved?
    A. The knowledge would be useless.
    B. There were potential ancestors all over the world, so the location was impossible to discover.
    C. Knowing where humanity originated would threaten his theory of evolution.
    D. He knew the location would be easier to discover later with the development of new technology.

3. Victoria Woodhull would have been most likely to agree with which of the following statements?
    A. Discovering the Garden of Eden should be a top national priority.
    B. Discovering the Garden of Eden would bring huge benefits to all people.
    C. The Garden of Eden is probably at the North Pole.
    D. The Garden of Eden did not actually exist.

1st Ed. © ibidPREP llc

4. For which reason does the author suggest that the theory of evolution was problematic for Christians?
   A. Christians had been claiming that man had devolved from a perfect state in the Garden of Eden, but evolution suggested that humans had, in fact, evolved from humble roots.
   B. Evolution showed that there could be no God.
   C. Science and religion are always entirely incompatible.
   D. Evolution showed that other major religions were closer to the truth.

5. Why did William Fairfield Warren conclude that the Garden of Eden was at the North Pole?
   A. Its present climate was similar to the way the Garden of Eden is described in the Bible.
   B. It was the only uncharted land remaining.
   C. He visited the North Pole and found evidence of the Garden of Eden.
   D. The North Pole had the highest concentration of fossils of any place on Earth.

6. What does "depraved" mean in the context of the fourth paragraph?
   A. sinful
   B. penniless
   C. greedy
   D. hungry

NATURAL SCIENCES

TIMESCALES OF EVOLUTION

The evolution stories that people are most familiar with occur at a glacial pace. Over millions of years, water creatures shed their ties to the ocean and colonize the land. Later, over several more millions of years, the dinosaurs rise and fall, and little scurrying mammals take their places. Eventually, those little rodents become you and me. Yet, as humans have brought staggering changes to the natural world, we have discovered that evolution can take place in the blink of an eye.

The fastest examples of evolution occur in the microscopic world of bacteria: humans are in the process of creating extraordinarily strong "superbugs." Here's how it works. If a doctor administers an antibiotic (a drug meant to kill infectious bacteria), the medicine will sometimes fail to kill all of the infectious cells. Those surviving cells, through their exposure to the antibiotic, develop resistance to the drug. They pass that resistance on to their offspring, their baby bacteria. Therefore, when those progeny infect the next unsuspecting person, that original antibiotic will not be effective in treating the disease; the bacteria have evolved in the span of days! Such adaptation is why you should avoid using antibacterial soap unless you work in a hospital or some other similar environment where the spread of infection is of special concern.

We do not, however, need to look to the microscopic world to find evolution on a human timescale. A famous example of contemporary species adaptation occurred over the past two centuries in England. Prior to the Industrial Revolution, nearly all Peppered Moths were light-colored with a few dark spots (thus the name "peppered"). Their coloring helped them hide amid similarly colored lichens on trees. When pollution from the rapidly increasing number of smokestacks and other industrial sources killed these lichens, the pale moths stood out and became easy prey. As a result, any Peppered Moths that were born even a little bit darker than the others were suddenly harder to spot as the trees got sootier. Soon the darker Peppered Moths became the dominant type. Just like that, over the course of a few decades, the coloring of a complex organism evolved to adapt to a new environment.

That, of course, is the essence of evolution: successful species are those that change with their environment to

Practice

survive long enough to reproduce. If the environment does not change, a well-adapted species will not change. That is why some shark species, for example, have been largely unchanged over many millions of years. But when environments change quickly, some species can change just as quickly.

1. Which of the following best expresses the author's purpose?
   A. To show that bacteria and moths evolve over time.
   B. To argue against pollution in order to protect the habitats of many species.
   C. To show that evolution takes place on many different timescales.
   D. To convince readers not to use antibacterial soap.

2. Which of the following is not presented as a form of evolution?
   A. The change in color of the peppered moths.
   B. The increased resistance of bacteria to antibiotics.
   C. The colonization of land by life from the sea.
   D. The study of evolution by humans.

3. In what way does the author suggest that bacteria can evolve?
   A. They successfully manage to locate new hosts, often going from species to species.
   B. They pass on to their progeny a resistance to antibiotics.
   C. They are clever enough to evade antibiotics.
   D. The use of antibacterial soap actually helps them to reproduce.

4. What can be inferred about the darker peppered moths?
   A. They were more visible after the Industrial Revolution.
   B. They became healthier after the beginning of the Industrial Revolution.
   C. Part of their success was due to their awareness of their new situation.
   D. If the pollution of the Industrial Revolution were to disappear, the darker moths might once again be highly vulnerable to predators.

5. What cause does the author suggest for the evolution of both the bacteria and the peppered moth?
   A. The Industrial Revolution
   B. Antibiotics
   C. Drastic human alterations of the environment
   D. A gradual shift in the natural world

6. What explanation does the author suggest for the lack of change in some species of sharks?
   A. They lack the capacity to evolve.
   B. They are evolving, simply very slowly.
   C. They are one of the species doomed to extinction.
   D. They fit well in their environment, so there is no pressure to evolve.

1ˢᵗ Ed. © ibidPREP llc

DUAL PASSAGES

When you read dual passages, the THEME will be the same—the points the authors make about that THEME will be different and your job will be to see that.

Whether the dual passages are short or long readings, the process is the same.

1. Read Passage One
   a. Before answering the questions for Passage One, determine Passage One's POINT [thesis, why, etc.] toward its subject.
   b. Write down POINT and tone.
   c. Answer Passage One questions.
2. Read Passage Two
   a. Before answering the questions for Passage Two, determine Passage Two's POINT.
   b. Write down point and tone.
   c. Answer Passage Two questions.
3. Compare POV Passage One to Passage Two – Answer questions pertaining to BOTH. Remember when comparing the two sections:
   a. Passages may relate in only a few ways:
      i. One passage opposes the other [less frequent than you might expect].
      ii. One passage serves as an illustration of the point made in the other.
      iii. One passage builds or continues on a specific part or point of the other.
   b. When asked how one passage's author would respond to a point in the other passage, the question is really asking what is the POINT of that passage.
   c. When asked on what both passages would agree, look for the most general answers to which no one would really object. I.e., if these two passages are fundamentally different, then if they ask you what they would agree on, it would have to be something NO ONE would disagree about! [the sky is blue, water is wet, stars are distant from us, evolution is a controversial topic for some...]

The passages below are followed by questions based on their content. Answer the questions on the basis of what is stated or implied in the passages and in any introductory material that may be provided. Questions may also be based on the relationship between the paired passages.

Practice

DUAL PASSAGES
Passage 1

We might as well call the color "Universal Recycling Blue." It is ubiquitous. Bins, bags, boxes, in stores, fast food restaurants, subway stations—they are everywhere, waiting for us to deposit our recyclables and give ourselves a little morale boost. "There! I'm helping," we say to ourselves, and we feel so much better! Unfortunately, we've only scratched the surface, providing a little local band-aid for a global wound. All this recycling has two main effects: it gives us the feeling that we are taking action, and it allows us to avoid the deeper issues.

Passage 2

There is no question that most people want to do their best to help out. They care about the effect they have on the ecosystem, and they genuinely believe that each effort to recycle has a positive impact on the environment. Instead of focusing so intently on the products we discard and how to recycle them, we need to look at how much we consume in the first place. There are many simple steps we can take. Use less water each time we shower. Use both sides of each piece of paper. Take our own bags to the supermarket instead of continually using more paper ones, even if they are recyclable. The possibilities for reusing everyday products are endless and cost nothing to implement.

1. The author of Passage 1 would most likely argue that people who "believe that each effort to recycle has a positive impact on the environment" (Passage 1) are
   A. misguided and are mistaking the feeling of doing good with making actual positive environmental impact.
   B. justified in feeling that way because their efforts are noble.
   C. well-meaning but foolish to continue a useless endeavor.
   D. in denial that their efforts do more harm than good.

2. It can be inferred that the author of Passage 2 believes that one of the disadvantages of recycling programs is
   A. that such programs produce too much waste.
   B. their costliness.
   C. that they actually contribute to the world energy crisis.
   D. the lack of uniform standards across such programs.

3. Which statement best characterizes the relationship between Passage 1 & Passage 2?
   A. Passage 2 supplies evidence that rebuts the argument made in Passage
   B. Passage 2 offers a specific example to support the argument made in Passage
   C. Passage 2 supplies an explanation for a state of affairs described in Passage
   D. Passage 2 generally agrees with Passage 1 but offers an alternative way of looking at the argument.

4. The authors of Passage 1 and Passage 2 are likely to agree that:
   A. those who currently recycle lack awareness of how their actions fit into the bigger picture of environmental conservation.
   B. there are no instances in which using recycled products is a good idea.
   C. the effect of recycling on the environment is unquestionably positive.
   D. recycling programs only exist to make people feel good about themselves.

1st Ed. © ibidPREP llc

LONG PASSAGE COMPARISONS

The passages below are followed by questions based on their content. Answer the questions on the basis of what is stated *or* implied *in the passages and in any introductory material that may be provided. Questions may also be based on the relationship between the paired passages.*

Passage 1

Food will win the war, and the nation whose food resources are best conserved will be the victor. This is the truth that our government is trying to drive home to every man, woman and child in America. We have always been happy in the fact that ours was the richest nation in the world, possessing unlimited supplies of food, fuel, energy and ability. But rich as these resources are they will not meet the present food shortage unless every family and every individual enthusiastically co-operates in the national saving campaign as outlined by the United States Food Administration.

The regulations prescribed for this saving campaign are simple and easy of application. Our government does not ask us to give up three square meals a day—nor even one. All it asks is that we substitute as far as possible corn and other cereals for wheat, reduce a little our meat consumption and save sugar and fats by careful utilization of these products.

There are few housekeepers who are not eager to help in this saving campaign, and there are few indeed who do not feel the need to conserve family resources. But just how is sometimes a difficult task. A little bit of saving in food means a tremendous aggregate total when 100,000,000 people are doing the saving. One wheatless meal a day would not mean hardship; there are always corn and other products to be used. Yet one wheatless meal a day in every family would mean a saving of 90,000,000 bushels of wheat, which totals 5,400,000,000 lbs. Two meatless days a week would mean a saving of 2,200,000 lbs. of meat per annum. One teaspoonful of sugar per person saved each day would ensure a supply ample to take care of our soldiers and our Allies. These quantities mean but a small individual sacrifice, but when multiplied by our vast population they will immeasurably aid and encourage the men who are giving their lives to the noble cause of humanity on which our nation has embarked.

Passage 2

The group of nations that can make the greatest savings will be victorious, counsels one; the group that can produce the most food and nourish the population best will win the war, urges another; but whatever the prophecy, whatever the advice, all paths to victory lie through labor-power.

Needs are not answered in our day by manna dropping from heaven. Whether it is food or big guns that are wanted, ships or coal, we can only get our heart's desire by toil. Where are the workers who will win the war? We are a bit spoiled in the United States. We have been accustomed to rubbing our Aladdin's lamp of opportunity, and the good genii sending us workers. But suddenly, no matter how great our efforts, no one answers our appeal. The reservoir of immigrant labor has run dry. We are in a sorry plight, for we have suffered from emigration, too. Thousands of alien workers have been called back to serve in the armies of the Allies.

In my own little village on Long Island, the industrious Italian colony was broken up by the call to return to the colors in Piedmont. The country calls for everything, and all at once, like the spoiled child on suddenly waking. It must have, and without delay, ships, coal, cars, cantonments, uniforms, rules, and food, food, food. How can the needs be met with a million and a half men dropping work? Those are the horns of the dilemma presented to a puzzled America. Labor we must have. Will American women supply it, or will they accept the optimistic view that lack of labor is not acute?

Practice

Scarcity of labor is not only certain to grow, but the demands upon the United States for service are increasing by leaps and bounds. America must throw manpower into the trenches, must feed herself, must contribute more and ever more food to the hungry populations of Europe, must meet the old industrial obligations, and must respond to a whole range of new business requirements. One of the things which stands in the way of the United States reaching a more worthy position is reluctance to see its women shouldering economic burdens.

1. In Passage 2, the author refers to his or her own village on Long Island (paragraph 3) in order to
   A. suggest that Italian immigrants are most responsible for the shortage of labor in America.
   B. provide an example illustrating how immigrant laborers are no longer available to work because they have gone back to their original countries to serve in the armed forces.
   C. support the point that food shortages are not the most pressing issue in war time.
   D. show one way that the country is calling for everything, all at once, and cannot supply its own needs.

2. Which best characterizes the attitude of the author of Passage 1 towards the "the noble cause of humanity on which our nation has embarked" (paragraph 4)?
   A. The author of Passage 1 believes the cause involves an unnecessary loss of human life.
   B. The author of Passage 1 respects the contributions of the men giving their lives for this cause, but believes that more women should be involved as well.
   C. The author of Passage 1 feels that the United States' motives in entering the war are suspect, and should be questioned.
   D. The author of Passage 1 believes that the cause is worth a small sacrifice on the part of the citizens at home.

3. In the point of view of the author of Passage 2, why is the United States like a spoiled child (paragraph 4)?
   A. Because the women in the country don't want to become part of the labor force.
   B. Because the country expects to win the war without any sacrifice.
   C. Because the country has had its needs easily satisfied in the past, and expects the same thing to happen now.
   D. Because the United States is in need of more help than Europe.

4. In Passage 1, "one teaspoonful of sugar" represents what?
   A. The easiest way for the United States to "swallow its medicine."
   B. The amount of sugar used to make a loaf of bread.
   C. The ration of sugar allowed by the United States Food Administration.
   D. The small individual sacrifice which, when multiplied by the large population, can provide enough for the soldiers overseas.

1st Ed. © ibidPREP llc

5. The author of Passage 2 believes that the question, "Where are the workers who will win the war?" is best answered by which of the following?
   A. They are the women of the United States.
   B. They have emigrated back to the European countries from which they came.
   C. They will appear when we rub our "Aladdin's lamp," as they have in the past.
   D. They are fighting in the trenches.

6. Which of the following best describes the relationship between the two passages?
   A. Both authors agree that the United States can no longer depend upon the resources it has relied upon in the past.
   B. Neither author is willing to acknowledge that the other has a valid point.
   C. The author of Passage 2 is attempting to disprove the existence of the problem outlined in Passage
   D. The passages offer similar solutions to the problems facing the United States.

HOW TO AVOID EXAMICIDE

PART II—TIME & THE STUDENT MIND

1. TIME IS AN ILLUSION—REALLY

Teenagers are fascinating creatures. They are a hybrid blend of child and adult, and you seldom know when you're going to get which—except when it comes to matters of time. When it comes to matters of time, teenagers are infants. I have yet, even after thousands of students, to come across a teenager who had an accurate sense of time when it came to tests. Most students are freaked out about time from the start, so they rush—really, really psychotically and brutally rush. I have seen some kids so spooked about time they won't even take the time to work out 2 + 2 or read through to the end of a simple sentence.

Often kids have received these notions of time through their parents, who have told them, "You read too slowly." BAD PARENT! Most students who think they read too slowly actually read too quickly and don't have any idea what the heck it is they just supposedly read. So, when they get to the questions they have NO IDEA how to answer them, and that is where they lose time and points! All because of NOT, NOT, NOT reading slowly and carefully.

It's the same for math. Oftentimes, I show students the proper way to answer a math question only to hear them say afterward, "But I couldn't do that on the test, that would take me forever." To which I answer, "You're right. Let's just go back to getting it wrong quickly."

1ˢᵗ Ed. © ibidPREP llc

HOW TO AVOID EXAMICIDE

2. INDECISION IS THE ULTIMATE TIME SUCK

While it is true that time is an illusion and that attempting to save time results in loss of time or points and usually both [rushing wastes time], still it is possible to save time [life is a paradox[24]—get over it]. Students waste more time resisting doing the thing than doing the thing itself would take. When students give me the "Oh, I knew how to do it, but it would have taken too much time" line, that is when I feel myself growing older and when that small vein on my temple begins to throb. DO NOT MAKE DECISIONS BASED ON HOW LONG YOU THINK SOMETHING IS GOING TO TAKE. IF YOU HAVE ANY IDEA HOW TO SOLVE A PROBLEM, START DOING IT. JUST GETTING GOING WILL SAVE YOU ALL THE TIME YOU'LL NEED TO SOLVE IT. TRUST ME ON THIS. REALLY!

3. YOU CAN GET FASTER AT GOING SLOWER—THE SLOWER YOU GO THE FASTER YOU GO

This is another one of those time paradoxes that I spend an inordinate amount of time trying to prove to my students. First, I need to slow my students down enough for them to do the thing the right way. Then I really, really have to convince them to write everything out and not skip steps. Once they get used to not rushing and being thorough, they're amazed: most problems take no time at all!

It is like learning to play a piece of music. You don't begin at full speed. First you learn the notes and the phrasing and then, as you become familiar with playing the song, you get up to speed. If you try to play a piece quickly from the outset, you'll never learn it properly. If you rush through every math problem and every reading passage, you will never learn how to read or do the math properly. Once you know how to do a thing right, you will begin to go quickly naturally and it will never feel rushed. It will feel smooth, efficient and right. As Goethe[25] said, "Never rush; never rest."

---

[24] something that seems to be a contradiction but is still true
[25] old, dead German writer, thinker, colorist

SEE NEXT EXAMICIDE ON PAGE 334!

1st Ed. © ibidPREP llc

1st Ed. © ibidPREP llc

CHAPTER FIVE

SCIENCE

1ˢᵗ Ed. © ibidPREP llc

Section 4 – Science   40 Questions   35 minutes

Seven Passages
40 Multiple Choice Questions—5-7 questions per section
Four Choices per Question

You Call This Science?

It should be called CHARTS, GRAPHS, TABLES & DATA.

You have been taking the test for over two hours plus however long it took you to get set up. You're probably more than a little burnt out. And now you have to face the SCIENCE Section—7 passages of 5-7 questions each [40 questions total] in 35 minutes. Ugh.

Some students are frightened by this section right off the bat. "Science! I don't know anything about science. I've only been taking it for 6 years or so!!"

That's absolutely fine. If you tanked bio or chem or living environment [or whatever they call it]—it doesn't matter because the science section has LITTLE OR NOTHING to do with any of your science curricula.[1]

What the SCIENCE section has much to do with, as ALL sections, is reading comprehension. You must be able to read the experiment description and get the gist of what it is about. Then, you must be able to read charts and graphs and get the gist of the story they are telling. Pay close attention to whether data is increasing or decreasing, or increasing, decreasing and then increasing again, etc.

12 Steps To Better Science

As much as a natural test taker as I am, there are certain kinds of questions I recoil at and resist naturally. Far from hurting me as a tutor, this helps me understand my students better most of whom recoil at a lot of types of questions. It also makes me follow my own rules in a pinch.

In order to get myself through **the SCIENCE** section, I have broken it down to 12 points that might ease the pain a bit.

1. The **SCIENCE** section is comprised of seven passages with five, six, or seven questions each. Breaking it down, you should allot yourself five minutes per passage. With so little time for each you must be very efficient in reading and processing what's going on. You must also be ruthless about answering questions. Take long enough to determine an answer for yourself then find it among the multiple choices and move on. If you can't find it, or can't determine and answer, or just don't get the question, BY ALL MEANS: Guess and move on!

2. You don't need to know science for the SCIENCE section. If you think you need to dig up your bio, chem, physics, earth science, living environment notebooks in order to do well on this section: RELAX! In fact, if you think that, they've already got you psyched out. REMAIN CLAM! Almost everything you will need to know for each SCIENCE passage is in that passage! All terms and formulas will be explained and there's nothing you need to study and there are no formulas to memorize.

[1] The fact that there is little to no knowledge required for the science section has always made it seem odd to me that the inclusion of the Science section on the ACT means that if you take it you don't need to take SAT2s in order to demonstrate specific subject mastery. The Science section on the ACT is about as subject specific as the Reading Comprehension.

Science

3. You don't need to know science for the SCIENCE section, but it will certainly help to know the scientific method. Most of the passages in the SCIENCE section are based on experiments or studies and almost all studies are conducted using the scientific method. The scientific method involves a precise order of going about testing ideas. The steps are:

   a. **Problem**—I wonder what happens when you turn off the lights at night?

   b. **Hypothesis**—It will get dark.

   c. **Experiment**—Find a room at night, turn of the lights in it, measure the amount of light in it as each light in the room is turned off.

   d. **Data**—Take light meter readings for each step in the experiment and record it in a graph.

   e. **Conclusion**—As more lights are turned off in a room at night, the room gets darker!

Each experiment involves variables and a control. The control is the thing that doesn't change, in this case—the room. The variable is the thing that does change, in this case the number of lights on in the room. The variable, generally speaking is the thing being measured—in this case, the amount of light a room.

Being able to zero in on the variables in an experiment will help you process what's going on in that experiment that much faster!

4. You don't need to know "science" for the SCIENCE section, but a little bit of scientific common sense will go a long way!

Just as in the reading comprehension passages, in the SCIENCE section you will not be given passages that contradict basic truths and common sense. That means it's good to know stuff like:

MUST KNOW SCIENCE

[aka, You don't need to know much science for the SCIENCE section, but a little science goes a long way!]

- Fire gives off heat and water [steam] and consumes oxygen
- Hot air rises/Cold air sinks
- Generally speaking, solids are denser than liquids which are denser than gases
- Generally speaking, as you get higher above sea level:
  - Temperature gets lower
  - Air pressure decreases
  - Oxygen content gets lower
- The air we breathe is composed of roughly:
  - Nitrogen – 78 percent
  - Oxygen – 21 percent
  - Argon – 0.93 percent
  - Carbon dioxide – 0.038 percent
- Water boils at lower temperatures at higher altitudes
- Wind is caused by high and low pressure air mixing.
- Salt absorbs water
- Fat repels water
- The moon's gravitational pull on the earth causes tides
- The moon is a natural satellite
- Gravity is a force
- The sun is the star closest to the earth
- The color white reflects all light and indicates the absence of color
- The color black absorbs all light and indicates the presence of all colors.

- Objects that are green in color absorb all colors except green, objects that are red absorb all colors except red, etc.
- About 70% of the earth's surface is covered in water
- About 3% of the earth's water is freshwater
- The boiling point of water is 212° or 100°
- The freezing/melting point of water is 32° or 0°
- Salt raises the boiling point of water but it lowers its freezing point.
- The earth travels completely around the sun in one year
- The earth rotates completely around its axis in one day
- The seasons are caused by a tilting of the earth's axis to or away from the sun
- The polar regions are almost completely in the dark during their winter months because they are tilted furthest away from the sun.
- The polar regions are almost completely in light during their summer months because they are tilted to almost directly face the sun.
- The regions around the equator do not really vary much by season because only the poles of the earth tilt to and from the sun.
- Because of the tilt of the earth's axis, the Northern Hemisphere experiences summer when the Southern hemisphere experiences winter and vice versa.
- The center of the earth is very hot
- Earthquakes are caused by the shifting of giant plates beneath the surface of the earth.
- Atoms are composed of sub-atomic particle including protons, neutron and the much smaller electrons.
- Metals conduct electricity.
- The human cell is composed of a nucleus and cytoplasm.
                    ADD YOUR OWN COMMON SENSE SCIENCE FACTS HERE!

_____

_____

_____

_____

_____

_____

_____

_____

_____

_____

_____

_____

Keep in mind that there are always exceptions to rules [for examples ice is less dense than liquid water—ice cubes float] which is why it's always important to pay attention to the data. Often experiments are conducted to find these anomalies.[2]

In addition to these science facts, we've included a Glossary of Science Terms in the Apprendix. Don't feel compelled to learn or memorize them, they are there, like the facts above to make you feel comfortable when you're in the SCIENCE section. If you don't get to grasp them all, don't worry about it. Let common sense and good, close reading prevail.

5. You don't need to know "science" for the SCIENCE section, in fact, thinking you know too much about a topic can hurt you! If you hit on a topic you have recently covered in school, and it feels as if:
    a. You should know all about it,
    b. Or think your do know all about it.

    This first feeling is dangerous because it can lead you to get down on yourself for not having studied more or whatever. The second feeling can be dangerous because it may lead you to ignore the text in front of you, impose your own thoughts or, worse, half-knowledge on the topic at hand. Nothing is worse than partial knowledge! It is far better to:

    i.   simply read each experiment as if the topic is completely new to you,
    ii. absorb and process the information given to you, and then figure things out from there.

6. The **SCIENCE** section **does** require an ability to read and comprehend descriptions of experiments and studies, and an ability to read and comprehend charts, figures and graphs.

Reading and interpreting data principally requires the ability to follow the narrative of numbers. Are temperatures rising? Is mass decreasing and then increasing over time? It can be as simple as running your finger down a column[3] and saying, "Up, up, up, down, up...etc." It is also as simple as NOT seeing the trend in a column of numbers and ASSUMING it's just going up or down. Just like in reading comprehension when you read you must read ALL the words, in charts and tables you must scan ALL the data.

How To Read Graphs

Although you may have encountered graphs in math, you may not have dealt with too many in science. Graphs play a large role in recording science, economic data, and technical data. There's a good chance you're going to see a lot of them in your life [which is why they've become a bigger part of the SATs and Common Core as well], so you might as well get good at reading them.

Every graphs tells two stories at one time. The x story occurs along the x axis and the y story occurs along the y axis.

The way to remember which axis is which is pretty simple.

The letter x is a tilted cross and the x axis goes across.

The letter y comes from the Greek letter upsilon...which has up in it. The y axis goes up and down.

Before you set out to read or create a graph, you need to know which story each axis is telling. The x axis is often for measure of time or discrete events like each sampling, day or location at which something is measured.

The y axis is often good for quantitative measurements such as temperature, height, weight, or distance.

[2] Things that are out of the ordinary, exceptions.
[3] A row goes across. A column goes up and down. In order to know what each column or row measures, look to the top or bottom of each row or column for their headings.

1st Ed. © ibidPREP llc

Sometimes each axis represents quantities. See below.

Generally speaking, the x axis gives us our events and the y axis tells us what's happening over the course of those events.

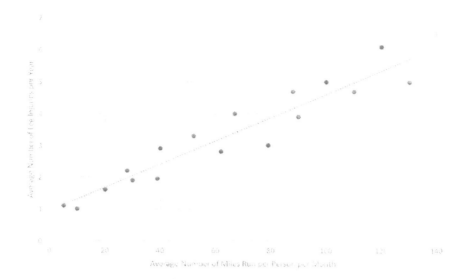

Once you establish what each axis is detailing, you can use that information to give two pieces of information about one event. In the chart above we know that people who run on average 100 miles per week also average 5 leg injuries per year. We also know that people who run 10 miles a month average about 1.5 leg injuries a year.

The two pieces of info per event are indicated by the point formed where the two pieces of information intersect on the graph. We record each point by noting its coordinate pair within a set of parenthesis. We write the x coordinate first and then the y coordinate and separate them with a comma. It's easy to flip the x and y coordinate, so remember, they're ALWAYS written in alphabetical order: (x,y). In our example graph, the number of leg injuries per runners who average 100 miles is written like this: (100, 5).

Besides getting information about specific events, the total image formed by a graph can show us trends, patterns, and, generally, the manner in which things increase or decrease. In our running graph we see that generally the more people ran the more they were prone to leg injuries. The data did not fit into the graph in a perfectly straight line[4] of course because there are other factors that contribute to people getting leg injuries besides running. All this makes perfect sense and fits in with our notion that most of the science that you'll need to know on the SCIENCE section will be common sense science!

LOOK FOR ANY AND ALL ANOMALIES IN THE DATA—YOU CAN BET YOUR BIPPY THERE'LL BE QUESTIONS ON THOSE ANOMALIES

[4] The dotted line that runs through the data is called "the line of best fit," it's drawn to run through the middle of the data to suggest the basic trend the data is following.

7. Don't fear formulas. Formulas are occasionally dropped into the descriptions of the studies. NO ONE is expected to know these formulas in advance. Merely, be aware of the formula and it's constituent elements [the variables within it]. E.g., if there's a formula with temperature in the denominator and they ask you what happens to the value of the formula when temperature increases, that's not a science question, that's math! The bigger the denominator gets, the smaller the value of the fraction!

8. Don't fear scientific jargon or complex words. Almost all specialized terms or names are defined when they are introduced. If species or chemicals are given complex Latin or Greek names, it matters not. You will not be tested on pronunciation or etymology.

9. Don't fear numbers—Even though the numbers in the tables and graphs may seem huge, clunky or decimal filled, you will never be required to do much with them arithmetically [you can't use a calculator on this section which means for sure you won't be required to do any heavy lifting with the numbers]. Generally you'll need to be able to tell if numbers are going up or down or, at most, roughly how they relate.

For example:

Model	Miles per Gallon	Weight in lbs
Car A	35.692	3,190
Car B	23.471	5,949

If you were asked to find the ratio of miles per gallon from Car A to Car B, you could put 35.692 over 23.471 and divide, OR you could simply put 36 over 24 and say that the ratio is roughly 3:2. Even easier is the ratio of the weight of Car A to the weight of Car B—basically 1:2. That's as close as you'll need to get!

10.   Fight Dyslexia BIG TIME

FIGHT DYLSEXIA—if you're dyslexic, fatigued, dyslexic and fatigued, stressed, stressed and dyslexic, stressed, dyslexic and fatigued, your tendency to flip numbers or confuse up and down will be shooting through the roof. The questions and the passages don't help in this fight either. They often ask questions or give you data in which up is down and down is up, they might ask you which value increased least or decreased the most—real head spinning stuff. If you don't slow down here and make sure you're looking for the right value, you're toast! Now is the time to *Remain Clammest!*

As in the math, these are the spots in which you must slow down and make sure you are correctly tracking up and down and more and less. Obviously, you want to fly on most of these questions, but if you don't untangle these questions, you're going to get them wrong and probably get other questions wrong to follow on. Taking the time to carefully untangle these kind of questions, will help you get them right and save you time on the rest of the passage.

11. Wordy Science Passages—Some passages, like the interpretive passages, are more words than charts, tables or graphs. Many students are scared off from tackling these because they believe that reading the passages and processing them will take too much time. Though these are usually dense looking paragraphs, the points they are making are usually as clear as the charts.

The Wordy Science Passages are usually Interpretive Science Passages—There are some passages in which an experiment and its results are presented and interpreted by three or so students or scientists. These interpretations are usually based on either correct scientific thinking, partially correct scientific thinking, or false assumptions and/or faulty logic. Mostly, with these passages, you are asked not only to interpret data, but you are also asked to interpret how other people are interpreting data. It's your job to draw conclusions about the logic behind each interpreter's conclusion and answer questions according the their logic.

1ˢᵗ Ed. © ibidPREP llc

For example, after checking over wordy paragraphs, you distill each idea to the following:

- Scientist A believes that in the experiment the pressure went up and the temperature went down.
- Scientist B believes that in the experiment the pressure went down and the temperature went up.
- Scientists C believe that in the experiment the pressure stayed the same and the temperature went up.
- Scientists A, B and C all agreed that the temperature went up.

There is generally at least one wordy passage per Science section, so find a way to power through them!

So really…Deep down, beneath the complex names and scary formulas, the science section is really a fairly straightforward exercise in reading charts and comparing results of experiments. Generally speaking , it's the story of up, down, positive, negative, higher and lower. Just Remain Clam and you'll be fine!

12. **Timing Science Section**—There are seven passages and 40 questions on the Science section, and you have only 35 minutes for the whole schmear—so you'd better move it. This doesn't mean you're not allowed to read what you need to read or process the charts and tables properly. It just means you should:

a. Read the experiment descriptions long enough to get the point of the experiments [what the passage it attempting to study: changes in climate, pressure, amount of stuff under certain conditions, etc.]

b. Review the charts and tables long enough to get a proper idea of what the data reveals about the topic being studied [e.g., it got hotter then colder than hot again!]

c. Go to the questions

   i. Read the question

   ii. Be clear on what the question is asking. Sometimes the questions can be very dyslexic making [how long was the grass when it was shortest, which element gave off the least heat, etc.].

   iii. If you cannot answer the question without looking at the answers, return first to the text to find an answer, THEN look at the multiple choice answers.

d. Move, move, move. No matter what, keep going and don't get discouraged. The passages ARE NOT in increasing order of difficulty. So, if the meaning of one experiment eludes you, ditch it and move on to the next. Better to sacrifice one passage or part of one passage then watch the rest of the section go up in flames!

Simple Science Glossary!

CHEMISTRY
proton—particle with positive charge in nucleus
neutron—particle with neutral charge in nucleus
nucleus—core of an atom, formed of protons and neutrons
electron—particle with negative charge that orbits the nucleus
atom—smallest part of an element (protons, neutrons, electrons)
element—chemical substance that cannot be broken down
molecule—groups of atoms
orbit—to circle around; electrons orbit at diff. distances from nucleus
circuit—connection for electricity to pass through
phase—state of matter, either solid, liquid or gas
solid—shape and volume stable, dense
liquid—definite volume not definite shape, not dense
gas—neither volume nor shape definite, least dense
melting point—temperature that a solid turns to a liquid
boiling point—temperature that a liquid turns into a gas

pH—measurement for how acidic a solution is, lower pH is more acidic

solution—a mixture of a solid substance(s) dissolved in a liquid

isotope—form of an element that has a different atomic mass

radioactive—a substance whose nucleus deteriorates and gives off energy

half-life—time taken for half the atoms of a radioactive isotope to decay

oxide—chemical compound of oxygen

BIOLOGY

protein—combinations of amino acids; helps growth and repair of cells

gene—unit of DNA that determines characteristics

enzyme—protein substance that promotes biochemical reactions

DNA—chain of acids that carries genetic information

chromosome—thin structure in nucleus of cell, formed of DNA

organism—life form able to reproduce and grow

organelle—any specialized structure within a cell

organic/inorganic—containing carbon/not containing carbon

bacteria—very small organisms

biomass—sum of all the living organisms in a given area

cell—basic independent unit of plant/animal tissue

mitosis—when a cell divides into two identical cells

prophase—first stage of cell division; nuclear membrane vanishes, chromosomes seen

metaphase—stage of cell division at which chromosomes line up

anaphase—after metaphase before telophase

telophase—new nuclei form around chromosomes at ends of cell

GEOLOGY

sediment—mass of solids that have fallen to the bottom of a liquid

deposit—a layer of a substance in the ground

molten—having turned into a liquid when heated

mineral—inorganic solid substance that occurs naturally

atmosphere—mass of gas surrounding the earth, with diff. layers

precipitation—water falling from clouds (rain, snow, hail)

erosion—wearing away of soil or rock

GENERAL CONCEPTS

soluble/insoluble—able to be dissolved/not able to be dissolved

radiation—energy spreading from a central point

viscosity—how hard it is for a liquid to flow

composition—make-up or structure of something

vertical/horizontal—up-and-down/left-to-right

buoyancy—ability to float

absorbance—ability to absorb

density—mass per unit of volume

volume—amount of space occupied

concentration—amount of a substance in a given mass or volume of a solution

pressure—force per unit of space

permeate—move through a layer of something

dissolve—to become a part of a liquid and form a solution

mass—measure of matter in an object

weight—force with which a body is drawn to the center of the earth

energy—capacity to do work

potential energy—energy waiting to come out (possessed because of its position)

kinetic energy—energy possessed by something because of its motion

momentum—measure of motion, mass times velocity

velocity—speed plus direction

wavelength—distance from one wave to the next

period—time from one wave to the next

periodic—happening regularly

frequency—how often something happens (like how often a wave passes)

compound—made up of two or more substances

supersaturated—when a solution contains more solids than will dissolve

spectrum—a range of different, but related things

core—center

insulation—prevention of heat/cold/sound/electricity from passing from one area to another

LABS

deviation—distance away from a usual position or path

variable—something that is changed in an experiment to give information

constant—something that is not changed in an experiment

net—amount remaining after all deductions have been made

MEASURES

amp—unit of electrical current

joule—unit of energy

angstrom—very small unit of distance

mole—measurement for the amount of a substance (certain number of atoms)

Celsius/Fahrenheit: $F = 1.8C + 32$, $C = 5/9(F - 32)$

1st Ed. © *ibidPREP llc*

Chapter Six

The Essay

1st Ed. © ibidPREP llc

Section 5 – Essay   [optional]   30 minutes

The ACT essay is an optional part of the ACT. Many students take it to show colleges what they are capable of, and many colleges require it not only to see what students are capable of but also to make sure that the person who wrote your ACT essay [you] is the same person who wrote your personal statement [hopefully you without too much help].

The ACT essay used to be a pretty simple affair. The prompt usually asked a question that had some sort of relevancy to most students [for example, "Should students be required to wear uniforms."]. Unfortunately for you, that has all changed.

The ACT essay **now** features a brief paragraph on a topic and three separate perspectives on that topic. Your job is to create your own perspective and use the given perspectives as touchstones upon which to build your argument. In a way that makes it easy for you as those perspectives lay out an argument for you and suggest a point of view for you if you lack one.

Scoring for the essay will now be based on four separate but equal criteria:
- Ideas and Analysis
- Development and Support
- Organization
- Language Use and Conventions

Each of these criteria can earn you up to 12 points for a maximum total of 48 points on your essay. That essay score is then cross-indexed with your English [Grammar] and Reading multiple choice scores to give you a Combined ELA score out of 36.

You are given 40 minutes for the essay section to read, think, write and proofread.

A sample prompt follows below, and after that, I'll walk you through how to tackle it.

Agri-business

Most of the food produced in the United States is produced under the control of agri-businesses. These large-scale, conglomerate corporations are highly productive, efficient and profitable. Their production guarantees that our nation and a good portion of the world has an inexpensive and plentiful source of staple crops such as corn, wheat, soy and hay and meats such as chicken, pork and beef. Many contend, however, that the ever expanding scale of agri-business has led to the kind of unregulated growth and excess that leads to large scale pollution, the destruction of the small farmer and unhealthy and unsustainable crops and meats.

Read and carefully consider these perspectives. Each suggest a particular way of thinking about the growth of agri-business.

Perspective One	Perspective Two	Perspective Three
Agri-business has brought innovation and efficiency to food production. If nations continue to support these efforts rather than try to regulate them into the ground, we stand the chance of wiping out hunger in the next generation or so.	There is no reason that regulation and good business practices need be in opposition to one another. With proper government oversight, agri-businesses can continue to thrive, but they can also be required to implement simple fixes that will protect our land, air and water from over-production and toxic waste.	Agri-business stands in opposition to the healthful production of food and a return to sustainable production methods that are good for consumers and the planet alike. Efforts should be made not only to reign in these businesses but also to do everything to supports small, organic growers.

Essay Task

Write a unified, coherent essay in which you evaluate multiple perspectives on the growth of agri-business. In your essay, be sure to:

- analyze and evaluate the perspectives given
- state and develop your own perspective on the issue
- explain the relationship between your perspective and those given

Your perspective may be in full agreement with any of the others, in partial agreement, or wholly different. Whatever the case, support your ideas with logical reasoning and detailed, persuasive examples.

In order to tackle these, it is best to follow our guidelines for all essays:

1. Read the prompt according to the Two T's. Once your know what it's about and its point,
   Agri-business is growing. That growth may be good or bad for the planet.

1ˢᵗ Ed. © ibidPREP llc

2. Come up with you own perspective on the topic. Although there will probably not be a direct question asked, you will still be asked to develop a point of view on the topic discussed. If you do not have a perspective on the topic, use one the perspectives offered and adapt it to your own needs.

    Agri-business has been great for production but is potentially very dangerous.

3. Discuss WHY you believe your perspective.

    The are many areas in the U.S. where ground water had been contaminated by uncontrolled run-off of fertilizer and animal waste. There are many simple fixes available, but the profit motive that controls all corporations makes agri-business stand in the way of any regulations no matter how mild and healthful.

4. Lay out your argument—Now easier than ever!

    a. Use the perspectives given—The new twist with these essays is that your body paragraphs are already lined up for you! Instead of having to tie each body paragraph to examples[1] of your devising, you may write each paragraph tied to discussing and assessing each perspective in light of your own opinion.

    Chances are two of the perspectives offered will agree with the other and the third will go off on its own. Read them closely and they'll lay out the road map for an argument for you!

    b. Organize the perspective given in an order that helps lay out your perspective best. For example:

    i.   Body Paragraph One—use the perspective that lays the groundwork for your perspective.

    ii. Body Paragraph Two—use the perspective that most supports your argument and will form the core of your essay.

    iii. Body Paragraph Three—use the perspective that most differs from your own and use it as a foil.

    Although some believe, ...

5. Conclude—Conclusions conclude. There is no need to get too fancy here.

    a. Re-state your WHY

    b. Sum up your argument and the points you've made to prove your WHY, and, if possible,

    c. Stress the implications of your WHY, beyond the scope of your essay.

Scoring

Scoring will be all new on the ACT Essay as well.

Instead of getting TWO overall scores of out of six each, you get four separate scores from 2-12 each on four separate writing categories.

The categories as defined by the ACT website [http://www.actstudent.org/writing/scores/guidelines.html] are:

Ideas and Analysis: Scores in this domain reflect the ability to generate productive ideas and engage critically with multiple perspectives on the given issue. Competent writers understand the issue they are invited to address, the purpose for writing, and the audience. They generate ideas that are relevant to the situation.

This means you will need to understand to THEME and THESIS of the prompt. You will need to address the point of the piece and its relevance to an audience in generating your own THESIS. It's not enough just to

[1] Examples are always great ways to support you perspective. Many students struggle to come up with specific examples [see box]; fortunately, the ACT is also fine with hypothetical examples [something young writers are more comfortable with].

restate the THEME, you must try to understand what the perspectives are trying to tell the reader about the significance of the topic.

Development and Support: *Scores in this domain reflect the ability to discuss ideas, offer rationale, and bolster an argument. Competent writers explain and explore their ideas, discuss implications, and illustrate through examples. They help the reader understand their thinking about the issue.*

Once you have come up with your own THESIS, you must develop a rationale for your THESIS [your WHY], and support it with examples, both specific and hypothetical, and clear reasoning.

Organization: *Scores in this domain reflect the ability to organize ideas with clarity and purpose. Organizational choices are integral to effective writing. Competent writers arrange their essay in a way that clearly shows the relationship between ideas, and they guide the reader through their discussion.*

Once you have developed a THESIS, a WHY, and established an argument to support them, organization reflects how well you lay out your argument through a cogent introduction, body paragraphs that build on one another and a conclusion that brings your point home as well as leads your reader to consider the greater implications of your point.

Language Use and Conventions: *Scores in this domain reflect the ability to use written language to convey arguments with clarity. Competent writers make use of the conventions of grammar, syntax, word usage, and mechanics. They are also aware of their audience and adjust the style and tone of their writing to communicate effectively.*

Here's where having learned to use grammar correctly comes into play. Your writing will be judged on your punctuation, word usage and how you put together sentences. You'll also be marked on your tone—whether you're able to avoid robot writing and address your audience as intelligent people you to wish to inform about your topic and your point of view and not as if they are your mommy and daddy, your idiot uncle or your warden.

Scoring The Essay

Once your scores in each of the four categories are determined, they are then added to give you a total score out of 48. That raw score is then scaled to a score of 36. This scaled score is then averaged with the scaled scores you received on the English and Reading Comprehension questions. That average is your ELA average and it is listed from your ACT average which excludes the essay and ONLY includes the scaled scores in the multiple choice sections: English, Math , Reading and Science.

Got that? No? Don't worry. Just write a good, solid essay and you'll be fine!

1ˢᵗ Ed. © ibidPREP llc

How To Write The Essay

Nuts & Bolts Procedure: The Essay

1. Read the question.
2. Think about question.
3. ANSWER THE QUESTION. That is, have an opinion!
4. Accept your opinion.
5. Make a list of things you were thinking about when you formed your opinion.
6. Use those examples WHETHER OR NOT you think they're "good" examples.
7. Start writing.
8. Leave time to REREAD YOUR STUFF!
9. REREAD YOUR STUFF!

ANSWER THE QUESTION

Most standardized essays set out to test your ability to prove a point, so the most important thing you need is **to have a point to make**. Having a point to make presupposes[2] having a thought in your head, an answer to a question about some aspect of the world around you.

So many students seem to have problems answering questions put to them in essays. I have generally found students' inability to answer a question is not because they are incapable of thought, but because, being teen-agers—those flickering wicks of blistering self-consciousness—they dismiss and disqualify their own thoughts as unsuitable or dumb.

Instead of thinking about their own opinions on these questions, most kids waste their time thinking:

> *Oh my god, I can't write about "X." That's not deep enough. And I can't write about "B" because "they" won't like it. I can't write about "C" because I don't know enough about it. Damn, I just can't think of any examples!!*

Of course in the "I can't think of any examples" scenario above, the student actually thought of three examples! He just couldn't ALLOW himself to use them. He disqualified all his ideas as he had them.

DON'T DO THAT!

No examples/proofs are perfect, so if you search for perfect examples you won't find them OR you'll wind up with examples so bland and generic that you're essay will read as if you didn't really have a thought in your head.

1. THINK ABOUT IT.
2. FORM AN OPINION.
3. THINK ABOUT WHY YOU HAVE THAT OPINION.
4. START MAKING YOUR POINT – AS YOU DO, GRAB ANYTHING THAT COMES TO MIND ON THE TOPIC AND USE IT. DON'T WORRY IF IT'S NOT PERFECT. [WHATEVER PART OF YOUR POINT ISN'T PERFECT, SHOW THAT YOU'RE AWARE OF THAT AND KEEP GOING ANYWAY!]

[2] assumes, supposes

The Essay

Here's what I mean by having a point [no matter how imperfect it might] and not having a point:

Question—Should the driving age be raised to 21?
Not an Answer—No, the driving should not be raised to 21 because it should stay at 16.
Also Not an Answer—The driving age should be raised to 21 because that would be better.
An Answer—The driving age should not be raised because I am really eager to drive!

You might think that the answer above is a bad answer because:

1. It used "I" in the answer.

   Using "I" in your essay is not horrible as long as you don't overuse "I". Try not to start every sentence with "I" or only talk about yourself.

   NO: *I think that the driving age should stay where it is because I think it would be better for me, and I've really been looking forward to starting driving soon.*

   It is generally better and stronger to make your point for a broader group than yourself

   YES: *Keeping the driving age younger would help more teenager become more responsible, more helpful and happier sooner.*

   But no worries if you start out personal!

2. It said what most teens probably actually think.

   Again, writing what you actually think is not bad—quite the opposite, it's terrific!—as long as you write your thoughts out well and give good reasons/examples:

Bad Writing—The driving age should not be raised because I am really eager to drive! I am really eager to drive because I really want to start driving, and the sooner the better.

Good Writing—The driving age should not be raised because I am really eager to drive! The sooner I start to drive, the sooner I start to become more independent, better able to help my family, and I'll be happier!

The above answer is personal, but it is supported with really good reasons. Even the third reason which is really honest is a perfectly fine reason to want something!

1ˢᵗ Ed. © ibidPREP llc

BEING HONEST IS OK!

FOR SOME REASON, HONESTY IS BEATEN OUT OF STUDENTS FROM THE BEGINNING OF THEIR EDUCATION. HAVING HONESTY REMOVED FROM WRITING MAKES IT THAT MUCH HARDER TO WRITE WELL; IT IS MUCH EASIER TO WRITE YOUR OPINIONS IF THEY ARE ACTUALLY YOUR OPINIONS. ANOTHER THING TO KEEP IN MIND IS THAT YOU'RE ALLOWED TO HAVE OPINIONS FOR SELFISH, PERSONAL, AND NON-GOODIE TWO-SHOES REASONS. YOU'RE EVEN ALLOWED TO HAVE NEGATIVE OR WHAT YOU MIGHT THINK ARE UNPOPULAR OPINIONS. THE ONLY THING THAT MATTERS IS THAT YOUR WRITE YOUR OPINIONS/THOUGHTS OUT WELL, BE RESPECTFUL AND MAKE GOOD POINTS TO SUPPORT THEM. WHO KNOWS? IF YOU WRITE YOUR OPINION WELL ENOUGH, YOU MIGHT EVEN CHANGE SOMEONE'S MIND—WHICH IS WHY ESSAY WRITING IS OFTEN CALLED "PERSUASIVE WRITING."

How to Write

Now that you know How to Answer AND How to Structure an essay question, let's learn How to Write!

Everything you write should have a beginning, middle and an end—from the shortest sentence to the longest essay. It all starts with the sentence.

Sentences

Every sentence must contain a verb and a subject. That's it!

I ran home.

In fact, with English sentences, the shorter the better. Some sentences may even have only one word. When the verb is a command, the subject is implied in the verb:

Stop! [It is implied that someone, YOU, should stop.]

The Essay

If, in your writing, you find yourself sticking together clause upon clause with lots of phrases sprinkled in your sentence, START ANOTHER SENTENCE. They're free!

NO: *I ran home, and then I got a drink of water because I was thirsty from running but the water was warm, so I spit it out!*
YES: *I ran home. When I got home, I got a drink of water. Unfortunately, the water was warm, so I spit it out!*

TREAT YOURSELF!

If when writing, you find yourself tacking together clause upon clause with lots of phrases sprinkled in your sentence, START ANOTHER SENTENCE. They're free!

Paragraphs

Paragraphs—the Beginning

We will deal with the essay later, but the first brick in the wall of the essay is the paragraph. The beginning of the paragraph may be called the TOPIC SENTENCE. This sentence usually connects to the previous paragraph (unless it's the first sentence of the first paragraph) and advances the essay (or story) to its next step. Here's an example:

Just as cotton was king in the South, manufacturing ruled the North.

After the TOPIC SENTENCE of a paragraph, the next sentence generally begins to explain the point of the TOPIC SENTENCE—we'll call it the POINT SENTENCE.

The Northern states did not have the best land for large-scale farming, but they did have many of the features needed to become strong manufacturing centers.

See? This second sentence explains and elaborates the TOPIC SENTENCE.

Paragraphs—The Middle

Now we're off to the races! Everything from here to the END of the paragraph is meant to provide specific examples to support the POINT SENTENCE.

Many of the Northern states had excellent harbors like New York and Boston harbors, which made it easier to sell their products. The Northern states also had larger city populations in which to find workers, such as those in New York, Boston and Philadelphia. Another common feature of the people of the Northern states was a strong belief in the value of work that came in part from their Puritan ancestors.

Paragraphs—The End

The thing to remember about all endings: conclusions conclude. The CONCLUDING SENTENCE should do what all endings do—wrap things up and leave us pointed toward the future.

1st Ed. © ibidPREP llc

All of these things made the North a strong manufacturing power and helped lead to the conflict of the Civil War.

All Together

Just as cotton was king in the South, manufacturing ruled the North. The Northern states did not have the best land for large-scale farming, but they did have many of the features needed to become strong manufacturing centers. Many of the Northern states had excellent harbors like New York and Boston harbors, which made it easier to sell their products. The Northern states also had larger city populations in which to find workers, such as those in New York, Boston and Philadelphia. Another common feature of the people of the Northern states was a deep belief in the value of work that came in part from their Puritan ancestors. All of these things made the North a strong manufacturing power and helped lead to the conflicts of the Civil War.

INTRODUCTION

Contrary to what you may have been taught, there are many ways to organize an introduction as long as you know where you're headed and what you're trying to achieve, and you let your reader know those things. Regardless of how you choose to bring your point to the reader, all intros, at some point, should drop the What/Why/How bomb. I.e. just like when you introduce yourself to someone you let them know who you are, why you're meeting them and how you're going to get to know them, the introduction to any essay should do the same:

Hi, I'm Stuart. I'm here to teach you about the ACT. I hope my instruction and stories will help you a lot with that!

WHAT I am:

- Hi, I'm Stuart.

WHY I'm here:

- I'm here to teach you about the ACT.

HOW I'm going to follow through:

- I hope my instruction and stories will help you a lot with that!

If I were introducing this book, I might write:

This book is ibidPREP's ACT book, Remain Clam! It will teach you about the ACT and how to be a better test taker. This book will review all the materials you need, tell you stories about test taking and give you practice, practice, practice.

What: the topic of your piece. This is your **THEME**.

- This book is ibidPREP's ACT book, Remain Clam!

Why: is why you're bothering to talk about them. This is your **THESIS**.

- It will teach you about the ACT and how to be a better test taker.

The Essay

How: is how you are going to set about proving your point. These are your examples/reasons.

- This books will review all the materials you need, tell you stories about test taking and give you practice, practice, practice.

You don't always have to come right out and state what your HOW is, but it certainly helps to know your HOW and to touch on it **lightly** for the reader.

Setting Up An Intro

Please read the following questions and write an introductory paragraph on the topic. You do not need to write an entire essay, just the WHAT/WHY/HOW.

Do you like school?

_____

_____

_____

_____

_____

_____

MAKING A POINT & HAVING AN OPINION

Please read the following question and develop an opinion on it. Decide what point you would make if you were writing an essay on the topic. Then explain your point on the lined paper provided.

Should teenagers be required to have at least two hours of screen-less time per day? That is, two hours without any computers, phones or tv sets on in front of them?

_____

_____

_____

_____

1ˢᵗ Ed. © ibidPREP llc

_____

_____

_____

_____

_____

HOW TO EDIT [THE SOUL OF WRITING!]

Many students look at writing essays the way most people would look at swimming through a lake of acid without goggles: the sooner they can get to the other side, the better.

Here's the problem, though. Writing an essay is actually more like cooking a delicious meal, which you are going to serve up to a panel of judges (readers) who will taste it and say things like "I loved the presentation!" and "It's so interesting what you did with the quail egg here!" You get the idea. So, think about it. Would you serve up a dish to that panel without first tasting it yourself? We hope not! So remember, on the essay, save a little time to TASTE YOUR ESSAY. What are you looking for?

First, do your paragraphs and sentences have clear beginnings, middles and ends?

Do your ideas build upon and flow into each other?

Are you repeating yourself and being repetitive and redundant, like this sentence?

BUILD AND FOLLOW

As the cars of a train go, so do your ideas. Each must **follow** the one before it. (See below.)

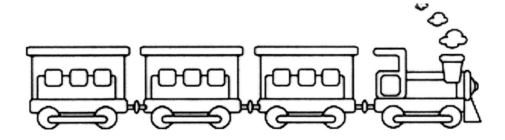

It does not **crash** into the idea ahead of it, nor does it **disconnect** from the one before it. (See below.)

Think of your sentences as being made of two parts, a first idea and a second idea. As you write, the second idea of your previous sentence becomes the first idea of the next sentence, and so on. This way, like the cars of a train, your ideas build upon and follow each other. By connecting sentences in this way, you ensure that you are not confusing (or boring) your reader (or accidentally hitting them with your crashing essay train).

Here's how this might work:

- The **man** went to the **store.**
  - The **store** was **crowded.**
    - **Crowds** had formed because a **storm** was coming.
      - **The storm was going to be bad.**
        - **Because it was going to be so bad, everyone went to the store to stock up.**
          - **Try writing something this way, and then go read one of the proofreading paragraphs (p. 110). It helps!**

Segues

Nope, not those weird people-mover things you see all over Washington, D.C., and other touristy towns. We mean the **words that connect** your ideas. Don't just start your sentences with "One example is..." and "Another example is..." [although that's better than just starting to talk about things out of the blue].

NO:
Paragraph 1: One example of why I like hot dogs is how juicy they can be.
Paragraph 2: Another example of why I like how dogs is how hot they can be.

NO:
Paragraph 1: Hot dogs are good because they are juicy.
Paragraph 2: Pretzels are good because they are salty.

YES:
Paragraph 1: Hot dogs are appealing for many reasons especially how juicy they can be.
Paragraph 2: Hot dogs are not just delicious because they are juicy, they also pack a salty crunch.

YES:
Paragraph 1: As much as hot dogs are maligned for being fatty and not nutritious, we all know they're delicious.
Paragraph 2: Just as hot dogs have a bad rep, pretzels also are put down for being too salty and fattening, but who cares? They are also a delicious treat.

As you see from our "YES" examples, you may use your intro sentence to sum up what's come before AND to

1ˢᵗ Ed. © ibidPREP llc

propel your argument to your next example. You may also use it to differentiate your examples.

Some Useful Segues...

Because	Therefore	Although	While	Similarly	Furthermore
Thus	As a result	However	First of all	Consequently	Alternatively

Essay Structure Summary

Please remember to try to keep things simple. Don't worry so much about the number of paragraphs or the number of sentences in your paragraph as about having a strong introduction, body and conclusion.

Here's basically what they all should contain.

Intro:

Just as it is important to make a good impression when you are introducing yourself to someone, it is very important to start your essays with a strong introduction. Please try to be clear and direct and make your points efficiently in your intro. Here's what is good to include:

- State your opinion on the topic:
  - *My elementary school dance was one of the most special events of my life.*
- Tell us why you have that opinion:
  - *The dance was so special because of my friends.*
- Specify:
  - *I got to spend time with old friends, especially my best friend.*
  - *I was also happy to make new friends*

Body:

Discuss each specific example in its own paragraph [or combine as needed].

1. My old friends [made me happy at the dance because...]
2. My best friend [made me happy at the dance because...]
3. My new friends [made me happy at the dance because...]

Conclusion:

Conclusions Conclude

No matter what you read or write on these tests, the last paragraph or lines are going to act like last lines and paragraphs. They are going to wrap up, however slightly, what has just been said, and draw a conclusion, however simple, from what came before. Once you have done that, you may point to the future.

Meeting new friends makes the dance special. Old and new friends alike come together for that great night. I look forward to the future evenings full of dancing and friends.

How To Be Your Own Editor

First, learn to read formally and for logic. This means read your own work word-for-word and make sure it connects on the page—not just in your head. One good way to connect sentences and thoughts is through something called normative and control.

Normative and control[3] is just a fancy way of saying subject and predicate which is just a fancy way of saying first part of the sentence/second part of the sentence. If you think of most sentences as being made of two parts, a subject and a predicate, a great way to connect the sentences is, as you go, to make the predicate of your first sentence the subject of your second. Then the predicate of your second sentence becomes the subject of your third and so on. By connecting sentences in this way, you ensure that you are not confusing your reader by referring backward or forward to subjects obliquely[4] mentioned elsewhere if at all. Remember no one—not even your mommy and daddy—are really inside your minds, so you HAVE TO BE CLEAR ABOUT WHAT IT IS YOU WANT TO SAY.

Connecting sentences in using normative and control way is also a great way to tell a story—and, in a way, even the driest essay in the world is a story of sorts, the story of your thought process.

Try reading the paragraph below. If you think sentences are out of order [hint: they are], try to reorder them using normative and control. Put them in number order, then check with the answer on the next page.

BEING HONEST IS OK!

[1] Having honesty removed from writing makes it that much harder to write well; it is much easier to write your opinions if they are actually YOUR opinions. [2/3] Who knows? If you write your opinion well enough, you might even change someone's mind—which is why essay writing is often called "persuasive writing." [4] For some reason, honesty is beaten out of students from the beginning of their education. [5] The only thing that matters is that your write your opinions/thoughts out well, be respectful and make good points to support them. [6] Another thing to keep in mind is that you're allowed to have opinions for selfish, personal, and non-goodie two-shoes reasons. [7] You're even allowed to have negative or what you might think are unpopular opinions.

Correct order for **BEING HONEST IS OK** paragraph : 4, 1, 6, 7, 5, 2/3

Now let's try to write a paragraph connecting all the nouns below in the same way. It might actually be fun! I'll go first. Let's start with a random list of nouns:

Boat/bird/breakfast/balloons.

> *The old Captain's boat dropped anchor in a cove filled with birds of all types. The birds flew to the deck of the boat as the Captain tucked in for breakfast. The Captain's breakfast table was set with salty fish and other seafood tidbits he'd caught; the birds drifted away with the tidbits like balloons cut loose from a fair.*

Now it's your turn.

---

[3] DO NOT be afraid of fancy terms. Any good writing will explain them a second after you see them.
[4] indirectly, not clearly, circularly

1st Ed. © ibidPREP llc

Captain/coffee/crows/crowns

_____

_____

_____

_____

_____

_____

_____

Now write a paragraph telling us about your dinner last night.

_____

_____

_____

_____

_____

_____

_____

_____

Now write a paragraph about your thoughts on texting in school.

_____

_____

_____

_____

_____

_____

_____

EVERYTHING YOU LEARNED ABOUT WRITING IS WRONG

For some odd reason, most students only remember having been taught two things about writing, and they're both wrong.

1. You can use I in your essay. It's not the greatest way to write something or the most necessary, but there are sometimes when there's no way around it, so just do it:

    - OK:
        During my trip to Florence, I learned just how vital creativity is to education.
    - GOOD:
        Just last year, I didn't understand the importance of creativity, but since my trip to Florence, I have begun to get it.
    - BETTER:
        The artistic wonders of Florence show just how vital creativity is to education.

    Often, however, using "I" is just weak writing. There's no reason to say "I think" in an essay because everyone knows that an essay is all about what you think!

    - NO:
        I think that studying creativity is a vital part of our education
    - YES:
        Studying creativity is vital to education.

2. You can start a sentence with because:

    PERFECTLY FINE: Because learning about creativity improves the mind in all directions, study of the arts is vital.

1st Ed. © ibidPREP llc

Teachers probably tell you not to start sentences with "because" because they get tired of seeing it at the beginning of EVERY sentence. So go easy, you don't want to end up sounding like that song from *The Wizard of Oz*,

Because, because, because, because, because of the wonderful things he does.

One thing to be aware of when you're using "because" inside a sentence: it's NOT a conjunction, so don't put a comma in front of it.

- NO:
    I really like hot dogs and pretzels, because they are salty and delicious.
- YES:
    I really like hot dogs and pretzels because they are salty and delicious.

Stop Repeating Yourself, Stop Saying The Same Things Over And Over, & Don't Be So Repetitive...

What makes English such a fabulous language in which to communicate [and American English especially] is that it favors conciseness[5] and clarity. You can get to the point really quickly. When you re-read your work, be alert for any sentences that do not progress your argument at all. As discussed above, as you build your sentences through normative and control, you want each sentence to move forward from the previous one. Even if that progress is only a centimeter or so. **Zero sentences** are those many students are so fond of; they simply restate the previous sentence. Students usually resort to zero sentences in order to fill space, or because they can't think of anything else to say. If you are repeating yourself to fill space, stop it—your readers aren't idiots; they will notice and tune out. If you are repeating yourself because you can't think of what to say next, look to the end of your last sentence. For example:

Sentence 1.
Computers are really important in life today.

Sentence 2.
- NO—
Sentence 2.
Zero sentence
    Not only are they important, but they mean a lot to people.

- YES—
Sentence 2
Progressing Sentence; Building on back of Sentence 1:
    They play a vital role in most people's daily work, play and social lives.

OR

Sentence 1.
Macbeth killed in order to get ahead.

- NO—
Sentence 2.
Zero sentence
    So he killed as a result of his ambition.

---

[5] succinctness, getting to the point, shortness, brevity

- YES—

Sentence 2.
Progressing Sentence
This ambition led Macbeth to his own destruction.

CZECH VS. ENGLISH

It is important to remember that not every language puts a high value on economy of words. Some value formal structures and niceties over getting to the point.

When I lived in Prague, I had a great apartment in the center of town and a great landlady who didn't speak a word of English. My friend Jan came by to translate whenever she and I had anything important to discuss that we couldn't communicate with hand gestures and my few words of Czech.

One day I asked him to ask her if she could find someone to clean the apartment for me [it was pretty bad]. After making some small talk, he repeated the question. It took him slightly longer to ask in Czech than it had taken me in English because Czech, I was discovering, is one of those languages that is far more formal than English and nowhere near as direct. Then she answered him.

Her reply and their back and forth conversation about it took about five minutes. Finally, very curious [I thought I must have offended her or something], I asked, "What did she say?"

Without taking a second to interpret, he replied, "She said 'Yes.'"

The Over-Read

Here is the hardest thing for young writers to learn, remember, think, motivate, push to do: REREAD THEIR OWN STUFF.

Remember: If you want someone else to read your stuff, you have to be considerate enough to read it first.

Once you have finished your piece, make sure you have left yourself 3-5 minutes in which to read it over. When you read it over, you are no longer the writer of the piece or even an interested reader, you are the editor, and you are reading for two things.
   1. Does this essay make and prove a point?
   2. Does it read correctly and well formally?

The reason I have not done more writing in my life is that I always took very seriously my 12th grade teacher's edict[6] about the heart of writing being re-writing. And re-writing is a pain. It would be nice if we could just blurt out our thoughts [as we are taught to do] and then give them to Mommy or a ghostwriter or a hands-on editor. Unfortunately, for most of your school and work lives, you will have to learn to be your own editor. Although it's always great to have a friend or significant other to bounce your work off, when the paper/report is due at 7am the next day, and you're still writing at 5am—you're on your own!

Does This Essay Make And Prove A Point?

Reread your intro first [makes sense as it is first]. Does it lay out your What, Why, and How? Then check your

---

[6] rule, order, law

1st Ed. © ibidPREP llc

other body paragraphs. Do they connect and propel your argument? If they don't, at the very least, shore up[7] your transition sentences [first and last in paragraphs].

Does It Read Correctly And Well Formally?

As you read your essay, pay particular attention to your pronouns, especially in the introduction and conclusion when you might be writing more generally. In those sections, there is often a tendency to slide pronouns from one to they to he and back. One great way to show command [definitely one of the criteria evaluators are looking for] is to be consistent in your use of pronouns AND use them correctly. It is one of those inconsistencies of the English language that test makers love to pounce on, but singular pronouns such as everyone, no one, none, one—all take singular pronouns in their predicates. That means if you want to write:

Everyone knows _____ must learn how to write better.

the pronoun in the blank must be he or she or he or she or it, but NOT they. No matter how much sense they makes [it maintains gender neutrality for everyone and is so much less clumsy], everyone is singular and so must be the pronoun that is renaming it. If you catch this in your writing, it will signal serious grammar chops!

---

[7] strengthen, support

Essay Process: Structure and Tips

1. Read the topic.
2. Think about the topic.
   a. Ask yourself what it really means.
   b. Cast about your mind for anything (historical, literary, personal—anything that makes your point) that has to do with the topic. It is not important whether it seems like a positive or negative example—just be **specific.**
3. Based on your examples, decide which point will be either easier or more interesting to make. Remember, <u>**any**</u> example can be used to make any point of view. You don't have to be "right" as long as you are consistent. Your examples don't necessarily have to be from literature or history, but they do have to be on point. Personal anecdotes should be used sparingly.
4. Begin writing:
   a. Intro Paragraph:
      i. [Sentence 1] <u>**WHAT**</u> YOU BELIEVE—Your opinion of the topic. It is not necessary to say "I believe...." You can just make a statement: *It is not true that...*
      ii. [Sentence 2] <u>**WHY**</u> YOU BELIEVE IT— *It is not true **because...***
      iii. [Sentence 3] <u>**HOW**</u> YOU WILL SET ABOUT PROVING YOUR WHY. *History and literature have clearly shown topic to be false....*
      iv. [Sentence 4] Introduce your examples. *The lessons of **WWII** and **Macbeth** provide clear examples of where history and literature prove topic false....*
   b. Paragraph 2—Example 1
      i. Example 1 proves that topic is false because...
      ii. Specific Example "A" from text or incident.
      iii. Specific Example "B" from text or incident.
      iv. *As shown in Specific Example "A" and "B," Example 1 proves topic false.*
   c. Paragraph 3 — Example 2
      i. Connect to Example 2 and then show how it further proves point....
      ii. Specific Example "A" from text or incident.
      iii. Specific Example "B" from text or incident.
      iv. *As shown in Specific Example "A" and "B," Example 2 proves topic false.*
   d. Paragraph 3a— Example 3 [if you have a good third example and time, use it. If not, just mention it as additional proof in conclusion along with any other possible examples you might have].
   e. Paragraph 4—Conclusion
      i. *As shown above through history and literature, the topic is obviously false.*
      ii. *It is obviously false because of the "because" stated above* [Paragraph 1, Sentence 2] *and proved with the examples above.*
      iii. *Although some may say it is true because of **"some contrary reason,"** this reason only serves to make topic even more false because **"some reason of your own to contradict the contrary."***
5. **Reread** what you've written.
   a. Make sure there are no blatant grammatical errors.
   b. Make sure that the essay is reasonably legible.

   c. Make sure that paragraphs are clearly delineated.

1st Ed. © ibidPREP llc

ROBOT WRITING

- ONE EXAMPLE OF THIS IS, ...
  - ANOTHER EXAMPLE OF THIS IS,.....
    - A THIRD EXAMPLE OF THIS IS,...
      - THIS IS TRUE BECAUSE...
        - I THINK THIS BECAUSE...
          - IN MY OPINION,...
            - ◊ I AM A ROBOT...

YOU MAY BE TAUGHT TO WRITE THIS WAY IN SCHOOL. OR, YOU MAY THINK YOU'VE BEEN TAUGHT TO WRITE THIS WAY. OR, YOU MAY THINK YOU NEED TO WRITE THIS WAY. YOU DON'T.

TELLING YOUR READER "I THINK," OR "THIS IS AN EXAMPLE," IS A VERY STIFF, MECHANICAL WAY TO WRITE. WHEN YOU WRITE AN ESSAY, YOUR READER KNOWS IT'S YOUR OPINION, SO JUST START TELLING US IT! ALSO, THERE IS NO NEED TO TELL US THAT YOU'RE GOING TO TELL US AN EXAMPLE, JUST TELL US THE EXAMPLE AND WHAT IT DEMONSTRATES.

<u>NO</u>:

IT IS MY OPINION THAT KILLING IS BAD. ONE EXAMPLE OF THIS IS WHEN A YOU KILL A PERSON BECAUSE THEY MAKE YOU ANGRY. ANOTHER EXAMPLE OF THIS IS WHEN PEOPLE ARE KILLED BECAUSE OF WHAT THEY BELIEVE.

THAT IS MY OPINION.

<u>YES</u>:

KILLING IS BAD. IT'S ESPECIALLY BAD TO KILL PEOPLE JUST BECAUSE THEY MAKE YOU ANGRY. IT'S EVEN WORSE TO KILL PEOPLE BECAUSE OF WHAT THEY BELIEVE. KILLING IS NEVER GOOD, BUT IT IS WORSE WHEN DONE OUT OF ANGER OR JUST BECAUSE SOMEONE DISAGREES WITH YOU. NO FEAR!

FEAR IS WORTHLESS.

FEAR IS WORSE THAN WORTHLESS COME GAME DAY. COME GAME DAY, YOU KNOW WHAT YOU KNOW AND YOU DO YOUR BEST. IF YOU ARE AFRAID, YOU GET TIGHT. IF YOU GET TIGHT, YOU'RE UNABLE TO FUNCTION NATURALLY AND ACCESS THE KNOWLEDGE AND SKILLS YOU'VE WORKED SO HARD TO INGRAIN IN YOUR BRAIN.

SO TAKE EACH QUESTION AS IT COMES, TAKE YOUR BEST SHOT AT IT AND, IF YOU HAVE ANY DOUBT, SHRUG IT OFF AND MOVE ON. YOU ARE THE DESTROYER, THE PUNISHER, THE MASTER TEST-TAKER, AND THAT'S WHAT MASTER TEST-TAKERS DO: TAKE THEIR BEST SHOT ON EVERY QUESTION AND THEN MOVE ON.

NO FEAR!

1st Ed. © *ibidPREP llc*

HOW TO AVOID EXAMICIDE

PART III—TAKING THE TEST: BEFORE & AFTER

1. EVERYONE LIES ABOUT HER SCORES—

Keep in mind: no matter how well you do on your tests [unless you score perfectly], it will always seem like everyone else has done better. Things will seem this way for two very good reasons:

Kids who do well on their tests are much more likely to talk about their scores than kids who don't.

Also, kids who don't score well on their tests are much more likely to lie about their scores.

2. IF YOU RUN INTO PEOPLE YOU KNOW BEFORE YOU TAKE YOUR TEST, DO NOT TALK TO THEM!

The only motive other students have in speaking to you right before a test is to give you some of their anxiety. How much your friends love and support you doesn't matter; everyone is in survival mode, and everyone is just trying to unload anxiety as quickly and easily as possible. Short of throwing up, making other people nervous seems to help best. So kids will tell other kids things like "Did you hear there might be Roman Numerals on this test?" or "Did you hear that there might be poetry in the Reading Comprehension this year?" all in the hopes of seeing that burst of fear in their best friends' eyes. It doesn't even matter that you tell yourself they're full of baloney—it's too late—you just got a dose of their anxiety right into your veins. In order to avoid this happening, smile and wave to your friends and acquaintances before a test, but DO NOT engage them in conversation. Talk to them AFTER the test.

1st Ed. © ibidPREP llc

HOW TO AVOID EXAMICIDE

3. THE TODDLER & THE THRESHOLD

When my sons were just starting to walk, their balance was incredibly precarious. They toddled down our hallways, perilously[42] swaying from foot to foot until they reached the threshold to the living room. Invariably, stepping on and over that tiny threshold was, for them, akin to climbing Mount Kilimanjaro. That little bump would upset their tentative[43] balance, and they'd come crashing down on their diapered rears.

While you're taking the test, if you hit a bump, you must be more resilient than a toddler, if only because you have no diapered butt to fall on. If you see a new kind of math problem or there's a reading passage the meaning of which completely eludes you, DON'T FREAK. Just take your best shot at it:

- ELIMINATE bad answers,
- GUESS, and then
- MOVE ON and FORGET ABOUT THAT PROBLEM!

Don't let one tough question ruin the rest of the test—put it out of your mind.

---

[42] dangerously
[43] uncertain, faltering

1st Ed. © ibidPREP llc

CHAPTER SEVEN

GAME DAY

1ˢᵗ Ed. © ibidPREP llc

Ok—You've Earned It {At Last!}: Studatuta's Guide To Guessing

How To Guess

As I've gotten older and crankier, I have become less interested in teaching kids how to guess because, for the most part, it's really much more productive for me to spend my time teaching them how not to **have** to guess.

However, in spite of everyone's best efforts, sometimes there are those questions that we just can't figure out. In those situations, we need to grab our guts and guess! Below is a summary of some of the ideas I have touched upon throughout this book and a few new ideas on how to guess and how not to guess.

Ten Steps To Better Guesses

These guidelines are not always right, nor are they meant to overrule any answers you may have figured out on your own. These are just some ideas of what to do if you have no idea what to do!

1. In math: **Close is Wrong**! Unless you are rounding to begin with, if you get an answer, and your answer isn't among the answer choices, DON'T guess the number that's closest to your answer. Pick any other number.
2. In math: On a hard problem that you don't know how to solve, do not just guess the answer that turns out to be the sum or product of the numbers in the question. **Don't "just" do anything**.
3. In vocab: **Close is Wrong**! If you're trying to figure out the meaning of a word, don't guess its meaning because it sorta looks like another word. Guess anything but that!
4. In reading comprehension:
    a. **Guess the answer that is most wishy-washy**—contains words like "generally," "usually," and "often." (ACT test writers don't like to commit to extremes and absolutes, so the correct answer will often contain a lot of qualifying statements and adverbs.)
    b. In reading comprehension: **Avoid absolutes**! Avoid answer choices that contain words like "always," "never," "all," "none,"...
5. In reading comprehension: **Don't guess the answer that has a lot of words lifted directly from the passage in it.**
6. In general: **If you are a lousy guesser, figure out what your guess would be normally and then pick something else.**
7. In general: **Don't plan to "come back later."** Guess right away, but put a little "g" next to the questions you guess on [in your test book, not your answer sheet]. That way, you can always go back.
8. In general: **Do not waste time guessing**. Instead of "thinking" about your guess, flip a coin in your head, pick that answer and MOVE ON!
9. In general: **Guessing should be fun** [about as fun as anything ever is on these tests]. Don't overthink it; just relax and pick the right one!
10. In essays: Even if you're not clear on a part of your essay, theme, thesis or text, be sure to write a fully structured essay [intro, body, conclusion], NO MATTER WHAT!

When In Doubt, <u>Don't</u> Choose "C"?

That ship may have sailed a while ago. Statistically, whatever edge "C" used to have, it's gone now. It's probably been gone since the big test prep companies started saying it! Mostly, because the test makers heard them too!

WHEN "E" OR "D" IS OK!

For some questions, like the grammar on the ACT on SAT, there is an option to pick "E" ["A" on the ACT] which is basically like none of the above [or "no change" or "correct as is"]. It is really scary for some people to pick this, so instead they hunt for something wrong until nothing seems right. Yeeeesh. Here's the rule of thumb for these kind of "E's": if you've checked through the sentence [let's say] and the verbs, pronouns, prepositions, numbers and usages all check out, then "E" is ABSOLUTELY FINE. Or, you have tested out all types of numbers, and you have come up with more than one answer. In either case, trust yourself and move on!

WHEN "E" IS NOT OK!

On really hard math questions, they will sometimes offer you the "none of the above" or "not enough information given to solve the problem" option. This option makes some students crazy. Here's the rule of thumb for these questions: If the math on these problems seems really, really hard: DO NOT PICK "E." Most times, students see these hard problems and reinterpret "E" to mean "cannot be determined by me!" It does not. The only time you get to pick "E" is if you've gotten more than one answer. [SEE TRY DIFFERENT NUMBERS] OR: Sometimes late in a section, you'll get an "E" question for which you get an answer REALLY quickly [too quickly]. In which case, I'll bet you dollars to donuts that the answer **will be** "E" because there is one type of number or one case you've forgotten to try, which would give you a different answer and therefore, the answer is "E." In grammar questions, if it's late in the game and it seems like no error, pick anything but "E." If the sentence is awkward and stilted and SOUNDS wrong but you can't pin anything down, it probably IS "E."

"E" IS OK ON READING COMP

For some reason, as students read down the multiple choices in the reading comp, they get progressively more nervous and lose confidence as each choice fails to be their answer. Some get so nervous that they end up picking "B" or "C" just to wrap things up. [There's even a type of student who grabs "A" any time it looks remotely reasonable].

Here's the rule: If your answer hasn't shown up by "C" or "D," KEEP READING!

There is no law against the answer being the last choice. If you're really too nervous to avoid this, perhaps read the answers in a different order [D,C,B,A or A,E,B,D,C or ...]. It's important that you get to "E" because the test makers do frontload wrong answers precisely because they know students will often prematurely grab the wrong choices.

 1ˢᵗ Ed. © ibidPREP llc

Don't Change Your Game

So you've remembered to bring your ID [if necessary], your pencil and your calculator. You've shown up at the right test center, found your room, and now at last you're ready to take your test. Remember: play exactly the same way you've practiced. DO NOT change your game just because "now it's real!" If you've learned anything through this book, it's that we always apply ourselves equally well whether we are doing a simple exercise or taking the ACT for the final time in your high school career. You've learned that doing better isn't about some Tiger Mom Schmiger Mom b.s. or about trying so hard that your brain pops and your personality falls out. You've learned that doing better on this and all tests and in all your learning is about slowing down and allowing yourself to think and process; it involves keeping all the extraneous thoughts, fears and rumors out of your mind and seeing exactly what's in front of you. This power will enable you to follow directions, read through difficult texts and ace your friggin' tests.

It's Not Roulette!! [And Roulette Isn't Roulette]

If you've ever been to a casino [and if you have, I don't want to know about it], you might remember that next to most roulette wheels are LED displays that list the last dozen or so prior winning numbers from that table. They might as well give you the last twelve winning numbers from the roulette wheel three tables away or from a casino down the street. Prior results HAVE NO STATISTICAL EFFECT on future results. The odds are exactly the same for getting three 5's in a row as they are for getting 3, 4, 5 or ANY RANDOM COMBINATION OF NUMBERS.

So: DO NOT WASTE ANY TIME LOOKING AT YOUR PREVIOUS ANSWERS AND USING THEM AS A GUIDE FOR YOUR NEXT ANSWER. DO NOT LOOK FOR PATTERNS OR TRY TO FIGURE OUT WHAT THE TEST MAKERS WERE UP TO. Doing so is a waste of precious time and brainpower.

For example:

You've just answered three questions, and they were all "D." On your next question, the answer you want to pick is ALSO "D." You freak out and decide something must be wrong—there can't be that many "D's"—so you talk yourself out of the fourth "D." The only problem here is, even if it were impossible to have five "D's" in a row, how do you know which is the wrong "D"? Kid logic always seems to have it that the last "D" must be wrong. It absolutely does not have to be.

WHEN I WAS WISE

I GOT TO THE TURNSTILES. MY TRAIN WAS ALREADY IN THE STATION, DOORS OPEN. I TOOK OUT MY WALLET TO GET MY METROCARD, BUT IT WASN'T IN ITS USUAL PLACE. FOR SOME REASON, I DID NOT RIFLE THROUGH MY WALLET LIKE A MADMAN AS I WOULD HAVE DONE THE OTHER 99% OF THE TIME. INSTEAD I SAID TO MYSELF, "THE TRAIN IS ALREADY GONE. PUT IT OUT OF YOUR MIND. WHAT IS THE MOST EFFICIENT WAY TO FIND THE CARD?" WITH A WEIRD POISE, I STOPPED, TOOK THE BUSINESS AND CREDIT CARDS OUT OF MY WALLET AND SYSTEMATICALLY FLIPPED THROUGH THEM. IN SECONDS, I FOUND THE METROCARD, SLID IT THROUGH THE TURNSTILE AND GOT ON THE TRAIN!

Test Taking And Time— More Thoughts!

WHEN I WAS NOT SO WISE

I TOOK THE WRONG SUBWAY LINE TO MEET A FRIEND IN LOWER MANHATTAN. THE STOP I ENDED UP GETTING OFF AT WAS NOT FAR FROM MY DESTINATION, BUT LOWER MANHATTAN IS FULL OF TINY, WINDING STREETS. I WAS ALREADY RUNNING LATE, SO I RUSHED OUT OF THE SUBWAY. AT THE EXIT WAS A LARGE YOU ARE HERE MAP OF THE NEIGHBORHOOD. I PAUSED FOR A NANOSECOND AND THOUGHT ABOUT STUDYING THE MAP. MY UN-CLAM MIND SHOUTED, "YOU DON'T HAVE TIME TO READ THE MAP!!" SO I DIDN'T.

OF COURSE, I GOT LOST. INSTEAD OF TAKING ONE MINUTE TO READ THE MAP AND ENDING UP MAYBE FIVE MINUTES LATE, I RUSHED AND ENDED UP TWENTY MINUTES LATE!

Subway Stories

1st Ed. © ibidPREP llc

THE LETTER: HERE'S WHAT I SEND TO ALL MY STUDENTS BEFORE THEIR TESTS. NOW I'M SENDING IT TO YOU.

To all my geniuses:

Congratulations on all your hard work and good thinking in the run-up to your test. You have prepped well, and now you're ready for the real thing. I just wanted to write you with a few things to be aware of come test day and the night before:

1. The night before, please relax. It is not the time to try to learn or review anything. Before dinner you might want to review your **MUST KNOW** rules, formulas, terms and words, but then: have some pizza, watch a movie and go to bed at a decent hour [but not so early that you end up tossing and turning in bed].

2. Game Day: Please arrive on time (or even early), and make sure you have with you:
   a. Photo ID/Test Ticket
   b. Pencils
   c. Calculator
   d. Snack
   e. Watch--You can't use your phone, and you can't trust your proctors to not be on theirs. Be your own proctor!
   f. Brain

3. If you see friends before your test, try not to speak with them too much. As much as your friends love you, they will mostly be looking to offload anxiety onto you. No one needs more anxiety.

4. Walk into the testing center like you own the joint. Float above everyone's anxiety. Whatever silly, annoying questions kids are fretting about, DO NOT ENGAGE. Everything will be sorted out, and you will be in your seat shortly.

5. If your proctor is a bit unreliable, rely on yourself. Keep track of time yourself and don't overreact to any errors said proctor may make. [see 2.e.]

6. Remember—Don't change what you've been doing! If your test seems different from those you have been practicing on, it's probably nerves. You have been working from real tests, and these things never vary that much! If something is different, it's different for everyone. Just keep going until you start to feel comfortable. If an early question seems hard, it does not mean that all the others ones will be harder; sometimes it's just difficult to get going. Try reading through the example problem or math formulas at the beginning of the section to get your head in the game. And remember: DON'T REACH FOR YOUR CALCULATOR FIRST--REACH FOR YOUR BRAIN!!

7. And also remember: It doesn't matter if you hit a bumpy patch—it matters how you respond to it!
   a. Guess and Don't Obsess.
   b. Forget about it
   c. Move on, because—
   d. All the questions afterwards are far more important!

8. You have practiced. You know the test...Now go out there, stick to your game plan and ace the test!!!

   Best,

   Studatuta

OUTRO

When I started tutoring, I was just a few years older than my students. I was a fine, if rough, writer and painter, and a wildly undisciplined and fairly indifferent math student. Now, I am more often than not a few years older than my students' parents, a somewhat more polished writer and artist, and a really excellent basic math kind of guy. In spite of what everyone likes to yammer about "Kids nowadays," I can honestly say that kids are the same. Mostly, as far as I can tell, only the nature of distractions has changed. It used to be more sex, drugs, and rock and roll; now it's more iPhones, Xbox and beer. Otherwise, the song remains the same: some students are engaged, some are checked out, some are only interested in hanging out. For many, education is something you get through or at best a means to an end. For others, it's a job: a responsibility you tend to during the day and evenings, and nothing more. In my experience, the rarest creature of all is the engaged student.

The engaged student is interested in the material either because she finds it interesting or because it might be interesting. The engaged student doesn't decide this is boring or that is boring or that isn't me. The engaged student samples everything, gives it a fair shake and moves on or not. The engaged student doesn't just learn stuff for a test and then do a memory dump the next day. The engaged student actually learns stuff.

As much as this book has been an appeal to students to REMAIN CLAM! on their tests, it has also [not so secretly] been an appeal to students to engage: to face the work in front of them head on and not spend all their time trying to find a way around it. I hope this book has inspired students to read in depth and write out and complete equations, to admit when they don't know something and figure it out or look it up or ask someone, to show enough care in their own writing at least to re-read the stuff they expect others to read!

The payoff for all this engagement is more than just a guarantee of marvelous scores on your tests; it is also a great way to learn how to use your mind—now and beyond these tests. So, by all means:

Engage!! [and REMAIN CLAM!]

1ˢᵗ Ed. © ibidPREP llc

APPENDIX A

GRAMMAR IN ONE PAGE

1ˢᵗ Ed. © ibidPREP llc

NOUN: person, place, thing, idea - **VERB**: action word - **ADJECTIVE**: word that describes a noun
ADVERB: describes verbs, adjectives and adverbs - Feeling verbs and the verb "to be" do not take adverbs
PRONOUN: takes the place of a noun

Subject Pronouns:		Object Pronouns:*	
I	We	Me	Us
You	You	You	You
He/She/It/Who	They	Him/Her/It/Whom	Them

An exception to the subject/object pronoun rule involves comparisons. - I am cooler than he/him.
In a comparison, always look for the word "than." Both nouns are subject nouns.

PREPOSITIONS: words that describe relationship between subject and object (usually place)—THERE ARE MANY WORDS THAT CAN BE USED AS PREPOSITIONS, BUT THESE ARE THE MOST COMMON ONES:

About	Below	From	Through
Above	Beneath	In	To
Across	Beside	Inside	Toward
After	Between	Into	Under
Against	Beyond	Like	Until
Along	By	Near	Up
Among	Down	Of	Upon
Around	During	Off	With
At	Except	On	Within
Before	For	Over	Without
Behind		Since	

PHRASE: group of words that does not possess subject or verb.

PREPOSITIONAL PHRASE: Preposition + Object

A Prepositional Phrase NEVER Contains THE SUBJECT

Each of the boys is/are tired.

CLAUSE: Group of words that contains a subject and a verb
   a. **Dependent Clause**—Cannot stand alone. When a sentence begins with a dependent clause, it [or long modifying phrase] is set off by a comma:
"Waking up this morning, I heard the telephone ring."
Immediately following the comma, the independent clause must start with the implied subject of the dependent clause.
   b. **Independent Clause**—Can stand alone. Must restate the implied subject of the dependent clause.

COMMAS: In addition to separating dependent clauses at the start of sentences, commas—
   a. separate items in a list of nouns or action—
      The hats, coats and scarves were in a pile on the bed.
      After school I like to change clothes, eat a snack and draw stuff.
   b. separate independent clauses when linked by conjunctions—
      I like cake, and I like beer. OR I like cake, but I hate pudding.
[When two independent clauses are in the same sentence and are not linked by a conjunction, the independent clauses are linked by semicolons—Stuart loves cake; he must weigh 290 pounds.]
c. set off appositive [descriptive] phrases within or at the end of sentences—
      There's nothing better than sleep-away camp, which is usually a bug-infested swamp of adolescent and pre-ad-olescent angst.
      My brother, by the way, is an idiot.
Fewer/more – fewer = countable things, e.g., French fries/ more = not countable, e.g., wind
Between/among – better/best == both of these are used for two, or more than two, respectively
Conjunctions: FANBOYS = for, and, nor, because, or, yet, so.

1ˢᵗ Ed. © ibidPREP llc

Appendix B

Oh, Calculator + Tips

1ˢᵗ Ed. © ibidPREP llc

Step Away From The Calculator

Unless you get a grip on the basics, you're never going to have a chance on these tests. The most basic basic is arithmetic. If you aren't comfortable adding, subtracting, multiplying and dividing WITHOUT A CALCULATOR, then you're starting out at a disadvantage. I know, I know, you're allowed to use a calculator on most tests, and it might seem like I'm being so old school hold-out, forcing you to learn your math tables for no reason, but trust me: knowing your numbers is VERY important. Here is the reaction I get from EVERY single student after I give them the little speech above:

> **THEM**: But we're allowed to use our calculators...[whine,   whine]

> **ME**:   AARGH! Yes. I know, but...

Here's why you should not use always reach for your calculator:

1. **Your test let's you use one**. I know that sounds a bit paranoid, but trust me, if the calculator were truly helpful, it wouldn't be allowed. Think about it. They don't let you use a dictionary on the sentence completions do they? Now that would be helpful!

2. **If you automatically reach for your calculator to solve a problem, you're hurting yourself.** Many kids reflexively reach for the calculator when a problem looks hard [like junkies reaching for their drug] as if the calculator will solve the problem for them if they just push enough buttons or wave it over the test. However, as with the reading passages, unless you process the problem FIRST, and set it up as much as you can without the calculator, you're probably heading down a blind alley or setting yourself up for EX-TRA work. The ACT is chock full of problems that look like they require the calculator for big complex numbers, and if you start punching them in: YOU'RE A SUCKER! These problems are called calculator busters.

Do You Really Need The Calculator For That?

Then next time you reach for a calculator to do a very simple multiplication problem, please stop and think. You may use a dictionary to look up hard words, but do you look up every word you read? Do you use a phonetic alphabet chart to figure out words? Then why use a calculator to do basic arithmetic? Know it or use your pencil!!

3. **The buried basics**: Remember, these are tests of basics. However, if the tests simply asked "What does 1 + 1 = ", everyone would get perfect scores. So how do they make the basics harder? They often bury them within scary, advanced looking problems. Just as they love the "Everyone thinks science is this, this, this and this, but really it's that [banana, banana, banana, but really strawberry]," they also love to ask questions like "What is the first digit in 398?", watch you scurry for your calculator and then pull your hair out when your calculator CAN'T SOLVE THE PROBLEM!! [Calculator Buster!] The reason your calculator can't solve this problem is that it's not really an exponent problem; it's actually a pattern problem. In this case, and for most cases, your pencil is your most powerful tool [the answer is inside it!]. Think about it. We'll explain the rest later.

4. **The College Board rewards students who know their numbers**. The College Board rewards students with a feel for numbers by creating questions with **Happy Numbers**. What are **Happy Numbers**?

   Numbers that work out evenly when divided, rational numbers, integers, or relatively small decimals. If you know your multiplication tables, you'll be able to identify those relationships FASTER than if you blindly punch numbers into a keypad. Try it. Divide 6 by 3. You're done, right? That took about a nanosecond [1]Now try to do 6 ÷ 3 on your calculator. Reach for it, turn it on, punch in the numbers, hit enter. That took

[1] One millionth of a second or, in NYC, the amount of time it takes the car behind you to honk when the light turns green

about 3 seconds. Later, when you prep for more specialized tests like the SAT Math2 Subject Test and deal with thornier numbers and terms, then you'll need the calculator, then I'll teach you how to really use that calculator, but I'll still make you set stuff up!

OH, CALCULATORS...

The irony of calculators is that students are given them to use FAR TOO EARLY [as early as 6th grade for some], and then never really taught how to use them when they really need them [in high school for things like trig, algebra2, calculus and stats].

I can't tell you how many students wield[2] these amazing TI 83's, 84's, and 89's and use them only for the most basic math—like using an Xbox 360 to play Pong [really, really simple, old video game—trust me]. I've even seen kids multiply $3 \times 3 \times 3 \times 3$ to figure out 34 because they didn't know what the exponent button was. I kid you not. I'm not saying you're that dude, but if you are, don't be. Put your calculator away. If you still need it later, I promise I'll let you have it back, AND I'll teach you how to use it really well..

5. **Knowing Numbers as More Than Just Buttons on Your Calculator Allows You to Spot Solutions & Mistakes You'd Never See Otherwise...**

   If you have no feel for numbers and just plug them into your calculator blindly, if you make a mistake punching them in, you will have no chance of catching your error. Kids with a number sense have a chance of realizing that their answer should be larger than the number they have, or that it should be negative, or that there's something wrong with the number they've gotten. Kids with no number sense will just see the number on the calculator and look for it in the multiple choice. If it's not there, they'll have no way of knowing where they've gone wrong and will just figure that's the way the math world goes and pick something close.

"All right, bright guy," you might ask, "So, when do I use the calculator?"

There are four occasions on which it is appropriate to use the calculator:

1. **After you've set up EVERYTHING—**

   and you're left with your final numbers such as $x = 5 \times 3^3$, then you can reach for your calculator and punch in 5×3^3, or since you know from your MUST KNOW MATH what 3^3 is, you can punch in 5×27, but since you also remember the rule of multiplying by 5's [see APPENDIX], you don't even need the stinking calculator [one half of 27 = 13.5 times 10 = 135!].

2. **To check yourself—**

   I am not an unreasonable man. I know that in the heat of the battle, we can lose our focus and find ourselves having problems adding 12 and 24 [I get much worse at arithmetic when money is involved!]. At this point, once you've set up the equation you want to solve, be my guest and check your numbers!

3. **As a tool [which is why it was built in the first place!]—**

   Students rarely think to use the use the calculator the way they really SHOULD—as a tool for testing numbers! Using a calculator to add $9 + 4$ is about as efficient as carrying around a bag of rocks and counting those. However, if for instance you, like most students, are not sure if $(2^3)^4$ is equal to 2^7 [add the exponents] or 2^{12} [multiply the exponents], for god's sake—just check it on your calculator! Like this:

$$(2^3)^4 = 4096$$

[2] use, brandish, ply

1st Ed. © ibidPREP llc

$$2^7 = 128$$

$$2^{12} = 4096$$

Therefore, $(2^3)^4 = 2^{12}$, which means that when a number taken to a power is taken to another power, the exponents are multiplied! That's using your calculator like a tool and not like a bag of rocks!!

4. **If you have Math Amnesia—**

It is deeply unfortunate that some students, try as they might, cannot hold onto math tables, retain squares, or turn to jelly whenever negative numbers appear. For these students, it is absolutely vital to use the calculator at every step of the way to confirm their process. If this is you, be sure to still set everything you can on paper first, then use your calculator.

QUICK TIPS!

1. When in doubt, use parentheses! Remember, your calculator is a dumb tool. In fact, if you plug in -9^2, your calculator doesn't know that you want $(-9)^2$. In fact, your calculator reads -9^2 as $-(9)^2$ and will give you -81 for your answer!

2. As you get results for each step on your calculator, WRITE THEM DOWN. After each long string of calculations, write down your result before putting it into a new equation. It can't hurt.

3. Do not clear compulsively! If an answer is 3.14175, don't clear and rewrite the number later on as 3.14. That would defeat the purpose of having a calculator capable of doing problems out to far-reaching decimal places, etc. If you need to clear, either store the number in MEMORY [ask your instructor] or WRITE IT DOWN! Don't round!!

> Say you need to multiply 8.256 x 8.256. Your answer should be 68.161536. Do not clear this and then write it down as 68! That's not the same thing! Use the long answer.

4. KNOW HOW TO USE IT!

   a. Learn the power button on your calculator [if you bang out 2 × 2 × 2 × 2 × 2 × 2 instead of typing in 2^6 or 2 x^y 6, you might as well just use your fancy calculator as a door stop].

   b. To find square, cube, and fourth roots of numbers, use fractional powers—it's much faster than searching for special root buttons if you even have them:

E.g. To find $\sqrt[3]{64}$, punch in 64^(1⁄3) to get 4.

   c. To find whole number remainders, especially for series or pattern problems:

   Divide the number using the calculator, subtract the whole number part of the answer from the answer, and multiply the decimal amount remaining by the divisor.

e.g.: $85 \div 7 = 12.\overline{142857}$

$.\overline{142857} - 12 = .\overline{142857}$

$.\overline{142857} \times 7 = 1$ R = 1

1st Ed. © ibidPREP llc

Appendix C

Multiplication and Division Tips

1st Ed. © *ibidPREP llc*

Multiplying by 2

Most everyone can multiply an even number by 2 fairly comfortably, but we often get stuck when multiplying an odd number by 2. One good approach is to simply double an even number just above or below your number and then add or subtract two.

E.g., 2 × 19
Think of (2 × 20) and subtract 2, so
2 × 19 = (2 × 20)–2 = 40 – 2 = 38

E.g., 2 × 37
Think of (2 × 36) and add 2, so
2 × 37 = (2 × 36) + 2 = 72 + 2 = 74

Of course you may also double the ten's digit and then double the one's digit:
2 × 37 = (2 × 30) + (2 × 7) = 60 + 14 = 74

Dividing by 2

Just as with multiplication, most of us can divide an even number by two fairly easily but have trouble dividing an odd number by two. One thing to keep in mind is that there are only ever two remainders possible when dividing by two: zero and one. An even number divided by two always has a remainder of zero, and an odd number divided by two always has a remainder of one (which becomes 0.5 if we continue dividing), so the best way to divide an odd number by two is to go to the even number below your number, divide that number by two, and add to your answer!

E.g., 45 ÷ 2

Think of (44 ÷ 2) and add .5, so

45 ÷ 2= (44 ÷ 2) + .5 = 22 + .5 = 22.5

Is a Number Divisible by 3, 6 or 9?

3

To determine if a number is divisible by 3, simply add all the digits in the number. If their sum is a multiple of 3, then the number is a multiple of 3.

E.g., 2,132
The digits of 2,132 are 2, 1, 3 and 2, and their sum is 2 + 1 + 3+ 2 = 8, SO 2,132 IS NOT divisible by 3.

E.g., 366
The digits of 366 are 3, 6 and 6, and their sum is 3 + 6 + 6 = 15; 15 is a multiple of 3, so 366 IS divisible by 3.

6

A number is a multiple of 6 if the number is even and its digits add up to a multiple of 6.

E.g., 846
The digits of 846 are 8, 4 and 6, so 846 is divisible by 6 because 8 + 4 + 6 = 18, and 846 is an even number.

E.g., 1,942
The digits of 1,942 are 1, 9, 4 and 2 so 1,942 is NOT divisible by 6 because 1 + 9 + 4 + 2 =16, and 16 is not a multiple of 6.

9

A number is a multiple of 9 if its digits add up to a multiple of 9.

The digits of 17,658 are 1, 7, 6, 5 and 8, so 17,658 IS divisible by 9 because 1 + 7 + 6 + 5 + 8 = 27, and 27 is a multiple of 9.

Multiplying by 9

To multiply a single-digit number by 9, simply make the ten's digit of the product one less than the number you're multiplying 9 by, and then make the one's digit whatever adds to the ten's digit to make 9. That sounds much harder than it is.

In other words, in 9 × 7, the ten's digit would be 6 [one less than 7] and the one's digit would be 3 [because 6 + 3 = 9], so 9 × 7 = 63!

NERD FACT: The digits of the first 20 multiples of 9 [except 99] all add up to 9!

Multiplying and Dividing by 5

All multiples of 5 have a units digit of 0 or 5.

To multiply a number by 5, simply multiply the number by ten and divide it by 2.
　　In 24 × 5, 24 becomes 240, which is then divided by 2 to give the product 120!

To divide a number by 5, simply divide the number by 10 and multiply that by 2!
　　In 245 ÷ 5, 245 becomes 24.5, which is then multiplied by 2 to give the quotient 49!

Multiplying and Dividing by 11

The first nine multiples of 11 are simply that number repeated: 11 × 2 = 22, 11 × 3 = 33, 11 × 4 = 44, etc.

To multiply a two-digit number by 11, simply split that number and put the sum of its digits in between the original digits.

$$
\begin{array}{rl}
\text{E.g.} & 15 \\
& \underline{\times 11} \\
\text{split the 15 to make it} & 1\_\_5 \\
\text{then take 1 + 5 [6] to make} & 165
\end{array}
$$

1st Ed. © ibidPREP llc

Other examples—

$$\begin{array}{r} 27 \\ \times 11 \\ \hline 2\_7 \end{array}$$

2 + 7 = 9, so   297

$$\begin{array}{r} 35 \\ \times 11 \\ \hline 3\_5 \end{array}$$

3 + 5 = 8, so   385

When the sum of the digits of the number is greater than 10, simply carry the 1 as you would in regular addition.

$$\begin{array}{r} 94 \\ \times 11 \\ \hline 9\_4 \end{array}$$

9 + 4 = 13, so 3 becomes the middle digit and 1 gets added to 9 to make 10:   1,034

1st Ed. © *ibidPREP llc*

Appendix D
Math in Two Pages

1st Ed. © ibidPREP llc

1. Write it out.

2. Break down problems sentence by sentence, clause by clause and set up problems/equations as you go. If you get stuck or get a wrong answer, REREAD—you probably just misread something.

3. FIDOE: FILL IN DIAGRAMS OR ELSE. Fill in everything you know about the diagrams given and everything given about the diagrams. Then try to answer the question.

4. If the figure given is NOT drawn to scale, redraw it in a way that is different from the way given. I.e., if a triangle looks like a right triangle, but they're not saying it is, redraw it as a non-right triangle.

5. To find the area of irregular shapes, look for the regular shapes and add or subtract their areas.

6. It is impossible to solve for 2 variables. If it looks like you need to, do one of three things.

   a. Put one variable in terms of the other.

   b. Stack and subtract (or add)

   c. Solve for two (or more) variables as one. I.e. if you are asked to look for "a + b," don't worry what "a" is or "b" is, you only have to concern yourself with what the sum of "a" and "b" are.

7. Solve inequalities as if they are equalities. That is, set "x" or the equation of "x" equal to its upper and lower values and solve. Once you have solved for "x," put the inequality signs back in. That gives you the new solution set, the new inequality. If you are comparing inequalities and some of the limits are negative, don't be afraid to mix it up. E.g.:-3 < x < 4 and -5 < y < 6 then ? < x - y < ? ...To solve, make x = -3 and y = -5 to get x – y = 2; x = -3 and y = 6 to get x – y = -9; x = 4 and y = -5 to get x – y = 9; and x = 4 and y = 6 to get x – y = -2. Therefore:-9 < x – y < 9.

8. Bouncy-Bouncy: To factor a number, create factor pairs, beginning with one and the number being factored, and work your way into the middle of the factor pairs. Remember, if a number is a perfect square, its square root counts as only one distinct factor.

9. Every average problem comes down to one simple formula:

   AVERAGE = TOTAL ÷ NUMBER OF NUMBERS

   Every problem will give you two of these variables right off the bat. Even if there are more parts to the question, immediately plug those variables into the equations to see what else you have.

10. Remember: you can reduce across a multiplication sign but NOT across an addition sign [or equal sign]. With addition, you can distribute the denominator and reduce.

    E.g.:

    $$\frac{3}{4} \times \frac{8}{9} = \frac{1}{1} \times \frac{2}{3} = \frac{2}{3}, \text{ but}$$

    $$\frac{(3+8x)}{36} = \frac{3}{36} + \frac{8x}{36} = \frac{1}{12} + \frac{2x}{9}$$

11. "Percent" means "per 100."

    a. Therefore, as much as possible, use the number "100" in percent problems because a "percent" of "100" equals the same amount of "100" (27.5% of 100 = 27.5).

    b. Also, remember that the same amount added or subtracted to different original amounts will give you different percents (25 = 25% of 100, but 25 = 20% of 125 - N.B.—the same amount is a smaller percent of a larger original amount).

12. Whenever you see quadratic equations, DON'T think quadratic formula or even necessarily factoring. Think of these few quadratic identities (have them memorized):

    a. $(a + b)^2 = a^2 + 2ab + b^2$

    b. $(a - b)^2 = a^2 - 2ab + b^2$

    c. $(a + b)(a - b) = a^2 - b^2$

13. The area of a right triangle is simply one half the product of the two legs that form the right angle. This is true even if the hypotenuse looks like the base...any leg of the triangle can be the base.

14. ZERO IS, WAS AND ALWAYS WILL BE AN INTEGER.

15. Any time you see "x^2," don't forget: a negative squared is positive, a negative squared is positive...

16. Never ever change π (that's pi) to a number. Leave it as π. The answers are always expressed as π. (FOR THE SAME REASONS, DO NOT CONVERT ROOTS TO THEIR IRRATIONAL COUNTERPARTS).

17. Begin at the beginning. When you are plugging in numbers, begin with the first (or last) of a set. Doing this makes guessing an organized and rational process as opposed to a random, chaotic and not particularly helpful one.

18. If you want to know how a large group of numbers behaves, extrapolate from a small group. E.g. If a pattern of numbers is odd, odd, even, how do you determine if the 1000th term will be even or odd? ANSWER: DETERMINE WHAT THE 10TH TERM IS.

19. To determine the nth term in a series, begin with the first term in that series. Continue determining terms until you find the repeating pattern. Patterns should generally repeat within ten terms, so you should never have to evaluate a series until its, say, 98th term. All you need do is find the pattern. Say the pattern is 1,2,3,1, 2,3... which gives you an interval of 3, then divide 98 by 3. In this case, it's 32 with 2 left over. Since the remainder is 2, we know that the 98th term must be the second term, 2.

20. **Possibility × Possibility × Possibility**: Arrangement problems usually come down to possibility times possibility with limited possibilities going first. What the heck does that mean? Here we go:

    a. Find the number of possible combinations of outfits you can wear over a three-day weekend if you have 5 different outfits—

       i. Figure how many possible outfits you have to choose from on Saturday (5), now that you've chosen one outfit for Saturday how many outfits do you have to choose from for Sunday? (4) and how many do you have to choose from for Monday? (3).

       ii. Take your possibilities for each day and multiply them together. That is your total number of possibilities:

$$5 \times 4 \times 3 = 60$$

    b. If there are limits to the possibilities, begin with the limited selections first: If there are 5 people in a car but only 2 of them can drive, how many different seating arrangement can there be?

    c. Figure how many possible drivers there are to choose from since that is the limited role (2). Now that one slot has been filled, how many people are there to choose from for the passenger seat? (4!) how many for the first back seat? (3); how many for the middle back seat (2); and how many for the last back seat? (1)

    d. Your total number of possibilities is:

$$2 \times 4 \times 3 \times 2 \times 1 = 48$$

21. And please, don't forget the two rules of fractions.

    a. **Reduce** (where possible: across multiplication signs and from top to bottom)

    b. **Eliminate denominators** (where possible, generally by cross multiplying or multiplying by reciprocals)

NO MATTER WHAT, REMEMBER: It's never as hard as you think. If you think you need to do some random geometry proof you have completely forgotten from 10th grade, you are wrong. Chances are, the solution lies in some basic fact about the shape before you. The same holds true for all types of ACT math. Believe this; It is true.

1ˢᵗ Ed. © *ibidPREP llc*

APPENDIX E

HOW TO READ

1st Ed. © ibidPREP llc

NUTS & BOLTS OF READING COMPREHENSION

1. Read the passage.

2. Keep reading until you've got your Two T's. Usually you'll know your Theme and Thesis by the first few sentences of the second paragraph, but sometimes the author doesn't spit them out until much later. Hang in!

   a. Make sure you are clear on what the topic [THEME] truly is: just because they're talking about *bananas*, it doesn't mean that the topic is really *bananas*.

   b. Make sure you are clear on what the author's viewpoint [THESIS] is: i.e., look for the "but." Just because the author writes "most people think bananas," it doesn't mean the author thinks "bananas." In fact he probably thinks "not bananas."

3. Once you've established what the "but" and/or author's point is, you will see that **every** body paragraph is designed to support that point.

4. Occasionally, authors will devote a body paragraph to a contrary example—something that seems to contradict their point of view. Authors do this in order to:

   a. Seem fair—they want to create the appearance of examining all sides of an argument and demonstrating their awareness of them, or

   b. Strengthen their point—by raising and then ultimately dismissing or diminishing contrary points of view, authors hope to reinforce the strength of their own point of view.

5. Every passage makes one and only one point, and most of the questions hinge on your being aware of what that point is.

6. Answering the questions:

   a. Read the question,

   b. Paraphrase the question so as to be sure you know what it's asking,

   c. Determine **your** answer to the question. If you don't have one, look back to the passage. Don't flip back to the question until you've figured something out. Then:

   d. Once you have an answer in mind:

      i. Read the answers given.

      ii. Eliminate any answers that seem wrong outright.

      iii. If you find the answer during your first read-through of the answers—pick it.

      iv. If you don't find the answer you want but have one or two choices left, look closely at the remaining answers and try to find one or two words in an answer that would make it **wrong.**

      v. If you are still left with more than one answer choice, pick the answer that seems qualified the most [some, often, occasionally, etc.] **and** the most like previous answers to other questions in the section, and then,

      vi. Move on! Don't spend too much time on a question you're totally clueless about. The longer you spend on a reading comprehension question, the more likely you are to waste time, energy and points. If you don't know the answer, guess and GTHOOT![45]

---

[45] Get the Heck Out of There!

1st Ed. © ibidPREP llc

APPENDIX F

THE ESSAY

IN ONE PAGE

1st Ed. © ibidPREP llc

Essay Process: Structure and Tips

1. Read the topic.
2. Think about the topic.
   a. Ask yourself what it really means.
   b. Cast about your mind for anything (historical, literary, personal—anything that makes your point) that has to do with the topic. It is not important whether it seems like a positive or negative example—just be **specific.**
3. Based on your examples, decide which point will be either easier or more interesting to make. Remember, **_any_** example can be used to make any point of view. You don't have to be "right" as long as you are consistent. Your examples don't necessarily have to be from literature or history, but they do have to be on point. Personal anecdotes should be used sparingly.
4. Begin writing:
   a. Intro Paragraph:
      i. [Sentence 1] **WHAT** YOU BELIEVE—Your opinion of the topic. It is not necessary to say "I believe...." You can just make a statement: _It is not true that..._
      ii. [Sentence 2] **WHY** YOU BELIEVE IT— _It is not true **because...**_
      iii. [Sentence 3] **HOW** YOU WILL SET ABOUT PROVING YOUR WHY. _History and literature have clearly shown topic to be false...._
      iv. [Sentence 4] Introduce your examples. _The lessons of **WWII** and **Macbeth** provide clear examples of where history and literature prove topic false...._
   b. Paragraph 2—Example 1
      i. Example 1 proves that topic is false because...
      ii. Specific Example "A" from text or incident.
      iii. Specific Example "B" from text or incident.
      iv. _As shown in Specific Example "A" and "B," Example 1 proves topic false._
   c. Paragraph 3 — Example 2
      i. Connect to Example 2 and then show how it further proves point....
      ii. Specific Example "A" from text or incident.
      iii. Specific Example "B" from text or incident.
      iv. _As shown in Specific Example "A" and "B," Example 2 proves topic false._
   d. Paragraph 3a— Example 3 [if you have a good third example and time, use it. If not, just mention it as additional proof in conclusion along with any other possible examples you might have].
   e. Paragraph 4—Conclusion
      i. _As shown above through history and literature, the topic is obviously false._
      ii. _It is obviously false because of the "because" stated above_ [Paragraph 1, Sentence 2] _and proved with the examples above._
      iii. _Although some may say it is true because of **"some contrary reason,"** this reason only serves to make topic even more false because **"some reason of your own to contradict the contrary."**_
5. **Reread** what you've written.
   a. Make sure there are no blatant grammatical errors.
   b. Make sure that the essay is reasonably legible.
   c. Make sure that paragraphs are clearly delineated

1st Ed. © ibidPREP llc

THE ANSWERS

1st Ed. © ibidPREP llc

GRAMMAR
SPOT THE SUBJECT/OBJECT—P. 40
1. S: Billy, O: gyro
2. S: gyro, O: pita
3. S: gyro
4. S: things, O: gyro
5. S: I, O: Billy, food
6. S: Billy, O: kid

PRONOUNS—P. 42
1. me
2. he
3. his
4. we
5. us
6. they
7. my
8. them
9. she
10. I
11. me
12. their

PRONOUNS & ANTECEDENTS—P. 42
1. <u>Maurita</u> always forgets to do <u>her</u> homework.
2. If <u>the fire department</u> faces any more budget cuts, <u>it</u> will be seriously hampered.
3. <u>Matthew and I</u> wanted to go to the pool, but <u>we</u> had to stay and clean the house instead.
4. <u>Ernesto</u> thought <u>his teacher</u> would give him a B on the test, but <u>she</u> gave <u>him</u> an A instead.
5. The program helps <u>citizens</u> learn <u>their</u> rights.
6. <u>Anyone</u> who wants to look better on the beach should improve <u>her</u> diet and exercise now!

CLASSIFY PARTS OF SPEECH—P. 46
Part A:
1. noun
2. proper noun
3. noun
4. adjective
5. noun/verb
6. verb
7. adverb
8. adverb
9. adjective
10. adjective
11. proper noun
12. noun
13. proper noun
14. adverb
15. noun/verb
16. proper noun
17. proper noun
18. proper noun
19. adverb
20. proper noun

Part B:
1. For
2. And
3. Nor
4. But
5. Or
6. Yet
7. So

SUBJECT, PREPOSITION & VERB—PART 1—P. 48
1. Gerald lives [above St. Nicholas.]
2. Nina's desk is [against the wall.]
3. When Sylvia goes to class, she always sits [between Shakima and me.]
4. [In the sand-covered parking lot], the tour bus idled as the group stopped to picnic [on the beach.]
5. I like all kinds of fruit [except tomatoes.]
6. I am now a health nut; I have not eaten a hot dog [since I was a little kid.]
7. [In the 1950's], the United States of America made cars [for the world.]
8. Please do not talk [during the movie.]
9. My brother and I like to ride our bikes [around the block.]
10. It is hard to believe there is another state [across the Hudson River.]

SUBJECT, PREPOSITION & VERB—PART 2—P. 48
1. <u>The pack</u> [of cards] <u>is</u> [on the table.]
2. <u>The basketball</u> <u>went</u> [through the window and under the couch.]
3. [Across the street from my apartment], there <u>are a grocery store and a dry cleaners</u>.
4. <u>Julio</u>, the ballet dancer [from Montreal], <u>has been studying</u> Mandarin Chinese [since 2010.]
5. Because she did so well [in high school], <u>Liz</u> <u>has</u> many colleges among which to choose.
6. Unfortunately, <u>each</u> [of the movies that David wanted to see] <u>was</u> playing [during the test.]
7. [Off in the distance], <u>three pigeons</u>, speckled [with coal dust,] <u>perched</u> [upon the roof.]
8. [After mowing the lawn,] <u>my mom</u> <u>drove</u> Kevin and me [to the mall] [in her pink Cadillac.]
9. <u>Darren</u> <u>amazed</u> his friends and <u>bet</u> Betty that she also would not be able to figure out his magic trick.
10. <u>The prize</u>, a trip to Paris, a treat [beyond my wildest dreams], <u>dangled</u> [before my eyes.]
11. [All along the watchtower], <u>princes</u> <u>kept</u> the view.
12. Detailed <u>study</u> [of the coverage of the event] <u>exposed</u> a certain bias [in the reporting.]

Answers

COMMAS—P. 53
1. Darrin likes to eat, to drink and to fly kites.
2. The way Bobby, my brother, talks, you would think he's from a different country.
3. Tomorrow will be July 4, 2020.
4. My favorite date is Wednesday, November 22, 1961.
5. Mr. Getz, my principal, also teaches math, science and gym.
6. Noah, shine the light over here, so I can see you better.
7. The kids were wearing fuzzy, wool hats over their big, round heads.
8. Even though you saved your money, you still do not have enough for a bicycle.
9. Since you are late, we had to start without you.
10. If you don't finish the project by tomorrow, you won't get a good grade on it.
11. Before we moved to the city, we had many animals on our farm.
12. Providing that you study for the test, I am sure you will do well.
13. No, there is not enough time to play a game of Monopoly before we leave.
14. Before we leave, we need to turn off all the lights.
15. Well, if you must choose the red dress, I guess that is all right with me.
16. The light, fluffy lemon cake was the hit of the party.
17. A new highway was built, so motorists can move around the city more smoothly.
18. However, we have tried to find our dog for two days.
19. Well, do you want to be a squirrel instead?
20. The last time you told me a lie, I believed you, but not this time.

COMMA, SEMICOLON AND COLON PRACTICE—P. 54
1. She wanted organic fruit and went to the other supermarket to get it.
2. Beyond the city limits, there is an abandoned chocolate factory.
3. This is what I like to take to the beach: a good book, sunblock, and two towels.
4. As I walked down the street, the strangest thing happened: I lost my way.
5. Out of all the coffee shops you could walk into, why did you choose this one?
6. If you didn't want me to find out about the surprise party, you should not have put it on Facebook; I am on Facebook all the time.
7. My favorite musicians, in no particular order, are Jimi Hendrix, Nina Simone, and Beyoncé.
8. There are so many good parts to that coffee shop: free wifi, great lattes, and the best cookies and scones in town.
9. Jackson loved to surf; rain or shine, he was in the water.
10. When I listen to that song, I feel like dancing; it is very catchy.
11. Riley loved going to the country, yet he seldom got to go.
12. I wanted to tell her one thing and one thing only: don't go shark diving.
13. Summer is my favorite season, and I love the month of July the most.

COMMA, SEMICOLON & COLON—P. 54
PART 1:
1. Turning up the stereo, I heard the speakers fill with static.
2. Before the race began, he drank a cool glass of water.
3. The panel seemed to prefer films that were well-written, funny, and uplifting.
4. I hope you like this song, but i also have other music.
5. Nina wore a big, blue hat and a pale pink sweater.
6. I loved the artist's funky color choices and how he mixed neon and pastels, and i also loved the incorporation of writing and photography on the canvas.
7. No one thought the Ramones would like Lady Gaga's music because they were so punk, but I guess everyone misjudged the situation.
8. During orientation, most campers were wishing the big, beautiful lake were open.
9. Will was normally up for any stunt, yet he lost his nerve when asked to tightrope without a net.
10. While in England, Anna called "soccer," her greatest passion, "football" because that is what the English generally call it.

PART 2:
1. As the kicker got injured right after the coin toss, the team had a rough start.
2. As usual, I had to go around seven o'clock, but i didn't want to leave this time.
3. It was such a long trip, not only because of the traffic and snow, but also because he had to go to the bathroom every five minutes.
4. I wish the park had a swing set, some sprinklers, and more plants and trees.
5. If you want a good seat at the movies, you should leave the house early and buy tickets online.
6. Do you really like both sweet and salty foods?
7. If you didn't know that fact, now you know it.
8. Green farms is a great health food store; however, it does not have many gluten-free options.

1st Ed. © *ibidPREP llc*

9. I like to run and bike, but because I don't stretch properly, I get injured often.
10. Although he had all his shots before he traveled, he still got sick on the trip.

COMMA REVIEW—P. 56
PASSAGE 1
"Come back in fifteen months, and I'll show you something special." When Paul Peters recalled these words, he returned to his doctor friend in Maine. The doctor, however, was dead.

Peters found a drawing on the doctor's table. When he picked up the drawing, he knew it was a map. The map directed him to a hole. Here, a few feet down, Peter saw a chain attached to the wall of the hole.

As Peters reached down for the chain, it was growing dark. The chain was very long and the "something special" felt heavy. A metal box appeared below him. Peters, however, was exhausted after this tiring effort. Peters reached for the treasure box, but it was still too far from his grasp. The weary man admitted defeat, and he dropped the chain.

Before Peters died from his exhaustion, he wrote this story in his diary. No treasure, unfortunately, has ever been found.

PASSAGE 2
As four men were walking around Pine Creek Island in 1796, they found a shallow hole. The hole was twenty feet wide, and a branch was stuck in its center. The men, unsurprisingly, became curious. They returned with shovels to look for what they thought was pirate treasure. After they dug ten feet down, they found a copper rod. A second marker appears at twenty feet and a third was seen at 30 feet. At this depth, however, the digging became impossible.

When a different group dug in 1815, they also found markers every ten feet. While they were shoveling, someone hit a stone at 100 feet. The stone had strange markings, but no one understood what the markings meant.

Other treasure seekers have tried their luck. One group, fortunately, met with some success. They discovered links of chain and pieces of paper, but nothing else was ever found. Pine Creek Island's secret, like so many secrets, is still a mystery. If the truth is discovered, it will be of great interest to the world.

CONTRACTIONS 1—P. 57
1. Sam isn't coming to the library with us.
2. Don't you want something to eat?
3. We've been working on this project all month.
4. It's starting to feel like spring.

CONTRACTIONS 2—P. 57
1. he'd
2. wouldn't
3. won't
4. he's
5. we'd
6. I've

APOSTROPHES—P. 58
1. it's/suitcase's
2. its
3. children's
4. Who's/party's
5. dog's/its
6. theirs
7. twins'
8. hers/manufacturer's
9. principal's/else's

POSSESSION 1—P. 59
1. All the boys' bicycles are gone.
2. The dancer's dress was made of silk.
3. Did the cat eat the Smith family's food off of the table?
4. Marta plays on the girls' basketball team.
5. Matthew's and Marsha's toys are all over the floor.
6. The hero's arrows aimed for the villain's heart.
7. The family of dragons breathed fire on the heroes' shields.
8. The heroes' horses' heads were covered in flameproof armor.
9. The boys went to the girl's party and danced with her friends.
10. Some of the girl's friends danced while her other friends played Frisbee.
11. Unfortunately, it was the girl's dog's Frisbee.
12. The girl's dog chased its Frisbee, much to all her friends' fear.

POSSESSION 2—P. 59
1. The team needed new uniforms. They were tired of ___their___ old uniforms.
2. You need to put the collar on ___your___dog. If it is not wearing _its_ collar, it may get lost.
3. The workers went on strike. The boss hoped __ their__ strike wouldn't last long.
4. The girl wanted to do better and asked Mr. Wil-

lard how she could improve ___her___ grade.
5. As the bus was idling, the kids breathed in ___ its___ toxic fumes.
6. The books were destroyed in a great fire, and we have lost ____their____ contents forever.

Quotation Review—p. 62
1. C
2. A
3. B
4. D
5. "Call your dad and tell him we'll be late," said Tom's mother.
6. "Make sure that he understands why," she added, "because I don't want him to get confused".
7. She switched off the radio, which was playing "Rolling in the Deep" by Adele.
8. I called, and my dad picked up after the first ring and said, "Hello."

Fewer/Less—p. 63
1. less
2. fewer
3. fewer
4. fewer
5. less
6. less

Superlatives—p. 64
1. most expensive
2. taller
3. fastest
4. most beautiful
5. reddest
6. better

Between/Among—p. 64
1. Between
2. among
3. Between
4. among
5. among
6. among

Misused Words—p. 66
1. eminent
2. shrank
3. swum
4. drunk
5. accept
6. incredible
7. affected
8. stationary

9. nauseous
10. nauseating
11. persecuted
12. not different from

Comparisons—p. 66
1. Virginia Woolf's writing style is harder to read than Henry James writing style.
2. I prefer eating at Jimmy's BBQ over eating at Roberta's because the food at Jimmy's is less greasy than the food at Roberta's.
3. The new biology teacher says that this textbook is much more up-to-date than last year's textbook.
4. Greek artists were far more innovative than Roman artists.
5. The rules of Go are far simpler than the rules of Chess.

Redundancy—p. 67
1. ~~The reason~~ she wanted to go to the dance is because Tim will be there.
2. ~~There's a good chance~~ it'll probably rain tonight.
3. I prefer strawberry ice cream to vanilla ice cream ~~because I like it better.~~
4. President John F. Kennedy was assassinated in ~~the year of~~ 1963.
5. Please meet me at the office ~~this evening~~ at 7pm.

Misplaced Modifiers—p. 68
1. While Henry got into bed, a horse galloped through his room.
2. After hanging out on the beach all day, Henry had a burnt back.
3. No change
4. To guarantee a spot on the team, players must complete workouts.
5. No change
6. After seeing the play, we named Shakespeare our favorite playwright.

That/Which—p. 69
1. As far as I'm aware, this is the only book (<u>that</u> / which) he's written.
2. This is just to say that I've eaten the plums (<u>that</u> / which) were in the icebox.
3. (That / <u>which</u>) of these is yours?
4. The car, (that / <u>which</u>) he had bought only a year ago, was completely totaled.
5. A bicycle (<u>that</u> / which) does not have air in its tires is essentially out of commission.
6. Font (<u>that</u> / which) is red or green colored will be difficult for the colorblind to distinguish.

1st Ed. © ibidPREP llc

PREPOSITIONAL PHRASES—P. 70
1. We agreed __on__ a theme for the party.
2. He lives ___on___ Windsor Street.
3. She used to live ___at___ 101 Corning Street.
4. They now live ___in___ the Park Plaza Hotel.
5. Her confidence ___in___ me is reassuring.
6. She is so different ___from__ me that I'm not sure how we ever became friends.
7. Her biting sarcasm puts __off___ a lot of people.
8. Her attitude towards me is always condescending; I don't like it when she talks __down___ to me.
9. __In___ time, you will no longer feel the pangs of heartbreak.
10. Ever since she lied about the incident, she has been afflicted __with___ guilt.

HOMOPHONES—P. 72
1. Which/witch woman was accused of being a which/witch?
2. In New York City, there/their/they're are many museums that are world famous for the quality of there/their/they're collections. There/Their/They're an important part of New York's international appeal.
3. To/Too/Two many people these days struggle when they try to/too/two choose among homophones. But hey, if there are only to/too/two choices, at least the odds of getting it right are pretty good.
4. If it's important to you that you right/write well, you'll have to develop the right/write editing habits.
5. It's/Its always funny to watch a dog chase it's/its tail.
6. Do you know weather/whether or not the weather/whether is suitable for a ski trip?

COMPOUND WORDS—P. 74
1. A lot/Alot of people like ice cream.
2. Some people would eat it every day/everyday.
3. Celery can not/cannot make people fat.
4. Altogether/All together, the team must decide if the sacrifice is worth the risk.
5. Booboo went some time/sometime without blinking his eyes.
6. Everyday/every day thoughts usually include imagining sometime/some time when everything will be perfect.

MATH
MAKE FRIENDS WITH 10s—P. 93
1. 9,600,000
2. 1,440,000
3. 1,320,000,000
4. 1,200,000
5. 0.00012
6. 0.039
7. 0.00000004
8. 1.818
9. 1
10. 840
11. 54
12. 363

DECIMALS TO FRACTIONS—P. 94
1. $\frac{8}{100}$
2. $\frac{9}{10}$
3. $\frac{6}{1000}$
4. $\frac{17}{100}$
5. $\frac{95}{1000}$
6. $\frac{32}{100}$

FRACTIONS TO DECIMALS—P. 95
1. 0.2
2. 0.03
3. 0.07
4. 0.3
5. 0.22
6. 2.2

FACTORING—P. 97
1. 1, 2, 3, 6, 9, 18
2. 1, 2, 3, 4, 6, 8, 9, 12, 16, 18, 24, 36, 48, 72, 144
3. 1, 2, 4, 8, 16, 32, 64
4. 1, 2, 4, 7, 14, 28
5. 1, 2, 3, 4, 6, 11, 12, 22, 33, 44, 66, 132
6. 7
7. 18
8. 72
9. 60
10. 9, 108

REDUCING—P. 100
1. 1/4
2. 1
3. 2/3
4. 1/36
5. ¼

Answers

PEMDAS—p. 117
1. 5
2. 6.8
3. 1
4. 35
5. –72
6. 24
7. 1
8. 5
9. 68
10. 10
11. 16
12. 29

NUMBER KNOWLEDGE—p. 118
1. A
2. D
3. B
4. C
5. D
6. C
7. D
8. D
9. C
10. C
11. B
12. A

ALGEBRA
SOLVE FOR x—p. 126
1. 14
2. 7
3. –1
4. 2/3
5. –3
6. –9/2
7. 5
8. –2.5
9. 12/11
10. 622

MIXED VARIABLES—p. 127
1. i. $a = bx + x$; $b = \dfrac{a-x}{x}$; $x = \dfrac{a}{b+1}$

   ii. $a = \dfrac{2b}{x-1}$; $b = \dfrac{a(x-1)}{2}$; $x = \dfrac{2b}{a}+1$

2. $\dfrac{a}{x} = \dfrac{1}{5}$

3. $\dfrac{a}{b} = \dfrac{7}{3}$

4. $\dfrac{b}{a} = \dfrac{8}{15}$

5. i. $xy = \dfrac{4}{3}$; ii. $xy = \dfrac{4+7x}{3}$

6. i. $2a = \dfrac{12b+3}{8}$; ii. $2a = \dfrac{16b+20}{3b}$

THE WORST OF ALL: ALGEBRA WITH FRACTIONS—p. 128
1. A
2. D
3. 1,800
4. B
5. C
6. E
7. C
8. 1/3

EVEN MORE WORDS TO MATH—p. 132
1. D
2. 8
3. C
4. C
5. D
6. B
7. E
8. D

ABSOLUTE VALUE ALGEBRA WORD PROBLEMS—p. 135
1. A
2. $4/3 < y < 4$
3. E
4. Any n for $-6 < n < -5$ and $1 < n < 2$
5. 2.5
6. D

MULTIVARIABLES—p. 139
1. B
2. D
3. E
4. C
5. C
6. C

POLYNOMIALS—p. 141
1. D
2. C
3. D
4. D
5. C
6. 1
7. E
8. A

6. 1/8
7. 5/7
8. 31/13
9. x = 27/28
10. x = 8/9
11. x = 1
12. x = 72

PERCENT WORDS TO MATH—p. 102
1. 100%
2. 12
3. 1,200
4. 225
5. 20%
6. 20
7. 36
8. 1,000
9. 20%
10. 200
11. 160

PERCENT WORD PROBLEMS—p. 105
1. E
2. D
3. E
4. D
5. D
6. B
7. A
8. C

PERCENT/AMOUNT—p. 107
1. 50%
2. 20%
3. 25%
4. 60
5. 31.5
6. 600
7. 501.6
8. $575

MEAN, MEDIAN AND MODE—p. 110
1. B
2. B
3. D
4. D
5. C

EXPONENTS—p. 115
1. 5^7
2. 3^8
3. 5^5
4. 15^3
5. 6^{17}
6. 4^2

1st Ed. © ibidPREP llc

9. C
10. C
11. B
12. D

ALGEBRAIC EXPONENTS—P. 143
1. B
2. D
3. C
4. D
5. E
6. A
7. E
8. E
9. A
10. B
11. 12
12. 728

GREATEST/LEAST—P. 147
1. 3
2. 37
3. 68
4. 11

RATIOS—P. 149
1. C
2. B
3. 747 girls
4. A
5. E
6. B
7. D

INEQUALITIES—P. 152
1. 2
2. 40
3. C
4. E
5. D
6. B

(T − 1)—P. 154
1. $496
2. B
3. D
4. E
5. 7
6. E

SERIES, SEQUENCES & PATTERNS—P. 156
1. B
2. 18.5

3. 2
4. 406
5. D
6. B

COMBINATIONS, PERMUTATIONS & ARRANGEMENTS—P. 158
1. C
2. D
3. 24
4. C
5. 160
6. 48
7. 40
8. D

PROBABILITY—P. 161
1. B
2. B
3. C
4. C
5. C
6. 3/10

FUNCTIONS—P. 164
1. 3
2. 1
3. 67
4. t = 12
5. D
6. B
7. k = 6
8. C

FUNKY FUNCTIONS—P. 166
1. E
2. C
3. A
4. C
5. B
6. C
7. B
8. C

CHARTS, TABLES, DIAGRAMS & GRAPHS—P. 169
1. A
2. 9
3. 1,400
4. 0

GEOMETRY
GEO WORD PROBLEMS—P. 181
1. D

2. D
3. D
4. D

LINES & ANGLES—P. 187
1. D
2. B
3. E
4. E
5. D
6. E
7. B
8. 135

TRIANGLES: AREA & PERIMETER—P. 191
1. B
2. C
3. B
4. C
5. C
6. B

PYTHAGOREAN THEOREM—P. 194
1. E
2. E
3. C
4. D
5. B

30°, 60°, 90° TRIANGLE—P. 197
1. $10\text{-}20\text{-}10\sqrt{3}$
2. $8\text{-}8/3\sqrt{3}\text{-}16/3\sqrt{3}$
3. $7\sqrt{3}\text{-}7\text{-}14$
4. $8\text{-}4\text{-}4\sqrt{3}$

SPECIAL RIGHT TRIANGLES—P. 198
1. A
2. C
3. B
4. D
5. D
6. B

SECTORS—P. 202
1. π; 3π
2. 8; 2π
3. 9; 27π
4. 40°; $\dfrac{2\pi}{3}$
5. 90°; 4π

Answers

CIRCLES—P. 203
1. E
2. C
3. 66
4. 18
5. B

CIRCLES WITH TRIANGLES—P. 206
1. C
2. D
3. B
4. E
5. 113
6. E

INSCRIBED SHAPES—P. 209
1. C
2. B
3. A
4. B
5. E
6. C

AREA & PERIMETER OF REGULAR & IRREGULAR SHAPES—P. 212
1. B
2. B
3. A

3D IS REALLY 2D—P. 215
1. B
2. B
3. A
4. C
5. B
6. C

3D GEOMETRY—P. 218
1. B
2. C
3. C
4. C

COORDINATE GEOMETRY—P. 222
1. D
2. E
3. A
4. 4/3
5. B
6. B

SPECIAL ACT MATH
MATRICES—P. 232
1. A

2. B
3. E

TRIGONOMETRY—P. 241
1. C
2. D
3. D
4. A
5. A
6. B
7. E
8. B
9. D
10. C
11. E
12. C
13. C

LOGARITHMS—P. 249
1. A
2. E
3. C
4. C
5. E
6. D

READING COMPREHENSION
HARPER LEE—P. 265
1. C
2. D

CICADAS—P. 265
1. B
2. D

IMPRESSIONISM—P. 267
1. A
2. D

COGNATES—P. 267
1. E
2. C

SIGN LANGUAGE—P. 268
1. D
2. A

THE BASQUE PEOPLE—P. 277
1. B
2. A
3. B
4. D
5. C
6. B

THE TURN OF THE SCREW—P. 283
1. C
2. A
3. C
4. C
5. D
6. B

FROM DWIGHT EISENHOWER'S FAREWELL ADDRESS IN 1961—P. 285
1. A
2. C
3. B
4. D
5. B
6. D

FROM "THE LAST GREAT EXPLORER"—P. 287
1. C
2. B
3. D
4. A
5. B
6. A

TIMESCALES OF EVOLUTION—P. 289
1. C
2. D
3. B
4. A
5. C
6. D

DUAL PASSAGES—P. 292
1. A
2. B
3. D
4. A

LONG PASSAGE COMPARISONS—P. 293
1. B
2. D
3. C
4. D
5. A
6. A

1st Ed. © ibidPREP llc

Acknowledgments

Translating more than two decades of teaching into a coherent form that includes equations and illustrations has proven a vast undertaking. Many people have helped make this book and the others in the series possible. Among them, in no particular order, are Ian Fiedorek, Paul Ketchum [especially Paul Ketchum], Eugenia Leftwich, Vadim Yerokhin and the great and powerful Beth Servetar. Over and above the brilliant contributions of these wonderful people, I am grateful to all my students past and present who have allowed me into their amazing minds long enough to learn how to teach them better.

Also available:

Remain Clam! Test Taking & the Student Mind: 4th Grade NY State Test Edition

Remain Clam! Test Taking & the Student Mind: Hunter Edition

Remain Clam! Test Taking & the Student Mind: Middle School Workbook Edition

Remain Clam! Test Taking & the Teenage Mind: 7th Grade NY State Test Edition

Remain Clam! Test Taking & the Teenage Mind: SHSAT Edition

Remain Clam! Test Taking & the Teenage Mind: SAT Edition

About the Author

Stuart Servetar is from Brooklyn, NY. He grew up in Rockland County, NY, and attended Wesleyan University in Middletown, CT, where he studied English Literature. After briefly studying fine art at Pratt Institute, Stuart settled in New York City to write, paint and eventually tutor. When the Berlin Wall came down, Stuart headed to Eastern Europe and lived in Prague for a number of years. There he painted, taught English and was the food critic for *The Prague Post*. Upon returning to New York City, Stuart continued to paint and became the art critic for *The NYPress*. From there he wrote art criticism for a number of local, national and international publications. He also resumed tutoring. In 2006, Stuart formed ibidPREP in order to bring his approach to tutoring and test prep to a wider cross-section of students. Today, ibidPREP offers classes and individual tutoring throughout the New York/New Jersey metropolitan area.

Like what you read? For more, register at <u>ibidprep.com</u> to access exclusive online content, flash cards and other goodies!

0816

1st Ed. © ibidPREP llc